T0069263

Karolinum Press

Josef Šafařík
Seven Letters to Melin
Essays on the Soul, Science, Art and Mortality

VÁCLAV HAVEL SERIES

Josef Šafařík

Seven
Letters
to Melin

Essays on the Soul,
Science,
Art and Mortality

KAROLINUM PRESS

KAROLINUM PRESS
Karolinum Press is a publishing department of Charles University
Ovocný trh 560/5, 116 36 Prague 1, Czech Republic
www.karolinum.cz

Originally published in Czech as *Sedm dopisů Melinovi. Z dopisů příteli přírodovědci*,
Prague: Družstevní práce, 1948

Text © Josef Šafařík – heirs, 2020
Translation © Ian Finlay Stone, 2020
Epilogue © Ivan M. Havel, 2020
Afterword © David Drozd, 2020
Photo © Bohdan Holomíček / Václav Havel Library, 2020, p. 371

Cover and graphic design by /3. dílna/
Set and printed in the Czech Republic by Karolinum Press
First English edition

Cataloging-in-Publication Data is available from the National Library
of the Czech Republic

ISBN 978-80-246-4375-5
ISBN 978-80-246-4701-2 (pdf)
ISBN 978-80-246-4703-6 (epub)
ISBN 978-80-246-4702-9 (mobi)

CONTENTS

1
SUICIDE

MY DEAR MELIN, – Well, well. Just look what has slipped off my pen! Melin, a name forgotten and left behind in some high school class, a nickname. God knows where it came from. I only know that you did not regard it as offensive; rather the opposite. You only used to frown when addressed in this way by someone from whom you would rather have kept as much distance as possible. This nickname was rather a sign of trust and intimacy, and it seems to me that it was exactly some such kind of feeling that guided my hand to write it and not cross it out.

Of course it is to you that I am indebted for this feeling. You would like us to discuss the case of Robert in the same unbiased and unconstrained frame of mind that, as young lads, we were once capable of talking about anything. You write that the more you think about the unfortunate end of our kinsman, the less certain you are about the 'true causes' of his 'injudicious act'. Oh truly, these our certitudes! For everyone whom it concerned and did not concern, Robert's death came as 'logically' and 'inevitably' as one and one equals two.

Our worthy aunt has decided that Robert was bound to come to such a bad end because he had forsaken God. Apparently Havlíček Borovský[1] also came to a bad end for the same reason. On the other hand, in the case of John of Nepomuk,[2] she claims that he came to a bad end because he did not forsake God. It was clear to our equally worthy uncle that Robert was spoiled by money. Indeed, money – the key to everything! As soon as money gets mixed up in human affairs, then all other reasons seem groundless and spurious alongside it. For you Robert was simply a creature without discipline and orderliness. 'Asocial inclinations' led him to run away from work in

1   Czech writer and journalist, important figure in the Czech National Revival, expelled from theology studies (1821–1856).
2   Also known as Jan Nepomuk, Czech saint (c. 1335–1393): according to some sources, drowned at the behest of Wenceslaus, King of Bohemia, for refusing to divulge secrets of confessional.

his father's factory – and in the end also from his home – to eke out a miserable existence as a vagabond.

However, Robert's deed has started to grow between us and has now even attracted your attention. You tell me that recently you have read a lot of specialist books and that as a result you are well on the way to understanding Robert not as a wicked person, but rather as a sick one. You divine 'demonic complexes' in his soul and restraints that human society placed on him. You want to rid yourself of all moral and conventional preconceptions and to examine his case as a scientist, unbiased by anything other than the will to understand and discover the truth. You admit that the term 'wicked' has no place in a scientist's terminology. But do you think that the term 'sick' has a place there? This is also something we will have to talk about.

And those demonic complexes! Society recognizes no other complexes than demonic ones. What is more disturbing is that neither does Freud recognize any others. At Calvary, society crucified three scoundrels. If you protest and claim that there were only two scoundrels and one saint, then you raise the question of what exactly a society is that does not distinguish between scoundrels and saints; that, among those who cannot get along with it, does not differentiate those who suffer demonic complexes from those who suffer angelic complexes. If it was difficult to answer this question truthfully in the past, then it is all the more difficult today, when society has become the ultimate authority and the final criterion not only in praxis, but also in theory. Nevertheless, in spite of this it will be necessary for us to reply to this question also.

There is one circumstance, I would say, that distorts your view of Robert and also of yourself. Your fortune, and also your misfortune, is that you are paid by society for your research activity regardless of whether you manage to find something out or not. I do not underestimate this material security, but neither do I overlook how, as over time your scepticism has been growing, you are becoming accustomed to stabilize your life more from the outside than from the inside. Service stripes on your sleeve, social and professional position, material security, a wife, children, and so on: all these are keeping you above water more than you are willing to admit. But I have a question for you: The less your life is driven from within, are not the truths that you produce thereby the less worthy of attention? In this way, do you not scoop water more shallowly from the pool of life? If you use scaffolding from outside as a support for your life, you can then of course permit yourself a descent into the lowest depths of scepticism without harming yourself greatly. But where, then, is this dreadful reality that is reflected in your scepticism?

None of us is in any doubt what to think about, for instance, the 'abysses of life and the rages of the soul' in the verses of a teenager who lives in affluence at his mother's, diligently attends the corso and visits the local cafe, and occasionally emboldened by alcohol sneaks through the red-light district. But what to think about this? Your searching and researching have led you to the conclusion that, for instance, 'Life is nothing other than a whirl of electrons' or that 'Life is nothing other than mutual devouring and being devoured'. And I ask: What now? What follows from this? And you: nothing. Your conscience has not moved an inch to the right or to the left. Your morals have remained exactly the same. Your everyday routine has not changed in the slightest. And I ask in amazement: Where is the reality of these newly found and hard-won truths? How can one believe in them if their black hopelessness has neither crushed you nor galvanized you? Has neither frozen you into a sacrificial animal nor transformed you into a wild predator? In what way is your pessimism less merely formal than the pessimism of the teenage poet?

Where exactly is reality in the flood of what is spoken, lectured, written, and thought? Take, for example, books. A book that I have not yet read haunts me as a reproach of an unfulfilled duty. And when I get hold of it and read it, I close the book – even if the author has excellently answered all the questions that I posed to him – with the feeling that the main thing, the final thing, the conclusive thing is still missing. This is not a rebuke to the author. It is a rebuke to books, to words, to ideas. An idea is evidently capable of accommodating more than it can bear, more than it is capable of delivering, of guaranteeing.

Professor Vladimír Úlehla[3] contemptuously assigns the moniker of 'Platonists' to those who lament over the successes of reason, while for him those who rejoice in the success of reason are 'Aristotelians'. If we call a success of reason the conclusion that life is nothing more than a conglomerate of physical-chemical reactions, then an Aristotelian has precisely as many reasons to rejoice over this as a Platonist. One thing is certain: if it was feeling or some other irrational thing that led me as a Platonist to this dismal conception of life and the world, then I would lament over this success of feeling in precisely the same way that I lament over this success of reason. As Pascal says: 'Do they profess to have delighted us by telling us that they hold our soul to be only a little wind and smoke, especially by telling us this in a haughty and self-satisfied tone of voice? Is this a thing to say gaily? Is it not, on the contrary, a thing to say sadly, as the saddest thing in the world?'[4]

Rarely elsewhere than precisely here are we confronted more forcefully by the question of whether this victorious cry about truth, about a truth so saddening and mournful for human beings, does not have its origin somewhere other than in this truth. If a person exults and rejoices over the discovery of a truth which – if it were to penetrate his heart and really become a truth for him – would necessarily paralyse him and suffocate every spark of joy and appetite for living in him, this cannot, I think, be explained in any other way than that this process of searching for and discovering truth has

---

3   Czech botanist and ecologist (1888–1947).
4   Blaise Pascal, *The Thoughts of Blaise Pascal*, trans. by W. F. Trotter (New York: P. F. Collier 1910), para. 194.

some other sense than truth itself. We can observe how, while this new truth depresses us and fills us with hopelessness and emptiness, on the other hand it gives its discoverer a feeling of self-realization, a feeling that from someone anonymous, from a nobody, he has become someone. The discoverer of this devastating truth draws from it the precise opposite of what this truth contains and of what he announces to us, the others. It is worthy of note that a person can acquire significance by proclaiming human beings an insignificant occurrence of the universe. Preaching about the insignificance of a person in the universe evidently does not have the purpose of renouncing a significant social standing among people. We should keep this in mind during the following deliberations.

It is possible to ask whether a person does not renounce one existence (a metaphysical one, for instance) only on the condition that he receives full compensation in another existence (a social one, for example). Or, to put the question in another way: whether, if he becomes at home in one existence, he does not die away in another existence; and whether, if he lives one existence, then he does not experience the other one only abstractly, in mere thought. Then we would understand how he can very easily allow himself the darkest scepticism in that existence that he experiences merely as abstract thought, given that the existence that he actually lives remains untouched by this scepticism.

Have you never paused to think sometimes, my dear friend, that among scientists, even though they are today the main producers of scepticism and pessimism, suicide 'for scientific reasons' is an unknown phenomenon, while for instance among artists, where the combination of words 'creation and doubting' results in a complete contradiction in terms, suicide is, so to speak, the order of the day? Is this not because, while the scientist thinks in a world in which he does not live, the artist thinks in the same world in which he lives? And, while therefore the former can permit himself as much scepticism in his thoughts as he pleases, the latter cannot do so with impunity?

15

It might seem that by this I am intending to show the falseness of the path that you are taking. In no way am I doing so. I know it is precisely this path that you have marked out as the only true path – as the objective path, as you say. One of the main principles of the scientific search for truth is that we cut ourselves off from our entire lived experience and put our trust only in what we think and observe, or today even only in what we can measure and calculate. This maximum curtailment of the human being as a condition for finding truth will demand a lot of our attention here. For the moment let us merely affirm that the more ground is gained by this method of searching for truth, the more a person's internal and metaphysical existence is cut down to zero, and therefore a person tries all the more to catch hold of an external existence, a physical and social one. Internal props collapse; external props are sought. The emptiness that is left over after the disappearance of the soul is best suppressed when this emptiness puts on a uniform. A uniform is a magical means which compensates for the loss of internal reality with external reality. But one uniform alone is no uniform. A million uniforms increases the weight of each one of them tenfold compared to one hundred thousand uniforms. There is an instinctive enmity between a uniform and a personality. There is an essential dispute between convention and social morality on the one side, and a free and creative being on the other. Because – and let us make no mistake about it – freedom is merely another word for internal reality. We can observe the strange effort of modern science, which – while destroying our internal reality – proclaims the promise of freedom for us. It liberates us, but at what cost? Precisely at the cost of freedom.

In this bleak situation we place our hopes in the master builder's recipe: more shovels and less Latin! However, the question concerning whether there should be more shovels or more Latin entirely misses the point. The entire difficulty is concealed in the fact that it is only the attainment of freedom that leads most of us to a realization of what exactly it is that cannot live without freedom. The master builder's recipe – this is the redemptive slogan of all those who have been liberated without having 'internal reasons' for freedom. We expected freedom to tell us who were are and what we want, but freedom lets us run back and forth from Latin to shovels and from shovels to Latin, and thus shows us that it is a matter of complete indifference whether we do the one or the other. We do not feel in ourselves any urge to do primarily one, and not the other, and therefore we have elevated to a morality of life the opinion that the purpose of doing anything is making money. Profession – that is our uniform. Being a slave to money – that is the sense of our liberated life. We have convinced ourselves that we carry the weight of the world on our shoulders and that freedom is something like a well-deserved paradise. But, when we have acquired this freedom, we quickly renounce it again because we feel that there has never been a heavier burden on our shoulders.

No one personifies this strange state of affairs better than the so-called 'practical' person – that is, a moneymaking person. Without difficulty you can see that this person, who is today imposed on you as a model and an example – even a moral one – is without any shadow of a doubt a liberated person. What is more doubtful, however, is whether this person is also a free person in the true sense of the word. The ease with which such a person succumbs to despotism of all kinds (or even positively solicits such despotism) and the fact that the very word 'practical' in many cases means precisely this moral submissiveness – all this indicates a being who, even though he is begot by freedom, does not himself beget this freedom.

We are witnesses of the strange phenomenon that in the 'age of freedom' a truly free soul must try to win its freedom in a period under a commando of money-earning people with no less effort and sacrifices than was the case under the rule of despots. Indeed, in many ways the position of a truly free soul is even more problematical. In a state of political or clerical serfdom it is not easy to deny that a free soul beats for something 'higher' – the conscience of the serfs is on its side. What to say, however, about a person who ardently strives for freedom in the 'age of freedom'? This is precisely what is ridiculous and senseless: that so-called 'decent' and 'conscientious' people do not greatly differentiate individuals of the type like Robert from subversives, layabouts, and parasites; apart, of course, from those rare exceptions when the activity or works of such an individual become in good time a source of regular income. We see a source of anarchy and subversion in everyone who does not drag the burden of a profession, the horse-gin of regular working hours, on the back of his neck. Do whatever you like, but do it from eight until noon, and then again from two until six, except Sundays, and make sure you are paid for it. Because the circumstance that you earn money in some way assuages in us every concern about your activity. The revolutionary, the prophet, the reformer: each of these becomes harmless as soon as we award him a certification to carry on a trade. Today we would not regard it as necessary to crucify Christ. We would let him eke out a living as an 'officially authorized clairvoyant' at fairs and festivals. By this I mean to say that we would not deny him any of that indulgent respect that we show to this woeful but proper livelihood.

'The main thing is to make an honest living,' your servant was wont to say, as in the mornings she cleared away the used cups and test tubes with the same gestures and in the same state of mind as when she cleared away the plates and pans in the kitchen after lunch. At the time the theme of 'Robert' was a topic of daily discussion. According to this uniformed morality, it does not depend on what you do; it depends only on how much of it you do. It does not matter what you discover by your efforts, what growth you achieve, what development you undergo; it depends only on how much money you receive for this on Saturday or on the first day of the month. If you intend to protest, then they smash you down with a trump card: family, children!

Indeed, for the most part we marry in time for us, at an age when we can no longer pretend that life has not defeated us, to have something with which to reassure ourselves that life has not actually defeated us. Because a child is an acknowledged argument making sense of life. In addition, it is an animated and moving argument. In the warm glow of a family hearth and among the golden rays of children's smiles even an empty cellophane balloon shines like a mature and rich product. Robert could never understand why people who live only for their children are born as human beings, and not as rabbits or partridges.

Family and children do not support you in the slightest in your internal impulse to live and work as a researcher, and not for instance as a stockbroker, an advocate or a businessman. It can even be said that, although your feeling tells you that the activity that you pursue is 'more valuable' than other activities, morality tells you that, in the interest of your family and children, you should pursue something more lucrative. Family and children cannot serve you as a basis for evaluating what you do out of internal necessity, because their existence depends on your profession and not on your internal reasons. For your family, just as for your servant, the only important thing is that you are a state employee with a retirement pension; that you are a scientific researcher is a matter of complete indifference to them. Nevertheless, you find the entire value and worth of your life in the fact that you are a researcher, not in the fact that you are a wage earner. I am sure that, if it was to occur to the state, as the decision of some godlike or infernal conference, to pay a salary for instance to artists instead of scientists, then you would not veer from your path one iota, even if your researching was to bring you so little that you would have to live with the lot of – well, let us say Robert. However, even if this fate were a matter of indifference to you, it would not be a matter of indifference to your family, to your children, to your servants. And so, you see that family, children, and servants, and indeed all decent and proper people, do not deny respect to you as a soulless robot, but they do deny you this respect as a free and creative being.

We live in an era in which every activity that is carried out for money, career, and social success is regarded as excellent and sensible, while every activity for which a person has his 'internal reasons' is regarded as incomprehensible and suspicious. To perform any kind of activity as a gainful means of employment – whether it be science, art, or philosophy, or whether it means collecting mushrooms or bird eggs, reading cards, or performing somersaults on the horizontal bar – all this seems appropriate and reasonable to the human mind. However, to be an engineer and to simultaneously cultivate chamber music, or to be an officer with the dragoons and also be incapable of living without philosophy – this provokes amazement, indignation, sympathy, laughter. People have arrived at the conviction that the only activities that make sense are those that you do for money. You are troubled by the mystery of perception and truth? So, go and become a professor and earn some money with this. Your heart yearns for God? Then, become a vicar and collect a tithe for that. You love books? Then set up a bookshop or become a librarian – with a state pension of course!

And thus, disconnecting truth from the way in which we live leads us to a strange piece of wisdom: that only a madman does something really and truly. If we wanted to augment the number of definitions of a human being as a creature distinct from animals, then we could say that a human being is a creature in need of salvation – whatever meaning each of us imbues this term with. Every one of us wants to be saved in his own way and according to his own taste, and all his efforts, desires, and thoughts are directed toward this end. Or rather – were directed towards it, until modern science opened up in front of him an abyss that earlier ages did not know to such an extent: an abyss between desire and thought, between salvation and truth. Neither antiquity, in which philosophy played the leading role, nor the medieval age, in which theology played this role, knew such an abyss. A person of an earlier era believed that if he found the truth, he would save his soul; and a 'naive' person still believes this. However, a person, informed by modern science, who knows that life is nothing more than a 'whirl of electrons', nothing more than a 'conglomerate of physical-chemical reactions', nothing more than a 'mechanism for the transformation of energy', or simply and briefly a 'false problem' – this person knows that the cognizance of truth and the salvation of his soul are incompatible things.

Up until a certain time the church was the only institution of truth and also of salvation. However, the onset of modern science proceeded under the banner of truth, and the church, deprived of authority in matters of truth, also lost authority in matters of salvation. However, when it became apparent that modern science is indifferent and alien to human fate, human beings started on the one hand to flee to more tangible things, and on the other hand to turn back tentatively to the church, or in some cases to found new, more free-thinking ones. And so, on the whole, it can be said that we are in a situation in which we have a choice: either truth at the cost of salvation or salvation at the cost of truth. In spite of many attempts at reconciliation, what was written around half a century ago by free-thinking theologian Auguste Sabatier[5] still applies: 'The antithesis today is so acute that church theology, as it wanted to live in a certain arranged and interim peace with modern science, decided to ignore it, and modern science decided to ignore church theology.'

However, modern science and theology can succeed in living in arranged peace, when each cultivates its own world of ideas for itself. But how is peace possible between an intellect captivated by modern natural science and a heart rising upwards, when both – intellect and heart – have made up their minds to settle down in one body, in one being, and to struggle for dominion over this being?

---

5   French Protestant theologian (1839–1901).

I would say that it was precisely this impossibility of reconciliation between science and religion that contributed to a large extent to that fact that people started to grasp at more tangible things and to the fact that modern theories, which evaluate the world of the spirit as a mere ideological superstructure of material and economic reality, capture the state of affairs – even if not for the whole of human history, then certainly at least for the present. If such evident and irreconcilable opposites as science and religion are able to live side by side in peace, then I think that there is no better way to explain this than that they are conducting their real battle for existence and nonexistence on another field than the field of cognition and religious faith. For instance, you do not need to be endowed with any special power of sight to see that science and the church are actual powers precisely to the extent that they are material, technical, economic, and political powers. This strange human ability to think in one world and live in another world enables science and religion to live in mutual peace in the world of ideas, even though – and possibly precisely because – they are in conflict in the material world.

Humankind could not have produced the modern natural scientist as long as it both thought and lived in terms of religion. Therefore, when this scientist came on the scene, he gradually had more and more dealings with the church as a political and economic power than as a religious one. The victory of his science was more a question of conquering this material power of the church rather than its diminishing spiritual power. Until he had developed in technology an adequate weapon for this battle, he found himself more often in a real fire than in the fire of learned discussions. The behaviour of priests had no less influence on the creation of natural scientific methods than the behaviour of things did. Many scientific principles prescribe simply doing the exact opposite of what theologians do. Thus, for example, every orthodox scientist holds the conviction that 'the exclusion of the transcendent is a necessary negative requirement of any kind of scientific thinking'.

The necessity of the battle with the church gave rise to the fact that one of the leading principles of the scientific search for truth is defensive, negative: for science scientific truth cannot be in any way a revealed truth – that is, a truth spontaneously received from somewhere. This is the reason why, in the search for truth, science cannot share with anyone or anything; why in the search for truth it does not acknowledge a division of labour; why – for it – art, religion, philosophy cannot be regarded as knowledge; why science cannot recognize as true anything that makes a claim to truth until it has strained this claim through its test tubes; in short, why for the natural scientist there is no truth outside of natural science. Science cannot acknowledge as a reality anything for which internal affirmation, internal participation or faith are necessary; it cannot acknowledge anything that does not flourish under a sceptical approach. It has good reasons for this. It says: we are deceived by tricksters; we are deceived by our senses, by our own imagination and logic. However, all of these reasons are not enough to prove that it is not possible that there exists a certain reality that requires of us more faith than doubt.

To this day, many scientists in the course of their work do not neglect to refer to priests and the battle against them. American chemist Clifford C. Furnas in no way hides the source of his 'Aristotelian' joy over the success of reason. He writes: 'If life, even the very simplest form, is ever synthesized it will be a sad day for the clergy, because the implication that man is nothing more than a complicated form of laboratory product would be a little too much for even the most liberal cleric.'[6]

I guess, my dear friend, that the opposition of many scientists, including you, against the so-called spiritualist direction in current

---

6   Clifford C. Furnas, *The Next Hundred Years: The Unfinished Business of Science* (New York: Reynal & Hitchcock, 1936), p. 141.

science has the same roots. In a review of one popular science book you wrote: 'It is necessary to reject absolutely every inclination toward spiritualist and anthropomorphic science, if we are not to fall back once again into mediaeval darkness, under the yoke of a new mysticism, a new theology, new priests.'

My dear friend, let us try to foresee how the magnificent adventure of modern science may end – whether in mysticism or in something else. However, it makes no great sense to speculate about whether the mediaeval age or anything else is 'dark' or 'light', until we have established, on the one hand the share of what someone lives and experiences in the reality of the world, and on the other hand the share of what a person thinks in this reality.

I know that you are quite dejected at the thought that life and the world could be something that it is impossible to show to people during the light of day, without hypnosis and suggestion, without theatrical illumination, by a simple appeal to human reason. However, I ask once again whether in the end your explanation of life and the world are not determined more by the nature of priests than the nature of things; and whether the extremity of religion is not driving you to an opposite extreme.

In order for religion to save mankind, it proclaims this world a delusion; science, aiming to save this world, proclaims mankind a delusion. But at the same time it annunciates the truth to mankind. To whom? To a delusion?

You reproach religion for having, against all truth, torn mankind out of nature, out of its natural rules and order. But what does natural science teach us? That the human soul in the world is something so heterogeneous and alien that a human being must shed its humanness in order to approach the order of nature even a little; that the natural order knows nothing of human beings ('a false problem') and that the world does not need humankind for its harmony. Does not natural science build a higher barrier between man and the world than any religion has ever done?

There is no doubt that, if natural scientists were to imitate the behaviour of priests and were to use their knowledge for mysterious ceremonies, then we would kneel in dread and admiration before scientists and would laugh at priests as at pitiable bunglers. However, in this way I ask myself how it can be that the same mistrust that I hold toward the view of the world induced during mysterious ceremonies in the gloom of candles and the mist of incense, I also entertain toward the sober, dry words put forward by an honest man who is trying to make life and the world comprehensible to me by expelling secrecy and ecstatic rapture from thought.

A human being is simply not capable of belief. He is not capable of being convinced of something, as long as his being remains divided in two. And today it is not merely divided in two; today it is split into many parts, of which each part makes a claim for everything, for the entire human being. This corresponds peculiarly to the process of splitting up that has occurred at the same time in the field of science itself and which has led to the formation of numerous specialized fields of science, each of which lives more or less independently within its demarcated section of phenomena, but from there tries to explain the entire world. In this way, it makes all other fields of science merely a part of itself, in precisely the same way that each splinter of a human being declares the entire remainder as a part of itself. Even within the limits of science itself the division of labour is a deception.

To the fundamental questions of life and the world, today a human being receives such strange replies as: I, as a theologian, cannot truthfully say anything other than ...; I, as a biologist, cannot truthfully say anything other than ...; I, as a chemist ...; I as a psychologist, economist, statistician, lawyer ...; and so on.

I ask what should a being do who is neither a priest of this church or another, nor a biologist, a sociologist, an economist, a member of guild X or Y, but who feels that primarily he is a mere human creature and that he needs to hear something like this: 'I, as a human creature, cannot truthfully say anything other than …?' Oh yes, here is the stumbling block. A human creature who wants to live as though it has all its limbs in the right place, all directed toward one and the same purpose, all of a sudden feels like a monster, a freak, a conglomerate of separate pieces stuck together. A human creature who wants to believe that the elements of his soul were born and grew like the limbs of his body out of a natural need of cooperation, finds out all of a sudden that these elements of the soul and of the body became entangled with each other in order to mutually deceive each other, to fool each other, to throttle each other. He learns that, if he wants to attain the truth, then he must place on the throne of judgement his heart alone, his liver alone, his stomach alone, his sexual organs alone … and everything else he must silence, anaesthetize, and obliterate from himself. Are we born as freaks, or is this entire dance of truths a colossal monstrosity? Is the form into which we are born monstrous, or are our truths monstrous? The chemist, for instance, demands that feeling has nothing to do with chemistry. Very well! What, however, does chemistry have to do with feelings? What is very strange is this: one organ silences the other organs and arrogates for itself the right to produce its own truth as the truth of all. And a being who feels a desperate need to remain a whole being, not crippled, not eviscerated, who does not want to be a mere brain, a mere stomach or sexual organ on the flagstaff, receives from the guilds and the social associations the mark on his forehead precisely of being crippled, restricted, immature, the mark of dilettantism.

Tell me, Melin, if you feel the necessity to argue using the phrases: I as a biologist, sociologist, economist, and so on, cannot truthfully say anything other than … Do you not feel at the same time that in this way you are fleeing for help to a guild for it to give testimony about something on its responsibility, while within you yourself something categorically demands that you give a different testimony about this? – Is this not something like admitting: 'I do not entirely believe this, but I have given my word that I will not say anything different'? – Is it not like admitting: 'I, as a biologist, physicist, economist, am saying something which I could not say as a person'? – Not to give answers about matters such as other people have agreed to give answers to them, but rather to convey only your own feelings, this would place you in the ranks of fantasists and perhaps even liars. To answer something other than what you feel, this does not exclude you from the ranks of scientists, the experts of truth. What, then, is truth? Is it a monster produced by us, or are we monsters begot by it?

If a biologist speaks as a human being, he speaks thus: 'From a value so supreme as is the love of two people among others becomes in Christianity fornication.' (Úlehla) If a biologist speaks as a biologist, he says: 'The young man in spring will never believe that love is only a matter of molecules.'[7]

These two statements open up before us the entire abyss between the human world as a matter of thought and the human world as experienced. Here we have in a nutshell the spiritual crisis of modern man, a crisis comprising an incomprehensible conflict between truth and salvation. However, it is precisely in the fact that this divergence of truth and salvation is felt as something unnatural, something against sense, that we can find comfort that a human being in this world is not a monster or something deformed, an alien and disparate element, that the fundamental conflict between the world and the human soul is an artificial conflict, a deception. A human being can only be saved by values, but science has nothing other to offer him than molecules. However, humankind does not trust salvation without truth, and cannot reconcile itself with a truth that does not bring it salvation. That is why we can also see that preachers of salvation also preach truth, and that preachers of truth also promise us salvation.

The truth of the preachers of salvation – that is, the truth of theologians and priests – has not fundamentally changed since the times

---

7   Ibid., p. 50.

of the 'dark mediaeval era'. Accepting this truth entails dealing with science by simply turning one's back on it. It still presents itself as a *teaching based on faith* (that is, something that you should believe) and not as a *branch of knowledge* (that is, something about which you can and should persuade yourself). And where teaching based on faith shrouds itself in the vestments of scientific truth, bountifully substantiated by scientific literature, we learn things such as this: 'Against the direct creation of each human soul the objection arises that this requires from God constant miracles. A miracle is something outside of natural law. The creation of the soul is not anything outside of this natural law; on the contrary it completes the natural law. The Creator himself – the first cause – intervenes directly in a work that surpasses the forces of a secondary cause. The product of a birth is the body, as it is not possible to give birth to a spiritual soul. According to the natural law, which God himself established, at the moment when there is given a natural disposition and the conditions for giving life to the body, God creates the soul. In this way, *God acts in the physiological order, not the moral order, and so he acts in goodness according to the natural law even in cases when the begetting of people is against the moral law.*'[8]

Let us turn now to the salvation of the preachers of truth. We will leave to one side those who, in a similar way to Sir Oliver Lodge, attempt to reconcile science with religion and try to fool themselves and us into thinking that the truth of science does not contradict salvation through religion. About these people, Albína Dratvová[9] says: 'They devote the best energies of their youth only to their scientific research and turn to philosophy only in the period of their old age, of the deterioration of their powers. They often, then, view sceptically their own researches; they see the limits of knowledge and ex-

---

8   Metoděj Habáň, *Psychologie* [*Psychology*] (Brno: Edice Akordu, 1937), from the chapter 'On the Creation of the Soul'. (author's highlighting)
9   Czech philosopher of science (1892–1969).

press themselves pessimistically about the possibilities of the further progress of knowledge. And here in their senile weakness they seek peace for themselves in a faith in a higher being, in God. ... What they write about their world view is bland and jaded.'[10]

The remaining preachers of truth – that is, those scientists who promise salvation from science itself and not from religion – can be divided into spiritualists and materialists. The first group revive humankind's hope by attempting to show that there is no difference between the human soul and the basis of the world. Sir James Jeans, for instance, writes: 'If a certain kind of wave-motion seems capable of describing something in reality to a very high degree of probability, we may proceed to discuss the further question – "Waves of what?" Here, for the first time, we are confronted with difficulties, since the real essence of the "What" must necessarily remain unknown to us, unless it should prove to be of the same general nature as something already existent in our minds, such as a thought or mental concept, a wish or an emotion. ... We shall find later that the waves which are most important of all in physics can quite unexpectedly be interpreted as being of this type. They are waves of something which the scientist loosely describes as "probability". ... Present-day science adds that, at the farthest point she has so far reached, much, and possibly all, that was not mental has disappeared, and nothing new has come in that is not mental.'[11] Similarly, Bernhard Bavink writes: 'Matter will only be finally subjugated by mind when we are really able to understand it as the product of psychical powers. Merely to postulate this as a fact, which is all that spiritualism has hitherto done, is not of the slightest use; matter and its worshippers, the materialists, simply laugh us out of court saying: Here is a single atom, the simplest of all, the hydrogen atom. Show us what you can do! Show us how we are to understand it as the product of purely

10 *Český zápas*, vol. XXVII (official weekly of the Czechoslovak Hussite Church).
11 James Jeans, *The New Background of Science* (New York: Macmillan, 1933), pp. 62, 296.

psychical potencies – then we will believe you. Now it appears as if spiritualism today can actually pass this test. I will not maintain that it has already passed it, but I believe it to be undeniable that it is very close to doing so, and has every prospect of success.'[12]

Philipp Frank, who in his booklet *The Collapse of Mechanical Physics* cites this faith on the part of Bavink, adds sceptically: 'Let us hope that there are still enough people to be found who will deny this.' And in reality, we do not even need to be enemies of priests for us not to promise ourselves anything very encouraging from this test, which is supposed to discover the bridge from the soul to matter. Because if such a bridge from the soul to matter is demonstrated in a scientific laboratory, then all the reasons for jubilation will be on the side of the materialists. A bridge discovered in such a way will be evidence that the 'spiritual' and the 'material' occur on one level, and in every case that will then mean: *on the material level*. Because either there is no precisely ascertainable bridge between, for instance, love and the movement of molecules, or love is nothing other than the movement of molecules. The 'physical' level is immovable. Higher levels can only fall into it; however, no other level can lift this physical level up higher to its level. Just as the method of the spiritualist is the same as that of the materialist, so also is the currency of both the same. 'We will not understand anything until we express everything in physical-chemical terms,' says the materialist (C. Furnas). And the spiritualist: 'We must admit that the souls of our greatest geniuses – Aristotle, Kant, Leonardo, Goethe or Beethoven, Dante or Shakespeare – even at the moments of their greatest flights of thought or during their deepest mental and intellectual work were conditioned by causality and were merely instruments in the hands of the all-powerful law ruling the world.' (Max Planck)

12 Bernhard Bavink, *Science and God*, trans. by H. Stafford Hatfield (London: G. Bell and Sons, 1933), pp. 94–95.

And which law that rules the world? The one to which exact natural science wields the keys in its hands.

However, even if it were not for the materialist requisites that spiritualist natural scientists use, there is something else here that makes us sceptical toward them: this is their attempt to present to us the real world as a world that is exclusively a product of thought, a world that can be entirely conceived in logical and mathematical terms. And we have precisely characterized the crisis of modern mankind as a conflict between his world as a matter of abstract thought and his world as actually experienced. If we designate the whole of reality to the first world, not only do we not reduce this conflict, but on the contrary we intensify this conflict to an extreme.

It remains for us to take a look at how materialist natural scientists hope to bring us salvation. Because indeed our salvation – this is apparently their affair, not ours. Even though, for instance, in one book by V. Úlehla (who regards himself as an agnostic) we read that the author disapproves of the Messianic idea – that is, the idea that some third person will bring people salvation and that it is enough for them to merely wait and make no efforts – in another of his books the same author advises us to bide our time until the biologist has progressed a bit further. Biology certainly has enough time, but we must do something with our lives; we must decide immediately, incessantly, from one minute to the next. And what is strange: we must decide in such a way as though we already knew; we can only set out as though we were already sure what is at the end of the path. Is this self-deception, the wrong path? Do you think, then, my dear friend, that the task of all this endless procession of people past, present, and future was, is, and will be to wait with their hands in their laps, until this or that researcher solves the riddle? Until it is discovered, with final validity, what is truth, what is error, and what is a lie? What is correct, what deception, and what bad? But if it is not our task to sit around and wait for this, then in the final instance what substantial can we derive from the scientist's solution to this riddle after all?

So, it is not enough to give advice to wait. More is necessary; at least promises, and not any old promises. To promise more than religion promises is not possible. But people are far from giving preference to a person who promises less ahead of someone who promises more – even if 'less' means the truth and 'more' mere confusion and unclarity. From its very beginnings, science has not ceased to show that, even though it promises less than religion, in reality it gives more: that it gives reality instead of a phantom. And thanks to technology and its fantastic gifts, science is able to divert our attention to some extent from its gloomy conclusions. However, all the achievements of science, technology, and civilization take on the disturbing form of a phantom, as long as the unabating threat of death remains alongside them. Even you certainly see: as long as death is the unavoidable lot of humankind, consolation has more value than instruction, and religion is more essential for mankind than science. This is why all the magnificent gifts of technology are not sufficient; more than giving, science must also promise. And thus we see that the more popular that scientific treatises become – that is, written for a wider circle of people – the less sparing they are in making promises and offering rosy prospects. Here we hear from the mouths of scientists words such as these: 'For the meanwhile death appears to us as a necessary evil … but it does not appear to us as fate. The laboratory of the biologist and the biochemist can and must go into battle with it.' – 'Biology today cannot avoid the question of immortality.' – 'In its essence life is of cosmic character.' – 'Why should it not be possible one day to ascertain and calculate this spirituality?' – 'It is a fundamental characteristic of life not to die.' – 'Neither old age nor death is a necessary and unavoidable characteristic of life.' – Unusual phrases are beginning to find their way into the speech of scientists: 'the law of the conservation of spirituality', 'spirituality as a free state in space', and so on.

However, as we have seen, while the church offers – at least on its noticeboards – to bring salvation to people by its values, natural science has nothing more at its disposal for this task than molecules. While for religion the salvation of a human being is a matter of his soul, for science it is a matter of his body. A perfect opposition of extremes also occurs here. A biologist leaves the phantom of 'soul' to charlatans and dilettantes; he believes that he alone will reach the root of matters by himself, if he concerns himself exclusively with the body. The means of salvation in its essence cannot be of a different character than the means against a headache or against constipation. Perhaps the surgeon will also have something yet to say on this subject.

Dear Melin, give some thought to your work, to the method of your research, your approach, testing, the very principle itself of your science, which you cannot violate if you wish to remain a scientist, and indicate to me – even if only in the most general and notional terms – how you envisage such a redemptive work.

Maybe, after a pyramid of experiments, you will succeed in fabricating artificial life, uncovering its secrets, and putting together a recipe for immortality? What will happen then? Will this be followed by a debate at the Academy of Science and a discussion in the specialist and popular press? Imagine this world-shattering 'ultimate truth': How are you going to find a measure of sufficient reason to test it? And, when finally – 'even though relatively young' – you make a breakthrough with your discovery, what will happen after that? Will biologists confer immortality with an injection? Or will pharmacists reproduce pills of 'eternal life' in crucibles, and a human soul will receive salvation if a person swallows a tablet and drinks it down with water? And this without examining one's conscience, without repentance and confession, without self-flagellation? Or ... But no, my dear friend, I do not want to continue making facetious jokes at your expense. It is not a matter of jokes; in reality all these questions are posing you a serious question: Do you truly believe that something so revolutionary and miraculous for the human soul, something liberating it for eternity, is going to be obtained so cheaply? As you can buy a chocolate bar for a sixpence? As you can catch a bus for a few pennies? And is it going to be available for anyone whosoever? Wise and stupid, brave and cowardly, noble and base, industrious and lazy, believers and unbelievers – quite simply anyone who pays? Do you really believe that mankind can be saved by something that can be standardized and mass-produced like paper clips or lollipops? Does it not occur to you that, if you were right, then technology – that triumph of natural science – would already today offer humankind something entirely different from what it does in fact offer?

I recall that, when – while working as an engineer in the factory of our uncle – I built a tourist cable car to one difficult-to-reach summit, I had no doubt that by doing so I was contributing to the refinement and progress of mankind. Even though I know very well that, whenever I have honestly climbed up a hill somewhere, then the pleasure I got from reaching its summit – no! more than pleasure, something character forming, internally cleansing and uplifting – was directly proportionate to the effort that I expended in climbing up it.

Such, I think, is our problem: We have a mountain in front of us and we feel the need to climb it. Experience tells us that whoever reaches a higher point on its steep slope acquires more characteristics that make him 'more perfect' – as we say. And all of a sudden you have an idea: Why bother toiling to climb up it? We will build a cable car and everyone can reach the summit comfortably and without effort. As a scientist, you are convinced that the being whom you transport in comfort up to the summit by cable car will be the same being as if he had clambered up there himself. But, as a mere person drawing on your most elementary experience, you know that this is not true. Today I do not doubt that by my cable car I have not civilized any tourist; maybe myself a small jot. And

I think the same of you: even if you were to find the recipe for immortality in your test tubes, by this you will not save any souls – with the exception perhaps of your own. Precisely as you have not saved, or even civilized, humankind by the dynamo, elevators, aeroplanes, artificial silk, or aspirin.

Here you may perhaps object that this argument leaves the matter still far from resolved. It is not possible to give a serious reply to the question of the value of individual effort – and in essence this is what is at stake here – without at the same time dealing with the problem of development, heredity, and so on. We will really deal with this issue later, in its proper place. However, we can already say in advance that, for our task here – that is, for the question of human salvation or at least human perfection – eugenics is pretty much all that we gain from the field of development and heredity.

H. G. Wells's novel *Men Like Gods* describes a utopian society which owes its blissful existence to eugenics, conducted in an exemplary way for many ages. However, this is a fictional construction. Those who survived the Second World War are witnesses of the lamentable end of a society that wanted to make a eugenic utopia a reality. If we search for the causes of such deplorable ends, then this conclusion cannot escape us: before eugenics can really get started, it is necessary for some people to declare themselves as higher and more perfect than others, and by doing so to secure for themselves the prerequisite for denying others the right to life. In view of the fact that such self-preferment requires from people a quite specific nature and character, it seems almost impossible for a planned and munificent practice of eugenics to go down any other path than the appalling one that it has just recently gone down.

In the end, moreover, we can notice that the researcher's advice 'Wait until biology has progressed a bit further' can also have a different sense than the one that we gave it, and precisely the opposite sense: it can serve as an appeal to us, already born and living, not to wait for biology, because this 'further' does not concern us. Whom it does then concern, C. Furnas reveals to us, when he predicts a day when life will be designed like a laboratory product. Furnas no longer has anything to say about what will follow from that, but it is described for us in a very lively and intense way by novelist Aldous Huxley, grandson and brother of biologists with the same surname. He cannot, therefore, be suspected of insufficient scientific training. His novel *Brave New World* shows a blissful world of laboratory products. There is no pity in this world, no suffering, pride, envy, greed, desire – in short, none of those miseries that annoy us in life. Everything is mixed and prepared so excellently according to scientific recipes that, for instance, a garbage man, who is 'moulded' in an artificial hatchery, is the happiest person in the world only when he is collecting his garbage, while if you were to make him, let us say, a millionaire, then he would hang himself out of grief. Or a typist knows no greater delight than tapping her delicate fingers on the keys of a typewriter and would become despondent if you were to arrange a role in a film for her. In this world, therefore, 'climbing up mountains' is no problem. Any kind of effort is superfluous, because the cable car runs reliably from the bottom up to the summit and conveys everyone according to his liking. The most burning questions of moral, social, economic, aesthetic, psychological, and metaphysical nature have been solved and resolved by a chemist in his test tube. Molecules are sufficient for everything.

The truth, however, is that not even for a chemist are molecules sufficient for everything. Let us hear what Clifford C. Furnas himself has to tell us about this: 'True science shuts all doors against emotion from the very beginning. Usually there is a high wall with no door in it that rises between the emotional and technical fields of the scientist's life. But do not get the idea that the scientist is the unemotional fish that the caricaturist would make him. Outside working hours, he is, on the average, just as full of loves, prejudices, superstitions, likes, and dislikes as anyone else with the same degree of education. You will find a goodly proportion of them belonging to orthodox churches; not only belonging but attending, but that does not prove a thing. It does not indicate that there is no combat between science and religion, it just shows that there are two compartments in these men's lives and that they are supernaturalists on Sunday and naturalists on Monday.'[13]

We will not argue about who is a more appropriate object for a caricaturist: whether a person with one pigeonhole or with two. However, let us recall this: the end of ecclesiastical hegemony and mediaeval truth is posited in connection with the 'moral dissipation of the priesthood', with the fact that one day church dignitaries preach zealously against gluttony, fornication, and murder, and the next day themselves engage in fornication and robbery. 'Service to God' was an excellent wager for a priest who reckoned that the truths that he preached were guaranteed by God and a powerful church, and that he could therefore live in any way he pleased. Today it is possible to ask whether the scientist is not descending into the same mistake. Is he not shifting responsibility for the truth that he declares onto the 'all-powerful natural law' and science, while he reserves for himself the right to live in the way he pleases? Where is the guarantee that the reality of this law is composed of some other cloth than the reality of God once was?

The truths declared by the church collapsed as lies and deceptions, when it was shown that those who preach them do not live according to them. The truths declared by science vex us as mistakes and deceptions, when it is shown not only that scientists and scientifically educated people do not live according to these truths, but also that human life as such is absolutely not possible in accordance with them. 'The more and better I recognize the laws of the world, the less I have reason to live and act,' says Auguste Sabatier. And Tolstoy in *Anna Karenina*: 'The organism, its decay, the indestructibility of matter, the law of the conservation of energy, evolution, were the

---

13 Furnas, *The Next Hundred Years*, p. 136.

words which usurped the place of his old belief. These words and the ideas associated with them were very useful for intellectual purposes. But for life they yielded nothing.'[14]

Quite simply, a scientist is a person who has on his side all the reasons for putting a noose around his own neck. But nevertheless, as far as I know, so far no person has ever ended their life 'for scientific reasons'. And you say that I do not prove anything by this? I think that this proves this much: if findings such as 'life is nothing more than a whirl of electrons', 'life is a false problem', and similar reflect reality, then the only thing that must immediately follow from this reality would be extinction; at the moment when a person in accord with reality discovered that he is a mere delusion, he would breath his last. However, given that, even after this recognition, he continues to breathe and even goes forward with no less courage and no less effort, we can justifiably doubt that these findings capture reality.

Consider, my friend: If your reason comes to the conclusion that we are at the end, and despite this you do not throw in the towel, what do you prove by this? That inside us, inside our being, there is something that is very far from throwing in the towel when our reason comes to the conclusion that we are at the end; and that therefore in the final instance it is not reason that decides whether we are at the end, or we are not; and that therefore it is not a natural scientist who, with you as his mouthpiece, appeals to us not to lose hope. It is possible that physics and life mutually exclude each other, but everything in us revolts against acknowledging that life and truth exclude each other.

The question that caused the fall of theology was: Can we be saved by something that runs counter to the truth? The question on which natural science falters is: Can something which does not save us be

---

14 Leo Tolstoy, *Anna Karenina*, trans. by Constance Garnett (1901) (New York: Random House, 1965 – Modern Library edition, 1993), p. 888.

the truth? If mankind is not a freak in this world, then truth and life cannot be opposed to each other. Then reality is not merely a question of truth, but also a question of salvation. Then the nature of truth and the conditions of salvation are merely two different terms for the same thing.

The salvation declared by theology contradicts truth; the truth declared by natural science contradicts salvation. If a human being is not a monstrosity, then theology and natural science have deviated from reality to the same extent; then the nature of truth is deformed by natural science to the same extent as the conditions of salvation are deformed by theology.

My dear Melin, you are perhaps shaking your head at why I am writing all this to you? After all you wanted to hear about Robert. Therefore I hasten to assure that I am not writing about anything else than about Robert; more than that, my intention is nothing other than to let Robert himself speak. However, Robert's speech is not your speech; artistic speech is not scientific speech. Therefore it may seem that I am taking upon myself the role of an interpreter for you. Well yes, that is my intention, but I add immediately: this is an absurd task. Why, then, do I take it up? Precisely so that I can demonstrate to you its absurdity; and in order to demonstrate as absurd what you regard as possible and achievable, something that you also attempt as possible and achievable on a daily basis in your laboratory and that subsequently leads you to conclusions which are a source of misunderstanding, confusion, and iniquities, and possibly something even worse.

2
CRAYFISH MARCH

EVERY ONE of us who lived in Robert's milieu became accustomed to modelling his form for ourselves in accordance with a silhouette captured in the blink of an eye in the frame of a window of our offices, factories, chapels, or our peaceful homes. In the tough framework of our everyday order, this fleeting shadow incorporated for us the irresponsible and derailed life of a tramp, and we knew next to nothing (nor even wanted to know) about the fact that the old wooden shed in which he found refuge was also a workshop – a workshop with hard discipline and a workshop of values, albeit of values immeasurable by the mechanism of our values, by quantitative performance, and by items in ledger books of financial accounts. To translate these values into another form of speech – as we have said – is an absurd task. However, there is perhaps some kind of hope that that these values will became closer for you, and more comprehensible in your own immediate form of expression, if you do not decline to enter Robert's workshop with me and there – in its field of vision and with a kind of hindsight – you will look back at yourself and all those others of us who with our distorted mirrors shaped Robert's external form, and by doing so also shaped his external fate. Even if we are going to try to understand Robert's world in our own language, not in Robert's, we will not err in our judgements if we constantly subject to the test their suitability and load-bearing capacity for the task to which we have entrusted them.

At the beginning let us repeat this: the behaviour of priests has had no less influence on your research and on your language than the behaviour of things has had. Priests had the means of salvation, and for them this was at the same time also the means of explaining the world. You have turned their explanation into a delusion and have offered an explanation of your own. However, in the course of time it has become increasingly clear that the scientific explanation of life and the world leaves some kind of remainder, obstinately evading you, but on the other hand unusually welcome for a priest. The causal, or ultimate, explanation of life and the world has suggested the idea of the so-called first cause and ultimate or final purpose, and thus it has not only failed to eliminate a point of view that inclined to divide the world into a visible and an invisible part and to call the first the world of effects and the second the world of causes, but in the end even strengthened this point of view. You, who had your own good reasons to search in the visible world not only for effects but also for causes, have sensed the danger.

And that is why you have categorically pronounced that a cause cannot be of any other kind of nature than an effect, and therefore that, if an effect is a phenomenon, then a cause is the same phenomenon. This means: if there is no cause that has no further causes, then there is also no cause that is not at the same time also an effect. Or, in other words: the first cause and also the final cause have been removed. You have freed the straight line of causality, resulting in a mystical immeasurableness, from mysticism by turning it into a circle. From this moment on, explaining life and the world belongs to obscure actions; a scientist does not explain, a scientist describes. What is above description, that is anthropomorphism, and that contradicts the real nature of the world. The question *why* appears as a curse; only the question *how* remains.

Let us quote, from Úlehla's book *Thoughts About Life*, some citations that make clear what this orthodoxy aims to be and what it does not aim to be. 'Mathematical conditionalism leads to a mathematical understanding of all events. The last vestiges of metaphysical colouring that perhaps still adhere to the concept of conditions are removed when, instead of this concept, the mathematical concept of a factor, a coefficient, is introduced. Events are then divided up into factors that relate to each other functionally like variables in a mathematical equation. Factors in a certain group of factors change mutually with regard to each other, when one of these factors changes: these are dependent variables. ... However, inside the system there are also factors that change without regard to the system; with respect to this system they are independent variables.

With regard to the system they form a group which we call the external situation. In the external situation, therefore, every factor is an external condition with respect to the system and as a rule it is an independent variable. The system, then, appears with respect to external factors as a compound dependent function. ... According to mathematical conditionalism, all conditions are in essence equal; however, each of them can become more important, because each of them can become a limiting condition. There are no permanent causes. There is also no cause before the existence of general laws; causality is not the basis of general laws – in fact under mathematical conditionalism the principle of causality is abolished altogether. ... Every system is a function of (internal) structure and the external situation. ... It can be said that causality *explained*, while mathematical conditionalism *understands*. ... We should not ask why things happen, but rather how they happen. ... Mathematical conditionalism does not perceive any capitulation or resignation in such a decision. It derives its approach from its successes. ... For mathematical conditionalism, the problematic nature of life does not lie in its essence. It lies in the human incapability of discerning and expressing all the conditions from which the phenomenon of life is composed. ... Because not even when all the conditions comprising the phenomenon of life have really been discovered and the relations between them studied and expressed, will things turn out better for human beings. The phenomenon of life will be dismantled into its conditions; it will be dispersed in these conditions. ... Mathematical conditionalism, therefore, takes reality, empirical experience – as it appears to us – and tries to express it according to mathematical principles. It adopts a critical stance primarily toward the insufficiencies of human cognitive capability. Everything that appears to this human cognitive capability and that can be expressed in conditions, is in essence equally valuable and equally law based. ... This is not to say that colours are nothing other than a refraction of light in drops of water. ... This is not to say that if we were to close our eyes, then there would be darkness and emptiness and only the movement of atoms. This is not true. The refraction of light in drops of water is one of the conditions of a rainbow in just the same way that the these drops of water are a condition of it, just as the retinas in our eyes, and our mental capacity, our capabilities of perception and recognition, and many many other factors are also conditions of it. ... It is quite unjustified to extract any of these conditions and to say that a rainbow is nothing other than ... If we understand this implication of mathematical conditionalism, then all reality will seem to us even more beautiful, more colourful and rich than this reality seems to simple naïve thought.'[15]

I apologize, my dear friend, for this long citation, but I cannot shorten it in any way, if I am to remain fair to you and also to Robert. Mathematical conditionalism, therefore, promises us that, through a mathematical description, it will capture the reality of life and the world more perfectly than anyone could do in any other way. Let us investigate whether it can or cannot fulfil these promises.

A functionalist system, 'in order to get into operation', requires then at least one independent variable, which is usually posited outside the system; this is certainly correct, because inside a closed system no member itself can of itself become an independent variable. This would lead to a notion of some kind of mysterious source of power – that is, to mysticism. However, this notion of closed systems and external independent variable quantities is only a methodological aid. The demarcation of systems is artificial, notional. In the same scientific reality, every external 'independent' variable is a member of many other closed systems, or *de facto*: it is not really independently variable and the entirety of the world is one single closed system of dependent variables. 'It is certain,' writes Dratvová in her book *The Problem of Causality in Physics*, 'that the opinion that a cause is a sum of conditions has substantial deficiencies. It is

15 Vladimír Úlehla, *Zamyšlení nad životem* [Thoughts About Life], (Praha: Život a práce, 1939).

necessary to limit ourselves to necessary and sufficient conditions, but there may be so many even of these conditions that we could end up going on ad infinitum. Therefore, physicists have had no other option than to denote a cause as a sum of conditions which they have agreed upon as causal.'[16] And Jan Blahoslav Kozák[17] writes: 'As all things are in some way interconnected, there are no such facts as an elementary process in the universe.'

In fact, the principle of the conservation of matter and energy already says the very same thing. If, according to scientific faith, all substance is subject to mathematical laws, then there is really no self-contained system and external situation, but rather the whole world is a system. So, then: 'The refraction of light in drops of water is one of the conditions of a rainbow in just the same way that the these drops of water are a condition of it, just as the retinas in our eyes, and our mental capacity, our capabilities of perception and recognition, and many many other factors are also conditions of it.' – Take this statement seriously, think it over, and you will see that, without some kind of Laplacian formulation of the world, no thing of nature can be expressed mathematically completely and without remainder. That is: every kind of phenomenon of nature is a function of the whole remaining entirety of the world. Even according to mathematical conditionalism itself, it would be necessary to conceive the whole world as one single closed system for us to be able to deduct any phenomenon from its equation without remainder.

For a functionalist system, it also applies that we can replace any kind of condition with the explained phenomenon (and vice versa); thanks to this, a functionalist law is a 'perfect description, one that is precise in mathematical terms. However, it is not an explanation, because it is not possible to deduce from it which phenomenon is

---

16 Albína Dratvová, *Problém kauzality ve fyzice* [The Problem of Causality in Physics] (Praha: Česká akademie věd a umění, 1931).
17 Czech theologian, philosopher, and politician (1888–1974).

a cause and which is a consequence.' (Dratvová) But this is precisely the aim of mathematical conditionalism: to be a perfect description and not to explain; to be satisfied with *how* something happens and not to countenance the question of *why* something happens. But is it even true that this conditionalism succeeds at least in explaining to us *how* something happens?

We know that a closed system needs 'external independent variables' in order to get into operation. However, conditionalism itself does not permit in the entire empire of natural events any factors that do not depend on other factors. In actuality there is no closed system to which some kind of 'outside' – in the sense of natural scientific space-time – would belong. So, if space is a single closed system of dependent variables, then where is the constant impulse? Where is that independent variable that maintains it in motion?

Let us observe more carefully how it is that at least notionally – that is, in our thought – a mathematical formula is sufficient to bring nature into operation. After all, a mathematical equation as a schema for a system of dependent variables shows us only the conditions in which the world is in balance, at rest; what it shows is a world that is immobile, solidified, dead. In order for us to acquire the notion of a world that is in motion, in which things are happening, already in school we get accustomed to use the magic formula, which then functions quite automatically in us. This is the phrase that every student has heard countless times and has also parroted himself: 'Let us imagine for a moment one of the factors as an independent variable!'

What does this apparently innocent aid really mean? If we are requested – for the conception of some event – to regard one of the factors, which in (natural scientific) reality are all dependent functions, as an independent variable, then this means nothing other than that mysticism, which has been banished with such vehemence through the front door, is now being quietly allowed back in again through the back door. For us to explain natural events according to the instructions given in scientific textbooks, we are supposed to accept into our thinking as a 'didactic aid' something which otherwise a natural scientist rejects and pillories as 'metaphysics'.

In this way I come to the view that this conditionalism still owes us a reply not only to the question why something happens, but also to how something happens and even the question of whether something happens at all. Not only does it not explain, but neither does it describe, and nor will it describe until it shows us an 'independent variable' of the factual system of 'dependent variables' that we call the universe.

Nature seen through the eyes of a natural scientist falls apart into a duality: into a dead, passive material and into laws. In his opinion, an explanation that does not make exclusive use of only these two concepts is unscientific. A natural scientist also admits that the existence of the empire of laws is mysterious and problematic, but he 'draws his stance from his successes'. Experiment! he exclaims. Carry out an experiment and thus show that I am not right, even though I have such astonishing successes!

My dear Melin, allow me then an experiment, even if one of a rather unusual nature. Allow me to examine some machine, let us say a flying aeroplane, and while doing so to be guided by the same principles that you are governed by in your investigations of natural things. If, then, I did not know that a flying aeroplane is the work of human hands, then as a natural scientist I would proceed perhaps thus: First of all I would shoot down the plane, by doing which the pilot would probably be killed and would possibly also fall to Earth somewhere far away from his plane, which would make my work much easier. However, even if he remained in the plane, then sooner or later I would 'eliminate' him as an anthropomorphism, as a mere mirror of myself. Then I would dismantle the plane down to the last screw and I would carry out thousands of all kinds of different experiments and tests, during which I would doubtlessly shoot down a load more planes; I would describe them, compare them, and I would notice that in many respects they differ and in many respects they are similar and then I would certainly classify them. And in an attempt to provide a definition of a plane, after a series of mechanical, technical, physical, chemical, and other experiments and analyses, I would compile some mathematical equations as an equivalent of the thing called an aeroplane.

You will notice that we could not understand a flying aeroplane from these equations. Precisely thus we do not understand things of nature from similar equivalents of natural science: living and non-living bodies, wagtails, anemones, stalactites. You will possibly smile and ask what exactly I want to prove by such a simple-minded example. I do not want to prove anything; I only want you to stop and think about this: *the existence of a living being or any natural thing at all is precisely as incomprehensible to us, from the standpoint of natural science itself, as a machine that has been made and put into operation by human hands would be if we were to imagine it as a natural creation.*

A parallel between an experiment and a natural event turns out the same way. The circumstance that, for instance, you can induce or destroy the 'sacred feeling of motherhood' by intervening in the function of internal secretions, or that you can change a normal being into a madman, and vice versa, by adding or taking away a pinch of iodine, serves for you as eloquent evidence that natural science is correct when it explains natural events to us as an analogy of laboratory experiments, 'only with the difference' that what is unthinkable in a laboratory without an experimenter happens in nature 'of its own accord'. An experiment requires material, laws (at least hypothetical ones), and an experimenter. However, you say that for the same event that in one case requires three factors, in the second case (in nature) two factors are sufficient. Then, however, it is no surprise when *from the standpoint of natural science itself a natural event is just as incomprehensible to us as an experiment conceived as a natural event – that is, as an experiment without an experimenter – would be to us.*

A laboratory experiment in the final instance proves this and only this: *scientific laws and material and an experimenter – these allow us to make sense of a natural event.* The reason why we do not understand nature in the explanation of natural science is that it describes living and non-living natural things as machines without a constructor, and natural events as experiments without an experimenter.

Cognition, if we understand this as an explanation, necessarily requires three elements: materials, laws, and a prime mover. (It is necessary to understand laws in the sense of descriptive laws, not causality. The concept of a cause includes both laws and also a prime mover, and it is precisely this that in the eyes of scientists lends the concept of cause an 'obscure' character. Nevertheless, however, the scientist does not make too much effort to rid his new concepts – whether law, condition, or function – of this ambiguity, because this ambiguity makes it easier for him to ignore the prime mover even when he moves from causality to descriptive laws, or as he himself puts it: from mysticism to science.) If natural science has renounced explaining in favour of mere description, this means that it ventures to suffice with the two elements and to exclude the third – that is, the prime mover. And, if natural science has also been successful with this approach, this is because: 1. In the case of *explanation* it replaces the prime mover with the notional magic formula of an independent variable, and 2. In the case of *experiment* in practice it replaces the prime mover with the experimenter, but without actually reckoning him as one of the actors of the experiment. The lesson that follows from this is that it is not possible to describe without it also being necessary to explain.

It is not possible to talk about laws without it also being necessary to talk about prime movers. If a scientist says that 'all-powerful laws govern the world', then he is attributing to the concept 'laws' the full content of the concept of cause; he says laws, but what he means by this is laws and also prime movers. It is only the more solid sound of the word *law*, in contrast to the profaned *cause* – despite their identical content – that is supposed to arouse the impression that the prime mover has become superfluous.

If we inquire why science should want to make do with a means of explanation that is pared of one of the three necessary elements, we can reply easily. Firstly, this expelled third element points to a field that is inaccessible to the instruments and equations of science, and which has therefore been declared by science as illusory. And secondly, there is someone here who bases his raison d'être precisely on the existence of this third element and uses it as an argument – and correctly uses it as an argument – against science. And this someone is religion. Religious noetics has a firm buttress in the essential assumption that an explanation of the world and its events is not possible without a notion of a prime mover. However, despite this, a religious explanation is no less restrictive than a natural scientific explanation. This is because religion, for reasons of feeling and other motivations, attributes to the prime mover more than he *logically* has a right to. In the trio comprising material, laws, and prime mover, all members are equal to the extent that they are all equally necessary. This means that each of these three elements is in a certain sense contingent on and limited by the others. However, it is irreconcilable with religious notions and feelings for this prime mover – God – to be something contingent and limited, even for instance limited by a given material or by given laws governing the shaping of this material. A developed religious sentiment requires a prime mover as an absolute being, unlimited by anything. Therefore, a religious explanation must suffice not with two elements, but with only one. Because it has solely a prime mover, it must make do without laws and without material. The elements of the explanation then change thus: In place of a prime mover an all-powerful God, in place of laws God's will, and in place of material 'creation from nothing'. The prime mover becomes a creator.

If we return now to the elements of natural science, we can see that natural science insists precisely on those two elements that religion denies, and denies the sole element on which religion is based. We can surmise that both the natural scientific and also the religious explanations of life and the world are deformed, and this in some kind of opposite, competing, and mutually complementary sense. By the way: those who are tempted, in view of this 'complementary' character, to attempt a reconciliation between science and religion aimed at sticking them together in some way, overlook that science cannot in essence be other than it is, and religion cannot in essence be other than it is, and that therefore every reconciliation between them is at the expense of one or the other. The orthodoxy of religion depends on the fact that, apart from an all-powerful prime mover – God – it does not recognize the other elements; the orthodoxy of science depends on the fact that, in addition to the given materials and given laws, it does not recognize a prime mover, in whatever kind of form this presents itself.

The objects of natural scientific investigation are 'physical' – that is, weighable, measurable, and calculable – and they cannot be otherwise. Something happens with this physical thing, but in this physical itself there is no factor that is capable of providing a reason for, and a clarification of, this happening. And, even if such a 'physical' factor was to be postulated, this would mean that something originally entirely independent – something that cannot be captured and expressed in natural scientific terms, something non-physical – comes into connection with the physical; that is, it appears in scientific formulas, without any kind of justification or grounds being given for this. The non-physical becomes physical, the mathematically inexpressible becomes mathematically expressible. This is not only in evident conflict with the principles of research (for instance, with the principle of the conservation of matter and energy), but also from the scientific point of view simply nonsense. This would be the end of all researching and calculating. On the other hand, however, as we have seen, if we are to acquire some notion of events, then – in the equation of a natural system, none of whose factors is in reality an independent variable – we must assume one of them as an independent variable. This leads us to the necessary conclusion that the principle of events does not lie in transformations of the physical into the physical; that we cannot find the explanation, reason, and sense of transformations of the physical in these transformations themselves. Quite simply that the physical itself cannot give us an answer to the question as to what is happening with this physical, or as to why and how it is happening. Transformations of a physical substance and a quantitative order of such substances occur here because *there is something else here as well.*

This *something else* bothers many natural scientists and thinkers more than orthodoxy itself bothers them. And it bothers them rightly. Because not to concern oneself with this means giving the last word in everything – even in natural science – to theologians. But what should a natural scientist do here? His position is truly tricky. The less he restricts his explanation, the more he sins against scientific rigour. The conjectures of the vitalist scientists, or respectively the spiritualist scientists, about a prime mover and bearer of events are admissible for official science only as the private sphere of their authors. This 'private' prime mover of events, in comparison with the official God of theologians, indisputably has a greater logical justification so long as it presents itself as a third factor alongside material and laws, and not as an absolute of itself. However, it has practically no hope of ever being recognized '*de iure*' in its existence by exact science, even though '*de facto*' it is recognized (for instance in the magic formula and in the experimenter). The main difficulty lies in the fact that – as Professor Bohumil Němec[18] writes – 'we are not capable of envisaging how a factor without energy can intervene in a material event in which energy is present, given that every change of this event presumes the overcoming of a certain resistance and the performing of certain work.'

18   Czech botanist (1873–1966).

The scientifically most acceptable solution of this difficulty is offered, as far as I know, by the vitalist Hans Driesch[19]. We can envisage his 'entelechy' as a force that acts on a certain system without changing the system's 'energy balance'. Some well-known examples: 1. If a force acts perpendicularly on the movement of a physical system, then its work is zero. For instance, the sun's gravitational force bends the orbits of the planets without performing any work on them; or an electron is diverted from the direction of cathode rays by a magnet without its kinetic energy increasing or decreasing as a result of this. 2. Similarly, a miller can use a water surge and transform its kinetic energy into potential energy and then later free it once again, without the energy balance being changed by this. 3. Entelechy could add a certain amount of energy and then take it away again, so that the energy balance would be once again the same.

One possible objection that can be raised against the vitalists is that, though they explain 'living' matter with their prime mover, they neglect the fact that 'non-living' matter also moves and requires for its explanation a prime mover. The impreciseness of the concepts 'cause' and 'law' enables the vitalists to introduce a dualist conception of material – that is, a 'dead' matter that is governed by simple laws, and a 'living' matter that over and above this is also governed by an initiating prime mover. We know, however, that a prime mover is necessary in both these cases, whether evident or concealed in another word.

Driesch's examples show us a prime mover as a factor that can be eliminated from equations in the form of a force of zero value, but which cannot be entirely divested of its 'physical' nature. Therefore, it does not pass muster as a member of the trio of material, prime mover, and law.

By the way: notice how the expression 'independent variable' can become a new source of unclarity. As a member of a mathemati-

---

19 Biologist and philosopher (1867–1941).

cal formula it has the character of a rule, a law; as an *independent* variable it has the character of a prime mover – that is, something that cannot appear in an equation of exact science. We can see that 'independent variable' is virtually identical with 'cause' as whose demystified successor – that is, as a successor of the discarded prime mover – it is regarded.

Either a prime mover is a member of a natural scientific formula, but then it is not an independent variable, and therefore neither is it a prime mover; or it is not and cannot be a member of a natural scientific formula, but then it is not a scientific concept and natural science must ignore it, in whatever form it presents itself, whether philosophical, theological, or some other form. Very often, natural scientists are not sufficiently aware of this character of the prime mover. For instance, an increasing number of scientists do not avoid the concept of soul/spirit in their notion of a prime mover. If they understand this concept 'non-physically', then they are evidently philosophizing, respectively theologizing. However, if they want to count it, to trace it in some way in their laboratory, to record it, then – as I have already mentioned – they meet the materialist natural scientists on the same level. A spiritualist chemist expects that chemistry will explain everything to him, just as a materialist chemist does: even how the human mind, which thinks up chemistry, arises from matter; this chemistry, thought up by the human mind, is then used to help explain how the human mind arises from matter, and how this human mind then thinks up chemistry, which in turn … and so on, ad infinitum. This and also that want to calculate the prime mover of events; they want to calculate the one who … Do you not see this vicious circle? The prime mover of events, if he is proved in an exact way, proves by this that he is not the prime mover of an event. A soul, if it were ever to be measured and calculated, would by this only prove that there is something else further beyond it that cannot be measured or calculated. If we promise ourselves that one day we will even succeed in calculating spirituality, then we are merely deferring something that cannot be cleared away from the world: the question of just exactly *where* is that particular something that cannot be measured or calculated, but without which it would not be otherwise possible either to measure or to calculate.

A popular means of cracking this tough problem of the prime mover is to dispatch it from the world by simply attributing movement to matter as an 'original state'. The apparent simplicity and self-evidence of this thought is alluring for many. However, quite apart from the fact that in reality we become entrapped in extremely problematic metaphysics, we do not help natural science one jot by this, because we do not rid it of the need to use a magic formula and an experimenter. The prime mover continues to haunt us in an undiminished measure.

We have shown that cognition, if it is to be logically possible, requires three explanatory elements: materials, laws, a prime mover. To cognize 'nature' then means to divide it into its material, the rules for the formation of this material, and the actor that forms this material. Natural science, when investigating nature, measures and weighs matter, discovers and calculates rules, but does not find a prime mover. An attempt at an explanation using just two elements collapses; a mere description also collapses. All historical revolutions and reconstructions of the very bases and principles of natural sciences can be attributed to the account of this mysterious prime mover, which is not – and never can be – an object of exact research. It is this prime mover that with logical urgency barges its way into the workplace of even the most orthodox scientist and turns his science into 'mere' philosophy, a popular public lecture, a subjective opinion, a private matter. Later we will see what deeper connections lie in this phenomenon. But now let us look at the entire matter from another perspective.

Our hitherto deliberations have led us to the opinion that a prime mover is neither of a physical nor of a law-based nature, so far as we understand the terms 'physical' and 'law-based' in a natural scientific way. So, what then can its nature be? If a prime mover is neither a material nor a law, then it is something that should not be sought or found at all in the field of vision of natural science – that is, something that cannot be denoted other than as 'metaphysical' or 'transcendental' or, for instance, merely as 'spiritual' or 'mental'.

It is evident that this cannot be a case here of metaphysics or transcendence in that absolute sense as preached by theology and idealist philosophy of all times; this metaphysical, transcendent, or spiritual *something* is nothing more than an equal member of the trio comprising material, laws, and prime mover, and therefore not only does it not banish material and laws to the empire of mere appearances, but on the contrary assumes them as natural scientific objects and forms. An experimental proof of this prime mover is impossible, and a speculative proof is worthless. However, if we were to show that material and law in nature are the same as they are in natural science, then by doing so we would also prove this prime mover, and this in its metaphysical, transcendent, or spiritual character, or in short its non-physical character – for the meanwhile it is not important exactly what word we use.

However, before we attempt some such thing, let us consider one more possibility. Let us grant that a prime mover could also have merely a *logical* existence – that is, that it could be a necessary requisite of an explanation, but not a reality of what is explained. Let us ask what consequences this would lead to. This question immediately gives rise to a further, more fundamental, question: What is an explanation? What is its relation to the reality that it explains? If a prime mover is nothing more than a logical rule, if then a prime mover in reality corresponds to nothing, then material and laws, if reality is comprised of only these two, cannot be in this reality what they are in an explanation comprised of three elements: $a + b$ cannot equal $a + b + c$. Then material and laws in reality are something other than material and laws in the explanation of this reality. Or to put it another way: if a prime mover is merely a logical rule, then material is also merely a logical rule and laws are as well. You will perhaps remark that we thus find ourselves in a world marked by the name of Kant, in which explanatory elements correspond to *a priori* schemata and the explained reality corresponds to the unknowable 'thing-in-itself'.

However, this is not the case. If nature, on the one hand, is for us a problem of *cognition,* on the other hand it is for us *experience,* an unproblematic fact. The thing that, on the one hand, we ask about, is something that, on the other hand, we are accustomed to live, something with which we are intimately acquainted – we understand it, we comprehend it, we interact with it without difficulty. Therefore, this is not a case here of a Kantian opposition between phenomena and the unknowable, but rather of an opposition between a rational problem and an experiential fact. To speak of an explanation as a mere 'logical rule' does not yet necessarily mean understanding it in the sense of Kant's *a priori* concepts and transcendentalism; our deductions lead us to a quite different conception without this decreasing the 'distance' between the 'logical rule' and nature. If – as we have said – our interest is concentrated on the opposition between a rational problem and an experienced fact, an experienced event, then Kant's problematic exists entirely in one half of this opposition – the first half (from the *Critique of Pure Reason*). The second half of our opposition contains only concrete things and events; and if you want to make a problematic thing out of such concrete things, then it is necessary to shift to the first half and ask: What is this thing? It is only then that the world can divide into two parts for us: into a world of 'appearances' and a world of 'things-in-themselves'. But both these parts – that is, the entire Kantian problematic – takes place on one side of our problem. That Kant himself felt this 'halfness' we can see, on the one hand, from the fact that he wrote further critiques, and also from the fact that he subordinated his grandiose *a priori* cognitive apparatus to experience.

We have deduced that material and laws are to constitute nothing more than a logical rule on the assumption that a prime mover is nothing more than a logical rule. However, this was only an assumption that was dictated by the special character of a prime mover. This character leaves us no other possibility for its proof than a deductive, purely logical proof, which as a proof of an existence other than logical does not have any great value. Therefore, we have no other choice than to focus our attention on material and laws and – so to speak – to examine these things themselves in order to verify whether they are, or are not, more than a logical rule.

If we can prove that material and laws are the same in nature as they are in natural science, then by this we will also indirectly demonstrate the existence of a prime mover, and moreover in its nonphysical character. Then we have shown that theology and idealist philosophy may be correct, albeit with the proviso that then at the same time natural science and materialist philosophy are also correct. Because, if matter is really to be ascertained as 'matter', then this means that a prime mover will be ascertained as immaterial, but this without any damage to its reality. However, if we prove that material or laws are merely a logical rule, we will have shown that the prime mover – and thereby explanation – is also merely a logical rule; that the explanation of nature is one thing, and nature another.

What is material? Where does this question come from? If a 'naïve' credulous person finds himself face to face with some thing, he simply takes note of this, becomes conscious of it, or – as some psychologists say – he finds himself face to face with it because he has become conscious of it; for the meanwhile such matters of finesse are not relevant here. However, a doubting person, a thoughtful person who observes the flow of changes and is accustomed to reckon with the possibility of error and deception, is not always sure whether 'this thing' is this thing and whether it is not in fact another thing. Such a change of fundamental stance – and we will see later how decisive and revolutionary this change is – was taken to an extreme in an inquisitive and investigative person, and cultivated in a consequent method. For this person, for a thing to really exist, it is not sufficient simply to become conscious of this thing; but rather every thing, if it is to really exist, must be 'demonstrated'. The guiding principle of such a demonstration is the question: *Which other thing is this thing?* We can easily see that this principle leads to some kind of endless chain, reminiscent of the chain of causes and effects. And, just as in that case we were led with logical necessity to an initial cause, to a original cause, so here we are led to a notion of an initial material, an original material, an essence. In short, this principle expresses an identical principle. We can notice the similarity in character of these two endless orders, the 'material' and the 'causal'. In the case of the two original explanatory elements, material and cause, just as cause has proved to be composed of two elements, prime mover and laws, so material also shows itself to be composed of two elements: appearances and essences. These duos behave in a certain sense similarly. Laws are the parts of cause that are accessible to science, while prime mover represents the inaccessible part; similarly, appearances are the parts of material that are accessible to science, while essence represents the inaccessible part. This is enough for us to suspect that essence has a purely logical existence and for the meanwhile to pay no attention to it. It is also the case that natural science, by abandoning the aim of explaining, has renounced not only the prime mover, but also essence, as imperceptible, inaccessible things. However, naturally natural science could not renounce essence also as something perceptible, because, if it were to do so, it would become a pure tautology and would lose all theoretical and cognitive value. Therefore, it transferred essence to the world of appearances and is trying to discover it as an unchangeable 'ultimate reality', one that is no longer further divisible.

In his Prague lecture on the meaning and boundaries of exact science, Max Planck says about this: 'The aim is the creation of a depiction of the world, the reality of which depiction no longer needs any improvement and which, therefore, represents ultimate reality ('*endgültig Reale*'). For us it is a matter of indifference here if a natural scientist doubts whether this aim will ever be achieved by science. It is sufficient that his belief in absolute reality in nature is firm, unshakeable by any obstacles whatsoever.' However, this 'ultimate reality' represents – it seems – a similar magic formula in the 'material' order as an 'independent variable' represents in the causal order. It is supposed to be that exceptional place in the ring of things from which all things arise and to which they return again. However, there is no reason why any one place in this circle of things should have a claim to this special standing, just as there is no reason why any one variable in the circle of causes and effects should have a claim to independent variability.

It is worth embarking on a little retrospective to show in its broadest outlines how this special expedition in search of 'ultimate reality' in a world of mere appearances has proceeded and where it has ended up.

If we return in thought to the time when science, religion, and magic were merged in one, we will see that living and non-living things were on the whole what they appeared to be. And even after their perishing, they did not actually perish, nor blend into some kind of 'original material', but rather, in the form of spirits and similar entities, remained what they were until the process of forgetting eventually erased them from the world. There were as many ultimate realities as there were things. However, over time the number of these perceived ultimate realities decreased, as did the richness and variety of their forms. The ancient Greek philosophers, who already distinguished between philosophy (together with science) and religion, knew hardly four or five of them. However, thus far these elements retained a concrete, tangible character: earth, fire, water, air. However, the beginnings of modern-era science are already marked by an invisible reality: atoms and molecules. And today even these as a final reality have fallen; they have been dismantled into electrons, protons, and neutrons, or now even into even more ethereal things such as energy, waves, mathematical thinking. And what is characteristic here: in every period it has been true that the only thing that really exists is the only thing that there was at the beginning. For science today it also applies that *what really exists* (as an ultimate reality) *is what there was at the beginning.* What do we see here? It is as though natural science, hastening toward the decipherment of things, has not followed the direction of events, but rather has proceeded in precisely the opposite direction: the greater the progress made by science, and the newer, the more modern the picture of the world that it depicts for us, at the same time this picture is older, further removed in the past. For exact science, substance is always precisely what at that moment science regards as the initial substance. How can we explain this 'crayfish' – walking backwards – approach of science? Natural science, proceeding from more complicated things to simpler things (dismantling them into their conditions), from human beings to animate things, and then further through living tissue and cells to organic and inorganic materials, down to elements, atoms, electrons, and so on, eliminates things from the picture of the world precisely in the opposite order from that in which, according to the conjectures relying on science itself, they entered the world. Science, therefore, while desiring to arrive at an ultimate reality, gradually eliminates from nature everything that we could call its past, its history, its development. The search for ultimate reality conceals within itself the assumption that from the beginning of the world until now nothing real, nothing fundamental, has happened or is happening.

Let us inquire where this 'crayfish march' of natural science may end up. If we leave to one side Heisenberg's uncertainty principle, which for the meanwhile has announced the end of this march, the goal appears to be that notional state of substance, when none of the things of nature existed, and when therefore there was no difference between being and natural laws; that is, a state which – if we remain with the mathematical laws of natural science – strikingly resembles Jeans's 'thinking of the mathematical thinker', or quite simply: pure mathematics. What can we expect from the achievement of this aim for our understanding of the world, of life and of us ourselves? I think that the question that will be necessary to solve at this moment is the same question that we have posed exact science ever since that science has existed: Where is the logical bridge leading from a mathematical formula to a dandelion, to a fish, a bird, a human being? And we guess that, if natural science has not given us an answer yet, then it is all the less likely to do so in the future when – as can be judged – it will expel even more of that which it is supposed to explain from its laboratory.

We shroud the dark beginnings of the universe in the word 'nebula', a word that tells us nothing. This nebula, which tells us nothing and into which exact science is hastening to immerse and dissolve everything living and non-living, is – as it seems – mathematics. The mathematician and philosopher Bertrand Russell, for whom mathematics is otherwise 'absolute knowledge', has said that in mathematics we never know what we are talking about, but that it seems that what we say is true. Emanuel Rádl[20] puts it in this way: 'Why could we not substitute cabbages for people for some value in a mathematical equation? The accuracy of the calculation does not change.' Mathematics is valid for all things, and therefore it does not express any of them, just as the initial nebula is the 'material' of all things, and therefore it is also none of them. Mathematics as a text of substance is an equivalent to the notional germinal nebula; from this it is even further to real things and an understanding of these real things than it is from the heated ore in the crater of a volcano to a flying plane.

---

20 Czech biologist and vitalist philosopher, adherent of Masaryk's critical realism, opponent of positivism (1873–1942).

If a layperson speaks about a kilogram of plums, a certain amount of cement and so on, then the mind of an exact scientist perceives the words expressing weight and measure. However, for him words like 'plum', 'cement', and so on conceal a remnant of imperfect cognition and metaphysics, and he feels the need to express these words also in a mathematical way. Today the scientist regards it as necessary to capture mathematically – completely and without any remainder – even such abstract and bare concepts as electron, proton, photon, and others. And then finally nature and mathematics merge into one, or to put it more accurately, nature is replaced by mathematics. Natural science, which went out into the world in order to discover relations and laws among things, has perceived more and more clearly that the thing that hinders it the most are these things themselves, and it has concluded that if we want to achieve an exact and certain picture of the laws of things, then we must admit that these things really do not exist. And so, the situation today is such that, although we have perfect laws and relations among things, we no longer have these things themselves.

Let us hear Russell's own words: 'As a matter of fact, if anyone were anxious to deny altogether that there are such things as universals, we should find that we cannot strictly prove that there are such entities as *qualities*, i.e. the universals represented by adjectives and substantives, whereas we can prove that there must be *relations*, i.e. the sort of universals generally represented by verbs and prepositions.'[21]

In view of this, it is all the stranger that people and even scientists continue to live in such way as if the things around us and also we ourselves existed. And one can be surprised that, whether these things exist only seemingly or really, they exist at all. If mathematics is the only true substance, then it is difficult to understand why any-

---

21 Bertrand Russell, *Problems of Philosophy* (London: William and Morgate, 1912), p. 149.

thing at all exists outside of the mind of a mathematician, whether as an illusion, or in any other form; after all, mathematics attains its most perfect being in the mind of a mathematician, and so why then would it attempt to acquire a less perfect being anywhere else? If it is true that mathematics, in explaining itself, by doing so explains reality perfectly, then how is it possible that precisely 'less real' things seem to our minds to be the most real? How can we explain the fact that through the combination of some numbers an apple or a horse arises? If these things can be accounted for only by our imagination, by our figurative abilities, then it is clear that any kind of world discovered by mathematics, if we want to understand it in any other terms than mathematical ones, can only be accounted for by the use of our imagination; then it is simply the case that for everything that mathematics 'proves' it is not mathematics that is responsible, but rather the mathematician's imagination; then mathematics can prove everything for which a mathematician's fantasy is sufficient and which it dares to imagine. It is possible to understand why a natural scientist is reluctant to use any other language than mathematical language.

Mathematical judgements are extremely strange judgements. If a layperson says: this apple is red, ripe, tasty, the substance 'apple' remains an apple, and it is even the case that every further word makes the substance clearer, more definite and more indisputable. A mathematician, however, if he succeeds in assembling an apple with an algebraic formula, sees in this evidence that the substance 'apple' is a mere appearance, a false problem, and that in reality it is a case of something else. The more precisely you express a certain thing mathematically, the more clearly you prove by this that this thing as such does not exist.

If you ask exact science about a rainbow, for instance, then you will not receive a reply about a rainbow, but rather about a refraction of light rays. If you ask about the light rays, then instead of hearing about light rays, you will hear about waves and photons;

subsequently, photons and waves also disappear and are replaced by 'waves of probability', and in the end these also disappear and all that remains is pure mathematical thinking. A rainbow is at least a delusion merely of a 'naïve mind', but an entire branch of science is built on the delusion of 'rays': geometrical optics; the whole of chemistry is built on the delusion of 'atoms' and 'molecules'; and even physics itself is based on the delusion of 'waves', 'photons', and 'electrons'. If we arrive at a notion of the world as a pure mathematical event, then all sciences except mathematics must appear to us as a mere distraction with soap bubbles.

Today we view the mystic numbers of Pythagoras with an indulgent smile. However, what substantial difference is there between my saying that the key to understanding this nature is some mystical number *3* or *7*, or my designating as such a key the algebraic formula $a + b = c$, or the 'cosmic constants' – that is, the numbers *1,835*, *137*, *2 × 29 × 10^{39}*?

In reply to our anxious question concerning what the world is and the sense of all this, today we receive from an exact scientist the terse and Delphic answer: two and two are four.

This is how an expedition in search of 'ultimate reality' ends. And, if anyone still has the shadow of a doubt about the result of this expedition, then this doubt will be perfectly dispelled by Sir James Jeans. In a speech given in New York in 1931, he says: 'We can no longer, in the way that our fathers did, explicate the world as a mechanical game. We are ascertaining that an electron is not merely a solid part of a material or an electric charge, but is rather what physicists call a bundle of waves. ... A materialist will immediately ask: Waves of what? And the reply that we must give is: *waves of absolutely nothing*, because nothing has remained for science in which these waves could be transmitted or move forward. ... Therefore, we must conceive these waves as purely mathematical waves. They are, so to speak, a description, an explanation, and not a material. We can express them in mathematical equations; however, if in addition we attempt to express them as waves of some material, we at once find ourselves in a confusion of nonsense and contradictions.' (cited by Bavink in *Results and Problems of Natural Sciences*)

And after all, the famous Michelson–Morley experiment has even proved this 'nothing' experimentally. Here the emerging principle of a constant speed of light states that the bearer of light waves is something that can be neither carried away nor left behind, something which can be neither be added to nor taken away from (as in mechanics or in acoustics), something which does not exist, and yet nevertheless in some way exists – what, in short, is called a vacuum in physics, and by ordinary reason is called *nothing*.

In his book *Physics and Philosophy*, Jeans himself already talks clearly about material as a mere requisite of logic and grammar – that is, of an explanation: 'When it had become clear that light was of an undulatory nature, physicists argued that if there were undulations, there must be something to undulate: one cannot have a verb without a noun. And so the luminiferous ether became established in scientific thought as "the nominative of the verb to undulate", and misled physics for over a century.'[22]

If nevertheless the natural scientist's 'belief in absolute reality in nature is firm, unshakeable by any obstacles whatsoever', this certainty of his reflects a logical necessity, a necessity of an explanation, and not a reality of that which is explained. In short, the result is that *'material' as an element of explanation is merely a logical rule, which does not correspond to anything in nature.*

The simple consequence of this is that laws are also merely logical rules, which do not correspond to anything in nature. And, when we hear the natural scientist's creed that 'throughout the ages nature, both organic and also inorganic, has been guided in its creation, duration and extinction by a set of unchangeable and constantly

---

22 James Jeans, *Physics and Philosophy* (Cambridge: Cambridge University Press, 1943), p. 86.

identical laws'[23] (Professor Artur Brožek), then we can feel in these words – after all that we have already said – an all too evident logical insistence of the postulate, and not a natural immediacy of the given reality.

We are in Robert's workshop. Let us stand in front of his artistic works and ask ourselves what are the eternal and unchangeable laws that have created them. A chemist will reply that these are chemical laws, a biologist will say they are biological laws, a psychologist psychological ones, a sociologist sociological ones, an aesthetician aesthetic ones, a moral philosopher moral laws, a theologian God's laws, and so on. Let us not forget that all of these laws mutually exclude one another, because these individual special sciences can only continue to exist in that each of them postulates its own substance *sui generis*, its own 'ultimate reality', governed by a similarly specific set of laws. If any of these specific sciences was to concede that its ultimate reality, or respectively its set of laws, is transferable to a different specific reality and can be expressed by the set of laws of another science, then its theoretical and cognitive value would fall to zero. We have already seen that in the question of truth science does not recognize a division of labour even in its own field. This is also the reason why the positivist assessment of philosophy as the creation of a world-view and a life stance from the sum of the results of individual sciences makes no sense.

Let us agree that in the case of a work of art we will reserve competence for aestheticians, or possibly artists. What will we learn? That whenever someone has attempted to compose a work of art in accordance with some aesthetic laws that are given in advance, this will not give rise to a genuine work of art; even in the hands of a Goethe this will not be an original work of art. According to William Dilthey, 'The artistic laws set up by Lessing were *geradezu leitend* [directly guiding] for Goethe and Schiller. But anyone who believes

23 Artur Brožek, *Nauka o dědičnosti* [Theory of Heredity], (Praha: Aventinum, 1930).

that Lessing's views are realized in Goethe's or Schiller's tragedies, would be very much mistaken.' Hippolyte Taine dates the beginning of the creative decline of great artists (for instance, Michelangelo, Corneille, and others) from the moment when they started to work according to the rules that they had established in the course of their hitherto creative work. In other words, it is not only rules adopted from somewhere else, but even rules adopted from one's own completed works, that are insufficient for producing a work of art. Alois Vojtěch Šmilovský[24] writes to Václav Vlček[25]: 'Laws of fine art are all very well, but let the aesthetician seek them in me, and not I seek them in books about aesthetics.' Jan Mukařovský[26] states: 'The history of art, if we look at it from the point of view of aesthetic norms, appears to us as the history of revolt against the ruling norms.' About Leonardo da Vinci, Sigmund Freud notes: 'Solmi thinks that Leonardo's investigations started with his art; he tried to investigate the attributes and laws of light, of colour, of shades and of perspective so as to be sure of becoming a master in the imitation of nature and to be able to show the way to others. It is probable that already at that time he overestimated the value of this knowledge for the artist.'[27] 'The happy gift of the poet,' says Arne Novák,[28] 'is that he shows us life in its individual fullness and turbulent colourfulness; criticism, however, deduces from these living concrete experiences dry, abstract laws and general rules that apply for all. This activity of criticism seems to be absolutely deadly for every purely artistic conception, for every true poetic temper.'

There is no sense in multiplying the number of these testimonies. Books about art are overflowing with them. Let us also just recall the

---

24 Czech author (1837–1883).
25 Czech author (1839–1908).
26 Czech linguist and aesthetician (1891–1975).
27 Sigmund Freud, *Leonardo da Vinci: A Psychosexual Study of an Infantile Reminiscence*, trans. by A. A. Brill (New York: Moffat, Yard & Company, 1916), p. 23.
28 Czech literary critic (1888–1939).

fact of so-called folk art, and we can sum up that there is no artistic law before the birth of a work of art. However, just as we can say that there was no law of artistic works before a work of art, we can also say that there was no grammar of human speech before speech, no physical or chemical laws before matter, no biological laws before life, no psychological laws before the 'soul', and no sociological laws before human society. There is no law of things before the things themselves. Natural scientists have become accustomed to speaking about natural laws that govern the nature of things, even though the only speech to which their experience entitles them should be: the nature of things creates natural laws. Natural scientists try to persuade us that there are no things without natural laws, but the truth is rather that there are no natural laws without things.

However, if we prove that laws are only logical rules, then mathematics is not affected by this in any way, at least not for so long as mathematics itself remains a question for us and until we have resolved its relationship to the elements of explanation and logic in general. Until we have done so, then we will have nothing on which we could base an assertion such as this: 'Nature seems very conversant with the rules of pure mathematics, as our mathematicians have formulated them in their studies, out of their own inner consciousness and without drawing to any appreciable extent on their experience of the outer world. ... The universe appears to have been designed by a pure mathematician.'[29]

Let us return for a moment to works of art. Imagine, my friend, that as an exact scientist you listen, for instance, to one of Beethoven's symphonies, that you have the possibility of repeating it and studying it in any way and as often as you like, but that you know nothing about Beethoven, or about music and artists. In short, you approach it as a natural scientist studies a natural phenomenon and

29 James Jeans, *The Mysterious Universe* (Cambridge: Cambridge University Press, 1931), pp. 113, 115.

you try to comprehend its nature using the methods of your science. What do you ascertain? I would guess something like this: 'If two tones are to blend into one unified whole for our sense of hearing, then their frequencies must be in a relationship of small numbers. If, for instance, the relationship of frequencies is 3:4 (a perfect fourth), then for every three vibrations of a deeper tone, there will be four vibrations of a higher tone, and so they combine together in a consequent periodic vibration, which after a period equal to both the three periods of the first tone and also the four periods of the second tone is always repeated in exactly the same way. This calm merging in a new periodic event is then, in accordance with Euclidean geometry, the cause of the euphonious nature of this dual sound. ... We can easily ascertain that the fundamental consonant intervals are determined by individual prime numbers. ... In short, music is expressed in logarithmic intervals; for instance, the statement that a perfect fourth and a perfect fifth produce an octave can be stated numerically as $3/2 \times 4/3 = 2$ or $\log 3/2 + \log 4/3 = \log 2$.'[30]

This citation perhaps enables anyone to guess in advance what your reply would be in response to the question of the origin and nature of the 'unknown phenomenon' called Beethoven's symphonies. We can best understand it as the work of a brilliant mathematician: you would reply in some such way, if you did not know anything about Beethoven and his musical creation. However, as you know that mathematics was something completely alien to Beethoven, it would not occur to you even in your dreams to explain the creation of his works in this way. However, in the same way that in our example you have arrived at the idea of a musical work as the creation of a mathematician, natural scientists arrive at the idea of the works of nature as the creations of an (imaginary) mathematician. Well then, if a musical work is just as 'conversant with the rules of pure math-

30 František Nachtikal, *Technická fyzika* [Technical Physics] (Praha: Spolek posluchačů inženýrské chemie, 1931).

ematics' as nature is, and its creation nevertheless does not have anything in common with mathematics, where can we find enough support for the idea that the universe is the work of a mathematical genius?

And thus, even though we have not yet pronounced our final word about mathematics, nevertheless we can say in sum about its laws that they constitute a rule of the explanation of things, and not a rule of the formation and creation of things. The discovery of new laws in original works of nature and also in original works of humanity truly highlights in all its clarity the mystery of creation, because the true mystery here lies in the fact that a work is constructed according to laws that are comprehensible to our reason, even though real creation is absolutely unaware of these laws.

However, there is a type of work to which everything that we have said here about material and laws does not apply. These are human works of technology. In the case of a work of technology, material and laws are not merely the prescript of their explanation, but also the prescript of their creation and their 'performance'. A technician is a rational being who intentionally and systematically forms a *given* material on the basis of the *given* (discovered) laws of this material. We have seen that rational cognition requires a given material, laws and a technician. *Rational cognition is adapted to the explanation of technical works and processes.* Whatever our reason does not explain technically, it does not understand. Engineer Alexander Niklitschek in his book *Technology of Life* writes: 'To understand a fish as a submarine, a wild bird as a plane, a tree as a chemical factory, is easier than to follow an explanation that attempts to explain and describe living beings as, so to speak, themselves as such.'[31]

If a natural scientist says that an eye, for instance, is a masterwork of natural engineering, this means more than a mere metaphor. According to Niklitschek, 'In the development of an eye, na-

---

31 Alexander Niklitschek, *Technik des Lebens* [Technology of Life] (Berlin: Scherl, 1940).

ture has performed all the tests and gained all the experience such as a person does when he builds photographic and film equipment'. Either nature works like a technician, or a rationalistic explanation of natural events misses its aim. But nature does not work like a technician, because it is not a result either of a given material or of given laws. The principle of natural events must be different.

One of the most popular recipes of today is this: 'More technology, more technical thinking!' You are even no longer supposed to recount children fairy stories, but rather describe to them hydropower stations, blast furnaces, and so on. We can see that we are so suffused with technical thinking and technically viewing the world to the extent that we are almost no longer able to understand anything natural. The presumption of eternal laws of nature turns nature into a technical problem for us; the presumption of ethical norms with universal validity makes moral virtue into a technical problem for us; the notion of an all-powerful God makes religion into a matter of mere behaviour – a technical problem, and so on. Try to base your approach in any kind of thing whatsoever on given laws and act in accordance with them. Up until now, every law discovered has led to technique, and not to a new natural original; every artistic law discovered has led to a trade, and not to new works of art; every religious dogma has led to rites and ceremonies, and not to real piousness; every ethical, legal, social norm has led to nothing other than convention and social morality. A technical approach cannot get by without a notion of a rational law. And so an acting creature is either aware of the laws of his actions, in which case he has a command of these laws, as for instance the technician himself, or he is not aware of these laws, in which case the laws have a command of him, as for instance all 'lower' nature, but also artists and other people. A technician constructing a bridge is a master of natural laws, while Beethoven composing a symphony is a slave of natural laws, which he neither knows nor commands. This is the source of the inclination of technical thought to view contemptuously non-technicians, even if these happen to be Beethoven or Shakespeare, as blind kittens in the paws of their mother cat. A natural scientist who – as we have seen – needs to make do in his technical explanation with only material and laws, and without a technician, operates with an 'all-powerful' law. However, it is not possible to envisage laws as something that are effective and forceful in and of themselves; an all-powerful law can achieve precisely as much as an ordinance displayed at the town hall without any police force or goodwill on the part of citizens.

How can we understand that this all-powerful law, which is not even capable of causing a ripple on the surface of a puddle, is capable of directing the world and bringing life from its first primitive form to a fish, a bird, a human being? However, if you listen carefully to natural scientists, you will find that so far not one of them has successfully used this all-powerful law to explain the creation of anything living or non-living in this world; moreover, they have not even attempted to do so. Even though he has these all-powerful laws at his disposal, he nevertheless prefers to attribute the creation of all things, from the smallest to the largest and most complicated, to 'chance', 'coincidence', 'classification performed by little demons', 'probability', and so on.

The science of development teaches us that reason is the last segment of development. However, on the other hand, science explains natural events to us as events taking place according to rational laws for whose effectiveness and specific application – if it is thorough and sincere – it invents in addition some kind of transcendental brain. And thus, already at the beginning science presumes reason, which according to it is only supposed to appear for the first time at the end as the result of a process of chance and chaotic development. It is known that the higher the degree of development, the more difficult it is to capture this development in formulas, and therefore the less certain every prediction about it becomes. For instance, H. G. Wells writes about us human beings that 'we are pushed and driven by impulses and endeavours that have nothing in common with logic', but he silently accepts from science the idea that the lower a form of being is on the scale from a human being to atoms, the lower the form of substance, the more it is pushed and driven by logic. Human beings, who – as it seems – are the only creatures in nature to possess reason and the capability of logical action, are not governed by logic. However, in the case of other beings and natural things, the less they possess these capabilities, the more perfectly they are governed by them. A being with reason behaves illogically; a soulless piece of rock behaves 'logically'.

Natural science preaches to us that, in order for us to approach closer to the real nature of natural events, we should forswear anthropomorphism, that we should renounce the human element. This process of removing this human element lies in amputating our psychological properties to the extent that nothing else remains other than pure reason, mathematical reason. However, our hitherto deliberations force a different view upon us. We must ask: if a human being's reason is the final segment of the developmental order, then does not the insertion of this rationalistic principle into natural events constitute precisely this anthropomorphism?

Let us carry out a thought experiment. Let us try to de-anthropomorphize the world with this anthropomorphized reason. Let us take the brain of Jeans's imaginary 'mathematical thinker' and insert it into the head of the mortal person Jeans. We will immediately ascertain that this brain fits the head of the mortal Jeans much better than it fits the head of some kind of unimaginable and undefinable creature. It is simply the case – as we have seen – that there is absolutely no bridge between the mathematical thinking of this monstrous creature and the concrete things of our life and our world. We had to assign the task of bringing these concrete things into being to new creatures, little demons, and chance occurrences. However, if we know that Jeans, in addition to being a mathematician, is also a human being like any of us, then we also know immediately how it is possible that a group of numerals can represent a rainbow or an apple or a horse. To put this in another way: the formulas of a mathematician plus the experience and imagination of a human being give us a picture of a concrete thing. Everything 'human' that you have excluded in order to arrive at an equation of some thing, you unconsciously add in its full extent to this equation once again in order to obtain this thing. And it is only because of this that a mathematician, compiling his equation, sees the world almost just as richly and colourfully as a simple 'naïve' mind does. This is why a physicist bites into a nice juicy apple with the same gusto as a simple-minded child without having the concern that by doing so he will fill his mouth with grains of atoms. This is also why a biologist can find in love the 'highest value' in exactly the same way as a sentimental girl who has never in her life heard about the movement of molecules and internal secretions, nor ever will hear of them.

In the name of true cognition, human beings have set up a strange principle: the removal of the human element. However, much stranger is the fact that they regard this removal of the human element as consisting in the amputation of all their organs except the one that, among all creatures and things in the world, belongs to them and them alone: reason. The result of this is the only possible result: given that rational action is a type of action that is exclusive to human beings, there is nothing else that human reason can adequately recognize except for the creations of its own actions. And because reason is a technique that processes a given material according to given laws, it seeks to understand every thing as a technical work, produced by a technician from a given material and laws. However, we have seen that the attempt to explain a bird as a plane, a fish as a submarine, or a tree as a chemical factory collapsed, because it was shown that a natural process is not a technical process; it does not take place under the direction of a technician and it does not derive from a given material.

Natural scientific cognition started out from the things of the apparent world and by a 'crayfish march' eventually ended up at nothing. If we search for the reason why science went in this direction and arrived at this end, it becomes apparent to us that this is precisely because *it wanted to have everything given.*

Let us try to deduce from this the consequences for cognition and for natural events themselves.

3
FROM THE SURFACE
TO THE INSIDE

OUR IMAGINARY CONVERSATION with Robert is already indicating the direction in which we must go if we are to enter into his world. Let us follow it!

If, my dear Melin, we have concluded that 'ultimate reality' is only a logical prescription, then what we have actually shown by this is that among all natural things there is no one thing so privileged that – in opposition to all other things as transient and changeable – is itself intransient and unchangeable. The 'elements' of natural science, whatever they may be called in this or that period – today for instance atoms, electrons, photons, and other terms – are equal to all other things in being just as intransient and mortal.

Let us ask ourselves what this now means if I say that we will not understand anything until we have expressed everything, let us say, in physical-chemical terms. What am I saying when I say that I will explain, for instance, a frog in physical-chemical terms? To put this in everyday speech, it means that I am simply asking Peter what he thinks about Paul; that I am asking atoms and molecules what they 'think' about a frog. And molecules and atoms reply as much as they are capable of replying: that a frog is nothing other than a dance of atoms and molecules. If, on the contrary, we ask a frog what it thinks about molecules, it will say that they are dwarf-sized frogs. And it is the same with a human being: on the one hand a human being is merely a whirl of atoms, while on the other hand an electron is a miniature creature with rudimentary feelings, will, and thought.

Natural science investigates nature, natural things. However, if there is no 'ultimate reality', then the explanatory capability of all things is noetically equal: each answers for itself, or to put it more correctly each simply behaves according to its nature, and we take this behaviour as a reply to its questions. A human being, as physics depicts him, simply expresses the particular 'opinion' of an imaginary Mr. Electron on any matter of the world; a human being, as chemistry depicts him, expresses the same opinion of Mr. Molecule;

a human being, as depicted by biology, zoology, and so on, the opinion of Mr. Amoeba, Mr. Tadpole, Mr. Worm, and so on. We can free our opinion on life and the world from 'anthropomorphism', but only at the cost of submitting ourselves to 'molecule-morphism', 'frog-morphism', and so on.

If science awaits a final reply from 'ultimate reality', and this reality does not exist, then the reply toward which science is heading is the reply of *no one*, of *nothing*. But naturally science cannot pose questions to no one or nothing; it cannot observe the behaviour of nothing. It comes to its findings only by observing the behaviour of something, by investigating something. It is, therefore, evident that in expressing an 'objective' finding, it is always only interpreting to us the 'stance' of something. It is certainly correct, as H. G. Wells says, that 'in reality there is no possible view of the world from the point of view of an ant or a crocodile, because their interest does not reach that far'; however, it is sufficient that a human being is capable of imparting such an interest to crocodiles and ants. A molecule knows nothing about a frog, a poplar tree, or a stalactite; nevertheless, despite this, a researcher relates the answers of a molecule about a frog, a poplar tree or a stalactite. But let us proceed!

When discussing Bergson's '*élan vital*', Julian Huxley and H. G. Wells write that this *élan* is nothing other than 'the elementary chemical properties of living matter, idealized and personified.'[32] Let us leave *élan vital* to one side and inquire instead what the authors are really hiding under the term 'elementary chemical properties of living matter'. They say: 'Living matter has, as its basic property, the power of metabolism and self-reproduction; and it varies.'[33] That is magnificent. The basic chemical properties of dead matter were combinability, separability, valen-

---

32 H. G. Wells, Julian Huxley, and G. P. Wells, *The Science of Life* (New York: The Literary Guild, 1934), p. 638.
33 Ibid.

cy, and so on; the basic chemical properties of living matter are the capability of metabolism and self-reproduction, and variability. If we proceed further, then we will come to the indubitable conclusion that thinking, feeling, and desiring are the fundamental chemical characteristics of brain matter. In this way of course chemistry explains everything.

But what prevents me – in accordance with many examples – from starting this explanatory approach from above and from replacing the word 'chemical' with, for instance, the word 'spiritual' and thus coming to the conclusion that combinability and separability are fundamental spiritual characteristics of atoms and molecules?

According to Vladimír Úlehla, 'a chemist cannot bond an atom to another atom and is not even capable of doing so. He merely provides an opportunity, and the atoms bond themselves together.' If a chemist is not capable of this, then I ask what it actually means when it is said that something is happening in physical-chemical terms? A breeder of poultry or cattle does not himself give birth to new types of varieties; he also merely provides an opportunity and the varieties are born themselves. Do we, therefore, know what we are actually talking about, when we talk about gravitation, attraction, combinability, valency, and so on? And, if we say that life is merely a conglomerate of physical-chemical reactions, do we know what we are actually claiming and what we are denying? If I say that the 'soul' is a property of matter, then by this what am I saying in favour of materialism? What is any kind of thing without its properties? What remains of chemistry if, for instance, I say that love and hate are merely chemical properties of organic matter? What prevents me from taking as my starting point what is given to me directly and from looking at events in matter, in the way that Empedocles did, as expressions of love and hate? Is not, then, chemistry merely a new name for the soul? And if we speak about separability and combinability as properties of atoms and molecules, can we be sure whose position we are actually defending? A materialist one, or a spiritualist one? Or some third position? Therefore, we can say: as long as the chemist gives his elements the opportunity for them themselves to do this or that, as long as he does not do and collect everything himself to the very last hair, until then it is not possible with a good conscience to use chemistry as an argument in the disputes between materialism and spiritualism. And what if the chemist succeeds in this, and matter is reduced to a mere technician's material?

As we can see, if physics and chemistry do not explain even the events in their own fields, how could they then explain everything? Of course it is not only the ambition of physics and chemistry to explain everything, but the ambition of every science! Every substance *sui generis* has a tendency to be the only substance, 'the ultimate reality'. In the end, does this not merely show that every branch of science remains enclosed in the field of things and phenomena for which it was founded? And if each of these branches defends its raison d'être by a tenacious attempt to prove that the field of phenomena that it investigates is a substance *sui generis*, by this is it not actually defending the idea that things, respectively processes, are non-transferable?

Here we run into a question that has fundamental significance for us. This will appear in its full breadth for us, if we relate it to Robert's case and pose it in this way: What essential knowledge will we acquire about Robert and his work if we try to learn about it through chemistry, biology, psychology, sociology, ethics, religion, economics, statistics, and so on? Is it, for instance, necessary to search for what makes art art in physiology, sociology, ethics, and so on, or respectively in some kind of sum of all these things? Whoever answers yes to this question commits himself to demonstrating to us a traversable bridge between art and this or that, or possibly between everything. If the natural scientist, the moral philosopher, the economist, the theologian, and so on do not have such a bridge, then it is necessary to ask from where exactly they take their right to judge art by a scientific, moral, or economic measure and so on? Is this right not founded on an exclusive acknowledgement by any given discipline of its own autonomous existence, and a denial of autonomous existence to everything else? We should recall immediately that there are entire systems of thought that attempt to show that they have found a traversable bridge between various fields of being; the most systematic and serious of these interpret this bridge simply as natural and historical 'development' and endeavour to demonstrate their objective reality by gaining acceptance as a science, as a 'science of development'. However, if a science of development is possible, then how can specialist sciences, which are premised on the non-transferability of certain things and phenomena into other things and phenomena, also be possible? If a science of development is possible, then – so it seems – our hitherto understanding of science has been deceptive. We cannot proceed further in the matter of Robert until we have thrown some light on this mystery.

Researchers have assembled and sorted so much evidential material to this day that they no longer speak about development as a hypothesis or a theory, but rather directly as a fact. In accord with this, they are attempting to specify a natural classification of sciences in such an order that reflects, according to the current state of knowledge, natural and human development itself. The parallel nature of these two orders is supposed to speak in favour of a theory of development. However, it does not do so. In my opinion, if you place these two orders alongside each other, then one speaks for development, but the other speaks against; one speaks for the non-transferability of things, the other against. If we want to remove this contradiction, then we have a choice: either to pronounce the non-transferability of things as merely ostensible, or to pronounce development as ostensible. Either the specific substances of individual sciences are not *sui generis*, and specialist sciences are at most merely branches of some kind of single science, or what appears to us as development is merely an artificial classification of things among which there is no developmental connection. However, we should not overlook something that perhaps at first surprises us: it is not only the second possibility that consigns development to the realms of the merely ostensible; the first possibility also consigns it there. If the subject of the only single science is a substance *sui generis*, then this substance occupies the place of 'ultimate reality' and development is merely a succession of various different disguises of this reality. We can see, then, that development requires not only the transferability of one thing into another, but also the denial of these things as things *sui generis* and also as modifications of one single thing. In short, the idea of development is defensible only when we admit that there are not things that develop. This paradox appears to us as an echo of one earlier paradox: if exact relations between things exist, then we must admit that things themselves do not exist.

And indeed these two contradictions are closer to each other than it may seem, in that the science of development represents a special case of relations, of a law that is in a certain way directed and guided.

This is because, if a developmental law is to be a bridge between the substances of specialist sciences, then it must in some way combine the specific laws of these sciences 'crosswise' and bind them to itself in terms of development. Without such a law, there is no science of development. However, in addition to its own laws, every science also needs its own material, its own substance *sui generis*, in this case the thing that develops. So, then, where is this law and where is the material of the science of development? As far as this material is concerned, we should recall that expedition we made in search of 'ultimate reality', when together with science we followed – in a 'crayfish march', that is in the opposite direction – the trail which, according to the contentions of natural science, development itself left behind. The material that we encountered there, and which bit by bit dissolved into nothing in front of our eyes, were the substances of individual sciences; we did not encounter anything that we could call the specific material of development. If we inquire of the specific developmental system that is closest to natural science – that is, Darwinism – about its subject, we ascertain with surprise that it really has no subject matter of its own. It has a name for it – 'species' – but it does not recognize this either as a sensory fact, or as an evaluation and a definition; it has neither a concrete subject nor an abstract one. How, then, is a developmental explanation possible? It is possible in that developmental science borrows its subject from other sciences. It actually borrows *subjects*, not a subject, because this is a case of substances *sui generis*, not of one single specific substance. All kinds of explanations can then be used to arrange these substances alongside one another and bind them in an order of development. If, however, this explanation is supposed to be a science of development, it cannot be just any kind of explanation, but rather it must be an explanation with its own specific laws which in the form of certain formulations capture precisely the 'jumps' – that is, the events and processes between individual substances.

While the science of development borrows its material from other sciences, it cannot borrow its laws from them, because what we demand of laws of development is that they provide a bridge over the gaps that separate the laws of individual special sciences. In the course of our 'crayfish march' we have not encountered any such laws. It is true that mathematics is often designated as the law that connects individual sciences, but what conclusion can we infer from this? The only thing that mathematics is capable of in this respect is of going through the world of things in a 'crayfish march', liquidating one thing after another, and eventually ending up at itself as the only universe. Mathematics: this is a law that – if we entrust development to it – destroys development, that undermines the world of things like a ladder or a staircase made from cards, and scatters these things around at the same ground level where it resides itself. Where, then, is the law that creates a developmental hierarchy of things? Where, then, in addition to physical, chemical, biological, and other specific laws, is there some additional 'developmental' law?

However, let us not hasten to any final conclusion. Every pupil today learns not only about one developmental theory, but rather about a whole range of such theories and developmental laws that all have scientific ambitions. We cannot pass over these in silence.

The majority of these developmental explanations are marked by the fact that they do not differentiate between two types of laws – that is, between the laws of individual sciences and developmental laws. This failure to differentiate is possible either by interpreting the laws of individual sciences as already also being developmental laws, or by establishing new developmental laws and by then presenting these new laws not only as developmental laws, but also as laws of all events, all sciences. In both cases all events are interpreted as a developmental process. The idea that 'everything is development' collapses as a consequence of the effort to squeeze all events into the narrow channel of one certain idea, direction, aim. If we have to assemble a stylish brooch from an inelegant pile of corals of various shapes and sizes, then we will make use of only a very small part of these corals and will simply ignore the others. If we then choose a different order, then we will assemble a different brooch, but in doing so we will disassemble the first brooch. For every idea and for every experience that we make into the content and tendency of development, there is a corresponding contradictory idea or experience that refutes our explanation.

It occurred to Hegel to make this contradictoriness itself into the principle of development. However, it was clear to him that he had discovered this principle as a principle of his own thinking, and therefore, if he was to make this principle a universal one, then he must insert it in an appropriate universal mind, into the mind of 'absolute spirit', which expresses itself through individual minds and attains the culmination of its development in human beings, in their highest actions and institutions.

The example of Hegel already makes us suspect the complete absurdity of the concept of development. As soon as I say 'development', I immediately want to know: *What* is developing? However, with this *what* I am inserting something constant, permanent, and unchangeable into the current of development; with this *what*

I place something substantial against the phenomenal and fictional nature of development. It is symptomatic that the most significant developmental theory, Darwinism, leaves us in the greatest uncertainty about exactly *what* is developing. In the case of Hegel, this *what* takes on the form of absolute spirit. We can surmise what will probably emerge from the combination of such an absolute with a development that actually wants nothing less than to sanction the variety of the concrete world, to make equal from the point of view of existence and reality all earthly things, all things being created and becoming extinct, all transitory things. While, on the one hand, absolute spirit favours a spiritualistic monism, on the other hand development favours a sensualist pluralism. In the light of the one, the other disappears, or possibly changes into a mere appearance. If we want to maintain both these things in one unity, then it is no surprise that this produces something like Hegel's obscure dialectic.

Dialectical materialists value highly Hegel's dialectic, but they claim that it is only compatible with materialism. Well, spirit or matter – this is not where the problem lies. The dilemma is this: either what develops, or development. Whoever wants to save both ends up either at obscurity like Hegel, or at claims that are mutually contradictory. Marxists are no exception. It is enough to look at the confrontation of these two statements by Engels: 1. 'The world is not to be considered as a complexity of ready-made things, but as a complexity made up of *processes* in which the apparently stable things, no less than the thought pictures in the brain – the idea, cause an unbroken chain of coming into being and passing away, in which, by means of all sorts of seeming accidents, and in spite of all momentary setbacks, there is carried out in the end a progressive development'[34] and 2. 'It already becomes evident here that matter is unthinkable without motion. And if, in addition, *matter confronts us as something given, equally uncreat-*

---

34 Friedrich Engels, *Ludwig Feuerbach: The Roots of the Socialist Philosophy*, trans. by Austin Lewis (Chicago: Charles H. Kerr, 1903), pp. 97–98.

able as indestructible (author's highlighting), it follows that motion also is as uncreatable as indestructible.'[35]

Engels, when he uses the term 'matter', in one case has in mind the momentary, coming-into-being and passing-away things of the world of experience, while in the second case he has in mind something 'equally uncreatable as indestructible', something not coming into being and not passing away. However, by such an ambiguity he has not of course resolved the dilemma of development. What is clear is that every thing of our sensory world comes into being and passes away, and therefore a specific concrete body, tree, crystal, or clump of grass is not indestructible, and therefore insofar as matter is indestructible, then this matter cannot be the matter of a body as a body, of a tree as a tree, and so on. Then it is necessary to ask what is the (indestructible) matter of a body, a tree, and so on. However, even though a Marxist can grant a competent answer to this question only to natural science, he is farsighted enough not to bind himself by this answer of natural science and to declare that the Marxist concept of matter is independent of the state of natural scientific research and knowledge. If, therefore, the Marxist indestructible matter is neither given in the coming-into-being and passing-away things of our experience, nor dependent on the results of natural scientific research, then – it seems to me – there is no other existence possible for it other than either a nominalist existence, or a metaphysical one. In the first case, things are real, while in the second they are 'mere appearances'. I have the impression that by the concept of matter Marxists often mean nothing other than precisely only the *reality* of things and processes, as this reality is given to us in experience. However, this reality is not a proof of materialism; on the contrary, it is an experiential fact, whose materiality the materialist is supposed to prove. And, if by 'matter' the materialist here means this reality itself, then he is sim-

35 Friedrich Engels, *Dialectics of Nature* (*Dialektik der Natur*). www.marxists.org/archive/marx /works/1883/don/index.htm.

ply stating a certain experiential fact, but he is neither proving it nor explaining it as 'materialist'; if, however, he wants to explain – that is, to deduce the reality of things and processes from 'matter' – then he necessarily finds himself in metaphysics, no differently, for instance, than Bishop Berkeley, who deduces this same reality of things and processes from the 'spirit of God'. This is why some people consider it more accurate to speak about Marxism rather as a form of realism than as a form of materialism.

Hegel's doctrine is a philosophy, not a science. It is a philosophy because it introduces on the scene something that science does not find and therefore does not concede the existence of: a prime mover. Because it does not find a prime mover, science makes do with a 'description' of natural events and leaves its explanation – that is, the question of a world view – to 'metaphysics', philosophy. In contrast to this, in Marxism the 'contradiction between science and philosophy is abolished. ... Dialectical materialism is a scientific doctrine about the laws of development of all things both material and also spiritual – that is, the development of the entire concrete content of the world and also the cognition of this world. Since thinking itself is merely a depiction of a real event, it too – just like natural and social motions – is also subject to these dialectical laws. ... Dialectical materialism, therefore, constitutes in the sum of its individual results a scientific world view. ... The materialist dialectic is not only a world view, but also a guide for action.'[36]

How can we now decide whether dialectical materialism represents a philosophy or a science, and moreover a science of development?

If the laws that are mentioned in the citations above were laws produced in the laboratories and workplaces of physicists, biologists, psychologists, sociologists, and so on, then there would be no doubt that dialectical materialism is nothing other than a philosophy, and moreo-

---

36 Kurt Sauerland, *Der dialektische Materialismus* [Dialectical Materialism] (Berlin: Neuer deutscher Verlag, 1932).

ver a philosophy of a positivist type. However, the citations do not talk about such laws. This is a case of different laws. Here they are:

'The law of the transformation of quantity into quality and vice versa;
'The law of the interpenetration of opposites;
'The law of the negation of the negation.

'All three are developed by Hegel in his idealist fashion as mere laws of thought.'[37] In the working version of his book, Engels added a fourth law: 'Spiral form of development'.

Abram Deborin complains that even though 'modern natural science by its own development brings the most visible proof of the fact that nature is also governed by a dialectic,' nevertheless 'in spite of this, natural scientists consciously reject the dialectic and continue to operate with metaphysical categories. However, unconsciously they are forced to adopt a dialectical standpoint.'[38]

The fact remains that natural scientists have achieved their triumphs when operating with 'metaphysical categories'. Let us try to see what we can achieve when we operate with dialectical categories. Let us take, for instance, the dialectical formula of motion, which is a central concept of both metaphysical science and also of dialectical science. 'Motion is itself a contradiction since simple mechanical movement from place to place can only accomplish itself by a body being at one and the same moment in one place and simultaneously in another place, by being in one and the same place and yet not there. And motion is just the continuous establishing and dissolving the contradiction.'[39]

---

37 Engels, *Dialectics of Nature*.
38 In *Under the Banner of Marxism* – Bolshevik journal published in Moscow (1922–1944).
39 Friedrich Engels, *Landmarks of Scientific Socialism: „Anti-Duehring"*, trans. by Austin Lewis (Chicago: Charles H. Kerr, 1907), p. 151. www.gutenberg.org/files/31933/31933-h/31933-h.htm.

If I did not know motion from my own experience, then I would hardly gain the correct notion of it from this formulation. In this respect, then, a dialectical formulation does not have any advantage over a 'metaphysical' formulation, which is at least comprehensible of itself – for instance, as a mathematical equation. The formulations of exact science arose as a symbolic form of a technical explanation of nature (material, laws; prime mover silenced) and therefore are predetermined to prove their worth in technical work. Even though science takes no account of a prime mover, applied science (that is, technology) celebrates triumphs, because in praxis the technician himself deputizes for the prime mover, either already in the function of a direct moulder, or merely in the role of an experimenter (that is, someone 'who provides an opportunity, and the molecules bind themselves together of their own accord'). And precisely the circumstance that the prime mover can be silenced in theory, but that in praxis it is 'always in place' enables natural science to be a science, and not a philosophy or a theology; it enables natural science to be universal – that is, not conditional on a prime mover, not conditioned individually, racially, locally, or in terms of class. However, this comes at a price, and a cruel one: that it cannot have any higher aspiration than to be the servant of technology. Such is the price that it must pay to the 'technician' for his silence, for the fact that he remains in the background and does not come forward with the claims of a prime mover.

Well, is a dialectical natural science capable of rendering to the technician the service that hitherto natural science has rendered to him? Let us listen to Engels's own words: 'To negate in the dialectic is not simply to say "No", or to describe a thing as non-existent, or to destroy it after any fashion that you may choose. Spinoza says "*omnis determinatio est negatio,*" every limitation or determination is at the same time a negation. Furthermore, the sort of negation here is shown first by means of the universal and in the second place by means of the distinctive nature of the process. I must not only negate but I must also restore the negation again. I must therefore so direct the first negation that the second remains possible or shall be so. How? Just according to the peculiar nature of each particular case. I grind a grain of barley, I crush an insect, I have certainly fulfilled the first act but have made the second impossible. Every species of things has therefore its own peculiar properties to be negated in order that a progression may proceed. ... With the mere knowledge that the stalk of barley and infinitesimal calculation fall under the principle of the negation of the negation, I cannot cultivate more barley nor can I differentiate and integrate.'[40]

If it is not possible to successfully cultivate barley or to perform integral calculus with the mere knowledge that both these things fall under the law of the negation of negation, but if I must additionally know how to cultivate a barley plant or how to integrate, then I think that, when cultivating barley or performing integral calculus, I can get by very well without the law of the negation of negation, and that knowledge of this law does not make these activities even the slightest bit easier for me. On the whole, this allows us to deduce that in a concrete case dialectical formulas provide me with no help whatsoever and that I have to run for help to 'metaphysical' formulas, which in Engels's terms I think would be stated as follows: that from a method of negation determined by the general nature of the process I switch to a method of negation determined by the particular nature of the process, or that 'every kind of thing therefore has a peculiar (its own particular) way of being negated', and that, therefore, I must always be governed by 'the particular nature of each individual case'.

If I do not have to use dialectical laws – or if I cannot even use them – for the activities to which they are connected, and this out of principle, and not merely because of some obstacles, then – it seems to me – I lose the last reason to call these laws natural scientific laws.

40 Engels, *Anti-Dühring*, p. 174.

By his reference to the cultivation of barley and to integral calculus, Engels admits that the so-called dialectical laws are actually only a mere schema, a cognitive vacuum that runs empty, unless it is filled with experiences, concrete events, and things. It is to this same condition – as is known – that Kant connects his *a priori* schemata. And are we supposed to deduce from this that dialectical laws are not from the same 'metaphysical' cloth?

For a 'naïve' person, every phenomenon is a fact; for a researcher, for science, it is a problem. However, let us be clear: it is a problem because it is supposed to be reproduced by a person, repeated, deliberately mastered – in short, a phenomenon is a problem for a technician. A scientific formula is supposed to be a 'resolution' – that is, it is supposed to be an instruction for a technician for the deliberate reproduction of a phenomenon, or possibly also for the suppression of this phenomenon. A law is the aim of theory, but a starting point for a technician. We choose an example in which the problem both for Engels and for natural science was motion. Natural science resolved this problem with exact laws, which serve a technician excellently. How does dialectical science resolve this problem? It does not resolve it at all. It simply concludes: 'And the continuous origination and simultaneous solution of this contradiction is precisely what motion is.' Well then, what use exactly is dialectical science? What work is it actually doing here? And what use is it to a technician? Can it really be a guide to action for him, as it promised? The problem poses itself; the problem resolves itself. But the matter is clear: the problem does not pose itself; the problem is posed by a technician, by human reason, and human reason also resolves the problem. Nature does not resolve problems, because it does not pose them. And it does not pose them, because it is not a technician, because the principle of its processes is different from a rational and technical principle.

What more can be said about dialectical materialism as a science of development? If we must disregard the textbook of dialectical materialism and resort to a 'metaphysical' textbook about, for instance, chemistry in order to perform even the most elementary chemical reaction, what will the use of this dialectical textbook be in our effort to – let us say – proceed from a chemical solution to a protoplasm? Or proceed from a protoplasm to thought? The law of the negation of negation is completely useless here. Is it possible that the 'the law of the transformation of quantity into quality' would perhaps be of more use here?

This law says that 'at a certain point mere quantitative changes are transformed into qualitative changes' (typical example: the boiling and freezing points of water) and it really makes a better scientific impression than the other dialectical laws. Why? Because it explains all events as mathematical events. It expresses in almost the same words what, for instance, James Jeans states when he oversteps the competence of an astronomer and a physicist, in short of a scientist, and turns into a philosopher: everything is mathematics. Here we must differentiate between philosophy and science, between an explanation and a description. If this is a case of philosophy, then if we accept that a quantitative process is the principle of world events, then we must also accept the consequence that Jeans honestly accepts: a subject conceived in this or that way, in whose consciousness it would be possible to localize mathematical processes, and thus to guarantee them at least in their abstract substance. This connection was evident already to Aristotle. The same thing applies to the law of the negation of negation. It is possible to admit that a thing exists objectively; however, it is only in someone's mind that a thing cannot exist. Only a mind endowed with memory is capable of 'seeing' some present thing as the negation of a non-present, past, not-being thing. Here for the first time is negation of negation! 'Objective' nature governed by this law can be more easily understood as an idea of the Hegelian Absolute Spirit than as the 'matter' of the dialectical materialists. (Here we are dealing only with dialectical materialism – that is, the explanation of nature; we are disregarding so-called historical materialism, relating to the explanation of social phenomena, because in this the representatives of processes are people, and negation as an effective factor therefore takes on some sense.) However, let us return to the law of the transformation of quantity into quality. We have already mentioned its philosophical aspect. And as far as the scientific aspect is concerned, the law of the transformation of quantity into quality simply states the existence of sciences comprised of mathematics, and apart from that, it does not contain anything else other than an appeal to have recourse to these sciences in every concrete case.

Apart from this scientific aspect, the interpretation of the law of the transformation of quantity into quality is usually mere arbitrariness and a play on words. For example: 'It is equally fundamental in such ethical systems as that of Aristotle, who pointed out that the difference between good and evil was largely quantitative. Thus the coward took too few risks, the rash man too many, and the brave man the right number.'[41] In this case, we actually use the indefinite quantitative terms 'too few' and 'too many' metaphorically to express moral quality directly, and not by means of quantities and amounts.

If our hitherto explanations have clarified the concept of science at least a little bit, then we can certainly agree on this: it is possible to believe that it will be a Marxist who will change the world; however, it is clear that if he makes use of science to bring about this change, then this will not be Marxist science, but rather universal science, for the simple reason that there is no other science. And I think that not even a Marxist will feel any regret about this, when he realizes what price science has to pay for its universalism: the loss of a prime mover, an impulse, an initiator. And this – as we will later demonstrate – is far from being the entire price. If Marxism was

---

41   J. B. S. Haldane, *The Marxist Philosophy and the Sciences* (New York: Random House, 1939). www.marxists.org/archive/haldane/works/1930s/philosophy.htm.

a science in the precise meaning of the word, then it would never occur to it to change the world.

We need not pause for long at the kind of developmental laws as represented by Herbert Spencer with his law of integration and differentiation and by Emanuel Chalupný[42] with his 'law of isolation', about which the author declares that it is 'not so much a sociological, biological, or psychological law, but rather the universal law of natural philosophy'. We explain development using laws of this type much in the same way as we explain the motion of a locomotive if we say that its wheels turn.

The developmental theories that are closest to natural science are Lamarckism and Darwinism, or respectively – in a newer form – neo-Lamarckism and neo-Darwinism. We can, therefore, expect that these will contribute the most to clarifying our question.

The thing that is especially valued about them is their 'naturalness, clarity, and simplicity'. If we go on to ask what exactly makes them natural, clear, and simple, we will find that this is the minimum of demands that they make on a person's ingenuity. Sufficient for these theories is the common and superficial human experience that can be expressed in these words: adaptation to given circumstances, the struggle for existence, chance. In principle, the two theories are mutually exclusive; however, when necessary, they have complemented each other. For a certain time Darwin himself explained the emergence of some new characteristics in a Lamarckian way, when he entrusted their selection and survival to the 'struggle for existence'; however, other than this, Darwinism attributes a decisive role in the emergence of new characteristics to mere 'chance' – that is, to factors that have nothing in common with the struggle for existence and with the survival of animal species. In contrast to this, in many cases Lamarckism is understood only as the current opinion known as so-called psycho-Lamarckism – that is, the idea that psychological

---

42 Czech sociologist (1879–1958).

factors have an active role in the formation of new characteristics. Neither Lamarckism nor Darwinism formulates any developmental laws; both of them simply appeal to our sober experience. If you systematically and recurrently use a hammer or an axe, then you will develop your arms; however, some of your other organs or limbs will atrophy. If you devote yourself to intensive study, your mind will become more powerful, but your muscles will atrophy. In such a way – so Lamarckism teaches – entirely new organs, characteristics, and capabilities can arise; even entirely new 'species' can arise, while respectively others can become extinct through this process. However, the main thing in this is the question of whether and how all these new characteristics are transferred to offspring. Today, Darwinism denies that characteristics acquired through this Lamarckian process – that is, acquired through the body (soma) or the psyche of the individual to whose benefit they serve – can be inherited. It emphasizes that many new characteristics – and possibly even a majority of them – are not beneficial for an animal species, but rather detrimental; that precisely through the 'struggle for existence' these unfavourable characteristics are eliminated, and the surviving tried-and-tested characteristics then support the deceptive Lamarckian idea that all new characteristics are 'purposeful', beneficial – that is, they arise either from the psychological effort of an animal, or through the adaptive reaction of its body (soma) to the environment.

According to Darwinism, therefore, individual effort, or respectively adaptation, is worthless for development. However, if an individual cannot change his innate faculties through his own exertions, then it is more logical if he also views the fruits of his own exertions as the refinement of his innate faculties, and not as the acquisition of something new. In this way, the price of individual effort even for an individual himself is reduced to the mere refinement of innate faculties. The Darwinist Sir Arthur Keith professes: 'I, for one, believe with Huxley that the government which rules within the body of the human embryo proceeds along its way altogether uninfluenced by occurrences or experiences which affect the body or brain of its parents. In short, man has come by his great gifts — his brain, his upright posture, his strange foot, and his nimble hand — not by any effort of his own, but, like a favoured child of the present day, has fallen heir to a fortune for which he has never laboured.'[43] And of course, for which none of his ancestors has laboured either. So where, then, does this richness come from? Darwinism replies: wherever it comes from, the creature that makes use of it cannot seek in it anything other than pure chance. For instance, a giraffe has not acquired a long neck because it needed it for its subsistence and has through its own efforts contributed in some way to its lengthening; only a Lamarckian or the bicyclist G. B. Shaw (see the preface to *Back to Methuselah*) could assert such a simple-minded judgement. The truth is that its neck has grown longer by pure chance. So be it! But, if I were a giraffe, then I would believe in Providence. Similarly, when the ancient lakes and seas dried up, it was those aquatic creatures who at an appropriate moment by a happy accident had acquired lungs and legs who were also able to survive on dry land; or a horse has managed to survive up until the present day not because through its own exertions it has developed its ability to escape the claws of predators, but rather only because a number of purely accidental changes have perfected its capabilities for running.

So, where do these changes come from? What is the source of the decision about what we are and what we look like? About the ways in which we resemble our ancestors and descendants, and the ways in which we differ from them? The science of heredity offers us some instruction on this question. 'There is not even the smallest part in the anatomy of a fruit fly, not even one single feature of its activity, that cannot be demonstrated to be governed in some way by all-important genes.' Each of us is assembled from these building blocks by someone about whom we must judge that he has less responsibil-

---

[43] Sir Arthur Keith, *Concerning Man's Origin* (London: Watts, 1927), p. 31.

ity and purposefulness than a frolicsome child. We are in the hands of imaginary card players who cast the dice that decide on our fate according to the rules of pure chance. Every one of us is mercilessly predetermined by the accidental result of this game.

However, the mere reconstructing and exchanging of building blocks does not explain development. Mendel's laws are not developmental laws. 'Mendelism as a developmental theory cannot at all reckon with cross-breeding as a sufficient principle of development,' writes Artur Brožek.[44] 'Under all conditions, if the developmental principle was supposed to be only the cross-breeding and combination of innate faculties, this could only be a case of a developmental change in a circle.' – It is evident that the building blocks are supplemented and replaced by new ones. How? By mutation! Bohumil Němec[45] regards it as debatable 'whether really new characteristics appear in the process of mutation'. What is mutation? 'These are changes caused by a wide variety of unspecified influences from the surrounding environment which directly affect not the body, but rather the constitution of the embryonic plasma,' writes Artur Brožek in his book *Theory of Heredity*. And similarly, Julian Huxley and H. G. Wells, the authors of a popular encyclopaedia of neo-Darwinism:[46] 'An exciting speculation, based on Muller's results, is that some at least of the natural mutation which is always in progress may also be due to X-rays. For X-rays do occur in the radiance that falls on our Earth. ... A disturbing idea, that life has evolved and is still evolving under the spur of those strange rays, shot casually into our world from unknown corners of the universe!'[47] However, 'Besides X-rays, it seems that chemical influences can produce mutations. An interesting example of this ... concerns the black or 'melanic' varieties of moths. ... The caterpillars of various moths

44 Czech entomologist (1882–1934).
45 Czech botanist.
46 Wells, Huxley, and Wells, *The Science of Life*.
47 Ibid., pp. 594–595.

[were fed] tiny quantities of heavy metals, especially lead and manganese, with their food. ... In the metal-fed cultures a few mutants with black wings appeared. Moreover, the colour, once it had been produced, bred true even without further metal feeding. The chemical agencies had induced permanent changes in the germ-plasm.'[48] According to Bohumil Němec: 'A majority of mutations caused by radiation have a *pathological* character. These are *detrimental* mutations. They do not go beyond the limitations of the species and they do not provide us with an explanation for the *ascent* of life from the simpler to the more complicated.' Similarly, Bavink: 'A large number of spontaneous and artificial mutations that have been observed can be characterized as detrimental mutations.'

However, the authors of the aforementioned encyclopaedia go bravely forward. With the help of the X-rays, they are capable of explaining not only the ascent from one form of life to another form of life, but also the creation of the living from the non-living. For instance, in their opinion, 'The whole of life upon Earth depends entirely upon solar energy. The sun's energy is the physical source of all life,'[49] while 'the Earth at that moment ... was a cosmic test-tube, whose particular brew led to the appearance of living matter as inevitably as an earlier and different set of conditions led to the formation of rocks and seas and clouds.'[50] Let us consider: if we are supposed to believe that a shower of dead sunrays knocks a creature with a human soul out of a pile of dead sand, then we are requested to believe that a shower of oil and diesel, or of whatever you like, will in time transform a pile of iron ore into an automobile. If during this process there is nothing in the sand, and everything in the sun; if the sand is a dead, passive material, and the sun an all-powerful moulder, then there is no reason not to identify the sun

48 Ibid., pp. 595–596.
49 Ibid., p. 962.
50 Ibid., p. 649.

with the mind of God. In truth, as long as people worshipped the sun as a God and called him the Creator of everything, then they understood what they were saying. We, however, who see in the sun merely dead matter and apply to it the same name of creator, do not have the slightest idea what we are talking about.

If Darwinism is favoured today in the dispute between Lamarckism and Darwinism, this is not on account of its merit. The core idea of Darwinism consists in the doctrine of natural selection – that is, the selection and survival of advantageous mutations through 'the struggle for existence'. This doctrine is necessarily convoluted. For instance, Bavink, who rejects Lamarckism but not Darwinism, enumerates dozens of natural phenomena that provide evidence against the theory of natural selection; and his list is not yet complete. How is it, then, that – in comparison with Lamarckism, which appeals to 'some significant current-day biologists' merely 'on account of the moral attractiveness of the idea that through our own efforts we attain permanent results' – Darwinism manages to retain its reputation of being scientific? This is because current-day science of heredity strengthens the Darwinist opinion that 'adaptation' to external conditions, which pointed to some kind of purposefulness of mutations and their direct connection with life, is a mere metaphor, and therefore that mutations are, with respect to effort and struggle in life, a purely accidental phenomenon.

'It is certain,' says Artur Brožek, 'that purposefulness cannot play any role in the process of mutations. It is also a matter of indifference whether the embryonic plasma is thus changed purposelessly and mutationally only in the sexual cells, or also in the nerve cells of the body. These changes are, then, also mechanical changes, and therefore undirected, and therefore quite different from those which Lamarck assumes and about which he teaches.' Today, then, the accidental nature of mutations is the most scientific argument of Darwinism. Therefore, let us look a little bit more closely at this argument.

The thing that gives the impression of chance here is the notion that changes that make sense only for a given living creature – that is, changes that are for this creature either necessary and desirable, or harmful and undesirable – arise without any kind of relationship to these needs and desires. It is evident that chance is not here an expression for acausality (absence of causality), respectively for indetermination, nor even for 'unawareness', as, for instance, Darwin himself said. If it is proven that mutational changes in genes are brought about through physical and chemical processes, then firstly this will prove their causality (regardless of the possible acausality of microcosmic phenomena, which have nothing to do with Darwinian 'chance') and secondly this will get rid of their 'unawareness', without anything changing in Darwinism concerning the accidental nature of mutation. Chance, therefore, is here an expression for something else. It is an expression of that fact that we are linking phenomena of one causal order to phenomena of another causal order; that we are trying to bring about a connection between two substances *sui generis*, and between two laws *sui generis*. We know that a scientific explanation of development has neither its own laws, nor its own material. Darwinism is no exception. It borrows its material from individual developmental levels; and for its own particular law, which is supposed to bridge the gap between specific laws of different levels, it can find no other expression than the concept of 'chance'.

Ignaz Lichtig, for instance, also interprets the Darwinist concept of chance as a meeting of two independent causal orders. However, if we consider that he nevertheless does not doubt the possibility of a science of development – on the contrary, he himself participates in this science – then we can see clearly just how little the Darwinian concept of chance tells us about the character of development. In his book *The Origin of Life Through Constant Creation* he writes: 'The reason why Darwinism makes chance responsible for the creation of purposeful organs consists in the fact that it accepts two causal orders that take place mutually independently of each other and that it cannot account causally for the meeting of these two orders: on the one hand, the occurrence of a purposeful organ, or in other words an organ that is especially suitable for a certain function – the first causal order; and on the other hand, the use of this organ, and the resulting benefit for the bearer of this organ in the struggle for existence – the second causal order.'[51]

We should notice how Lichtig's elucidation of the two causal orders is imprecise and how this imprecision is sufficient to make the impossible possible.

For Lichtig, the first causal order is the 'occurrence of a purposeful organ', while the second causal order is the 'use of this organ'. We should not forget that mutations arising through the first causal order are non-purposeful, undirected, and that if I use the term 'purposeful organ', then I already have in mind a directed mutation – that is, I already have in mind its use, and therefore the second causal order. If I have to acknowledge the mutual independence of the two causal orders, then this does not mean that in the first causal order it is not a case of the 'occurrence of a purposeful organ', but rather of something quite different. For instance, 'the lengthening of the neck' is something that makes sense for a giraffe, but not, however, for cells and molecules. Therefore, it is crystal clear that cells and molecules, in the process of extending the giraffe's neck, are not actually extending the giraffe's neck, but are rather doing something different, something which with respect to the giraffe and its struggle for existence is undirected and non-purposeful. If the changes that have their purpose, significance, sense, and use for a living individual are 'produced' without this purpose and significance, then these changes are not the same changes with regard

---

51 Ignaz Lichtig, *Die Enstehung des Lebens durch stetige Schöpfung* [The Origin of Life Through Constant Creation] (Amsterdam: Noord-Hollandsche Uitgevers Maatschappij, 1938) – my translation from Safarik's Czech.

to the origination of these features as they are in regard to the use of these features. If, for instance, a bird's wing arose 'undirectedly' (that is, not as a bird's wing, not as an organ for flying), then a 'directed' change expressed by the word 'wing' does not express (so long as we remain in the first causal order) a real change, but rather some kind of fictive change. If we pass over to the second causal order, then here we will now find a 'directed', purposeful organ, but not, however, its origination in the first causal order. So, the origination of an undirected organ, or even of any 'organ' at all, does not represent a real change, but rather only some kind of fictive change. However, given that according to Darwinism the origination of an organ is bound in every case to the first causal order, then if we try to transmit the mutation in its true reality – that is, in the reality of its origination – into the second causal order, then we come to the indubitable conclusion that a bird flies with fictive wings and a giraffe eats the leaves of a tall tree with a fictively lengthened neck.

What, then, is 'natural selection', if this is a case of a selection of fictions? To use the word 'development' means operating with directed changes. If the directed nature of changes is a mere metaphor, then development is also a metaphor. Lamarckism eschews these difficulties by remaining within the limits of one causal order, in our case the second order. For example, a giraffe has acquired its long neck *because* it has tried to reach food at heights, or simply *in order to* reach food at heights. However, the objection raised to this is that if Lamarckism was true, then it would have to explain how an animal's efforts induce physical-chemical, or respectively physiological, processes in cells and tissues that lead to a change of an organ; or to put it in another way, it would be confronted with the task of laying a bridge from the second causal order to the first, and it would not, therefore, be in any better situation than Darwinism.

The chance occurrence of mutations, therefore, captures the inconsistency that the law that creates them (for instance, physical-chemical) is not the law of the bearer (for instance, psychological) for whose benefit or to whose detriment they serve. The 'struggle for existence' is adequate here, for instance, for an antelope, but not for the cells or even the atoms and electrons of its body. It is the antelope that struggles for life; for atoms and electrons it can be a matter of indifference whether they exist as a part of the body of an antelope, or a lion, or no animal at all. By the way: in contrast to this, the philosophy of organism (process philosophy) of Alfred North Whitehead teaches that 'an electron within a living body is different from an electron outside it, by reason of the plan of the body. The electron blindly runs either within or without the body; but it runs within the body in accordance with its character within the body; that is to say, in accordance with the general plan of the body, and this plan includes the mental state.'[52] According to this, an electron in the body of an antelope would behave in such a way as the interest of an antelope demands, which I think is a Lamarckian stance. The question is what causes an electron inside an animal's body to behave differently than outside of this body, and whether its behaviour is not so different that it eludes any physical investigation. A falling stone behaves 'physically'; however, if a young boy is playing with it, then it no longer behaves 'physically'. In other words, the question is whether an electron exists at all as a physical element in the body of a living being. For the meanwhile, the natural scientist has found either an electron, or a body, but not however 'an electron in a body'. If Whitehead puts forward the concept of an 'organism' – and similarly J. C. Smuts with his concept of 'holism' – as something that is neither merely an electron, nor merely a body, but which represents 'electrons in the body', then both a natural scientist and also a layperson will object that, when using the word 'organism', Whitehead (or respectively Smuts with the word 'whole') is representing at

---

52 Alfred North Whitehead, *Science and the Modern World* (Cambridge: Cambridge University Press, 1926), p. 80.

best either electrons or a body, but never however both at the same time as one and the same thing, and a natural scientist will add, over and above this, that in his experiments this differentiation is an actual fact. And the layperson will go even further. He will point, for instance, to his dog Gnasher or his friend Bill and will say that Gnasher as an 'organism' ceases for him to be Gnasher and Bill as a 'whole' ceases to be Bill, and that therefore Bill is simply Bill and not some whole, and certainly not some whole of parts; there is simply no bridge from one to the other; to favour one means turning one's back on the other. According to Smuts, a 'whole' is not a 'substance' – that is, something that is added to the parts or something which is in some way alongside these parts. However, in truth it must be said that Bill is a 'substance' of his kind; however, he is neither added to the parts, nor is he alongside these parts – he is simply *outside of* parts. In this rejection by holism of the category of substance, we can see an attempt to resolve the developmental dilemma (development or that which develops) in the sense that only states of development (wholes), and the developmental principle immanent in these wholes (which Smuts also calls holism), are acknowledged. We need not examine Smut's resolution of the developmental dilemma any closer, because holism does not explain development: it does not lay a bridge between a whole as a 'whole of parts' and a whole as an 'individual'. All that it is capable of saying is that a whole of parts is a suitable 'basis' for an individual. The mutual relationship between them can be compared with the difference between a bird box and the bird that makes its home in this box. These two things are the same in name only.

Holism is not something that we ask about; holism is the reply that we give, the explanation that we put forward. If this is not sufficient for you, and you feel a need to ask primarily holism itself about its personal details, then it will refer you back to what holism was supposed to explain, to the world of experience: 'The concept of the whole means not a general tendency but a type of structure, a schema or framework, which, however, can only be filled with concrete details by actual experience.'[53]

The same witness testifies for Smuts's holism as also testifies for Engels's materialism and for Kant's transcendentalism, and even for the naïve approach of the simple person. A truly telling testimony; if only we do not remain deaf to it.

A different view from that of Whitehead and Smuts is offered to us by Pascual Jordan with his 'amplifier theory', according to which a living organism is not a macro-physical system, but rather a micro-physical, quantum one. In other words, we should conceive all expressions of living beings as amplifications of atomic events. A living creature is nothing other than some kind of amplifier that reproduces in an appropriate amplification what is happening in the molecular world of its body. How are we to envisage here that all the richness and variety of a human being's world is merely an amplification of the molecular world? For instance, you paint a picture of a landscape, or you organize an industrial company, or you think up the amplifier theory, but you are perhaps merely amplifying the quantum processes of your organism. What would constitute development according to this notion? A 'perfecting' of the amplifier? What would constitute the struggle for existence and natural selection? What would constitute mutation? If the lengthening of a giraffe's neck is merely an amplified reproduction of atomic events, then there is no other option than to envisage atoms as microcosmic giraffes; however, unless in addition to these rudimentary tiny creatures we can also envisage a microcosmic African steppe with the appropriate flora and fauna, then we must once again conclude in accord with Darwinism that the microscopic giraffes lengthen their necks non-purposefully, undirectedly, while however for the macroscopic giraffe, which is nothing other than an amplifier of the microscopic giraffe, this lengthening is purposeful. The fundamental

---

53 J. C. Smuts, *Holism and Evolution* (London: Macmillan, 1927), p. 125.

mystery – that is, how undirected events become directed ones – remains hidden somewhere in the depths of the amplification process. No bridge has been laid between individual levels of substances; on the contrary, all substance here is transferred to a substance of one level – the physical level. (Or to the biological level, or respectively the psychological one, according to whether the physical, the biological, or the psychological rudiment is taken as a basis. Jordan himself takes the last of these – the most suitable for the amplifier theory – as a basis, which leads to a kind of pan-psychism. However, this concept and the very question of whether physics, or respectively biology, should become part of psychology, or vice versa, is for Jordan merely a matter of terminology, as follows from his scientific noetics, which we will discuss further later.)

Finally, a mention about so-called emergentism. As developed by C. Lloyd Morgan, emergentism could serve as a sound argument against the claim that some real science of development already exists. What Morgan has done here resembles a clarification of concepts and a sorting of basic facts – that is, something that precedes a science, and not something that is its completion. If a true science of development had already existed, then it is difficult to imagine how and why Morgan's emergentism would have arisen. It does not have – as it seems – any greater ambition than to determine and classify effects that are predictable from causes (resultants), and effects that are not predictable from causes (emergents). The discontinuity of development – that is, ultimately its inexplicability, its inscrutability – can then be deduced from the emergents.

This makes it all the more surprising that many people consider that the concept of emergence explains development – and all kinds of other things as well. As at least one example of an emergent explanation, let us hear its reply to the question of the origin of reason and logical thinking: 'Reason and logical thinking are simply a new spiritual state for us, an emergence arising in reaction to the hitherto state of purely illustrative depictions, as they appear in the life of an animal, and this state probably arose as some kind of mutation during the formation of the species mankind.'[54] (Professor Josef Tvrdý,[55] who was tortured to death during the war, in his book *Contemporary Philosophy*) It is supposed to attest to the special character of human thought that it is capable of understanding not only explicable things, but also inexplicable ones. A fact being experienced – even if inexplicable – is apparently sufficient of itself alone for this fact to be consequently acknowledged as just as real as an explicable fact. What matters, then, in the end whether a fact is explicable or inexplicable? One way or the other a fact is just as real, and it is sufficient for a mere word to make it comprehensible and known. It is evidently also in this way that the concept of emergence was transformed from a mysterious concept into an explanatory concept. 'Emergent development becomes the sense of all world and living development. In this way the panorama of a magnificent future development of the world opens up for humankind, such as we can only guess at today.' If we grant emergentism the validity of a natural principle, the validity of a developmental law, then we may as well also grant the status of a natural principle and a natural law to such a simple statement as this: 'Every day brings something new.'

In conclusion to our comments on development, we can, I think, summarize: it remains evident that untraversable gaps gape between different causal orders – that is, between individual sciences – and that the range of special sciences is the most powerful argument against every science of development. The majority of developmental theories explain development by transforming it into a mere 'phenomenon' – that is, an appearance – to the benefit of *what* is developing. If, on the contrary, Darwinism gives the impression of being the soundest and most realistic developmental theory, then

---

54 Josef Tvrdý, *Nová filosofie* [Contemporary Philosophy] (Praha: Nakladatelství Volné myšlenky, 1932).

55 Czech philosopher, died in Mauthausen concentration camp (1887–1942).

this is because – to the benefit of the variety of things and events in the sensory world – it gives up on *what* is developing and, instead of annulling specific causal orders by some law of its own, it respects all of them and jumps about from one to the other by making use of the magic word 'chance'. In short, Darwinism provides us the most concrete description of the flow of changes, because of all doctrines about development it is the furthest from cognition and the closest to experience.

To make myself clear, if on the one hand I make mathematics the measure of scientific exactness, and make this exactness the measure of *cognition*, and on the other hand I regard the natural variety of things and processes as nature, and immediate participation in this nature as *experience*, then for me the natural ranking of sciences will look roughly like this: at the bottom of the ladder the world will be utterly devoid of anything, the exactness of science will approach the maximum, and science will be close to perfect cognition; at the top of the ladder, the world will fill up with things and processes, the exactness of science will fall to a minimum, and science will have an empirical character. The higher we ascend the ladder of sciences, the more the degree of exactness will fall – that is, the less it is possible to use mathematics, and the more it is necessary to appeal to experience. What science loses in exactness, it replaces with empirical findings. If perfect cognition involves the disappearance of 'things' and their conflation into mere mathematics, then it is possible that individual sciences retain their subjects, their substance *sui generis*, and therefore also their own existence, by not perceiving, recognizing, completely and thoroughly – that is, at the cost of their exactness. For cognition to be perfect, it must be devoid of things; it must be transformed into a mere relationship, a law. At the moment when cognition becomes perfect, nature disappears and only pure science remains – mathematics. On the contrary, at the moment when science changes over into mere experience and its connection with nature is the closest, it ceases to be science. Just as pure cognition is free of 'things', pure experience is free of rule-based laws.

What place should a science of development have in this picture? This science would have to contain all phases from pure cognition (mathematics) right up to the point when science vanishes in pure experience. It would be a science with a constantly decreasing exactness – that is, with constantly decreasing application of laws. However, this requirement has already been fulfilled by the 'natural' ranking of sciences, and – as we know – there are no crossovers between these sciences. Further, a science of development would be a science whose subject, whose substance *sui generis*, whose ultimate reality would also change. However, this requirement has also been fulfilled by the ranking of sciences, and we know that each substance *sui generis* of these individual sciences is not convertible to a substance *sui generis* of the others. Each of them acknowledges only itself and claims the right to explain the whole world. Therefore, we can conclude: in the picture of the sciences outlined above, there is no place for a science of development.

Let us return for a while to Darwinist 'chance'. It told us, for instance, that the path from the world of molecules and cells to the world of a giraffe leads only through fictions and metaphors. Whose fictions? Let us imagine a researcher who believes in the 'objectivity' of his cognition of 'nature'. This researcher wants to see things as they are, when no one is looking at them. He presumes, therefore, that nature is an objective reality to the extent that it is not perceived, or respectively does not have to be perceived, to the extent that it is not contingent on an observer, a spectator. Let us ask about the objective reality of some mutation, for instance a bird's wing. This arises undirectedly – that is, as a certain molecular process inside cells, which 'objectively' (that is, in the view from outside) we call a physical-chemical process. However, this physical-chemical process does not express the natural reality, because this reality evidently depends on the observer. If we move on to consider a directed mutation – that is, a flying bird – then the natural reality will be a certain internal process or state of the 'bird', which we express 'objectively' in zoological, morphological, psychological, and other terms, which are more or less dependent on the observer. In this way, then, we are led to the notion that what we here 'objectively' call mutation is composed in natural reality of certain processes or states which have nothing in common with the mutation, either directed or undirected. If, then, we adopt the stance of the researcher, for whom reality is what remains the same whether he observes it or not, then we come to the conclusion that not only mutations, but everything 'objectively' observed whatsoever, is a fiction of the spectator. Today the researcher also comes to a similar conclusion: we know that his objective observing ends up with him objectively no longer seeing anything and that he has ceased to seek objective reality anywhere else than in mathematical thinking alone. Why has he reached this end? Because he has obdurately sought natural reality in a view from outside, even though he has started out from the assumption that this reality is independent of the spectator, of the view from outside. Where there is no spectator, there is no fiction of objective reality; a scientist-spectator seeks objective reality as something that is independent of the spectator, but there is no objective reality, other than one for a spectator. For a spectator and only for a spectator is there 'ultimate reality', 'eternal law', 'substance of oneself', 'truth about oneself', and sometimes even 'a sentence about oneself', 'an idea about oneself', and other terms. If there is no spectator, then neither is there his requisite 'of himself'. Later we will clarify why he continues to believes so tenaciously in the eternal durability of his apparatus 'of himself', which does not survive him even for the slightest moment. Actually, he does not believe in this so surely; he is often tormented by a suspicion about the dependence of these things 'of oneself' on a spectator's thought, and since a spectator is a fragile and mortal being, he flees to a notion of an immortal spectator, in whose eternal mind he mummifies and stores his own thoughts.

Here I would just like to know whether the notion of an immortal spectator is also an 'idea of oneself' and in exactly what way its eternal preservation is accomplished.

The time has come for us to finally say plainly what we have been heading toward with all of our deductions: if there are no spectators in natural reality (that is, if there are no ultimate realities and eternal laws there), then this means that there is also no objective substance there (that is, *there is no view from outside there*); there are no things as mere objects of viewing and cognition there; there is a only a view from inside there, or to put it better, there is no view at all – *there is only an internal event, an internal process.*

4
THE TIGHTROPE WALKER
OVER THE VOID

OUR HITHERTO CONCLUSIONS have already indicated to us that we will not penetrate the true character of Robert's world – just as we cannot fathom the true character of nature – by mere observation, by a mere view from the outside, no matter what kind of glasses we make use of for this purpose. Remember, my dear friend, how the elements of what we call the human soul one after another fell into suspicion from the natural scientist and were repudiated as unreliable instruments of observation and cognition, until in the end only analytical and mathematical reason remained. However, at the same time the picture of the world became poorer and poorer until all that remained was pure mathematical thought, mathematical reason itself. What does this mean? This means that we have amputated from our soul precisely those organs that led us to the reality of things. What organs were in question here? If we designate those organs that the researcher has not renounced as the organs of *observation*, then the rejected organs represent the organs of *participation*. And, if their amputation has led to a loss of things, then it is necessary to conclude that things are not 'given', that mere observation does not have anything that it can see, and that *the reality of things is created by participation.*

If the so-called behaviourists reject introspection as a means of psychological research because the internal world – that is, spiritual states, feelings, emotions, will, and so on – disappear during observation, then it is necessary to add that nature, or the so-called external world, also disappears during observation, and that this is therefore actually a case of one single world, of a world that does not depend on that which is given, but rather on a creative process. The fact that the real world escapes us – this is neither a result of the view from within, nor a result of the view from outside, but rather a consequence of observation itself. The world is created by participation, and that is why it disappears during observation.

Now we already also understand why explanation as an instrument of the observer is merely a 'logical description', the elements of which do not correspond to anything in nature. A typical feature of explanation is that it speaks about each of its objects as about something objectively existing without in any way concerning itself with whether this objective existence is guaranteed. Everything about which it speaks it posits as 'given', and even when for instance it says that this or that thing is a mere fiction on the part of Mr. X or Mr. Y, then it is incapable of not positing even this hallucinatory process itself as objective, by which (whether it likes it or not) it concedes a certain objective existence not only to the subject who experiences the hallucination, but also to the content of the hallucination (that is, to the fiction itself). And, bearing in mind that our narration here is also an explanation – one which is supposed to interpret the world not as a something given, but rather as creative participation – it is evident that explanation represents the greatest opponent of what we have given it the task of interpreting; we find that it turns the principle that we entrust to it into its exact opposite for us. This is why, if we do not want to give up on words completely, we must remain systematically aware of this character of explanation and not miss any opportunity that helps us make plain its essential nature. One of the biggest cures that explanation tempts us with ends in solipsism, in that curse of the spectator. This is because, if a spectator sets as his main principle for understanding things a minimum of participation and a maximum of thorough and systematic observation, and then ends his path of cognition at nothing, then it is very easy for him to conclude that everything that exists is actually merely a figment of his own imagination, and therefore the only thing that 'objectively' remains is *nothing*.

It is evident that the relation of the explanation to the explained is taking on a fundamental importance for us and that the question 'What is the reality of explanation?' requires a very careful answer. Let us approach this gradually. Explanation itself will lead us to this answer and it depends only on us not losing sight of it. However, already now it can be said that, if the reality of the world is created by participation, then the burden of proof lies in the testimony of participants, and our explanation then has no more proper and higher task than to gain this testimony.

We have heard the following claim from the mouth of a modern biologist: 'Matter is a manifestation of a soul for a soul.' First of all, I would not say matter, material, object, because this is a 'logical description', an abstraction on the part of a spectator. For a participant a thing is not an object, but rather an *expression*; the way in which something or someone comes into contact with me and I with it, or him or her. If I search for 'matter' in the expression – that is, I revoke the bonds of a participant and adopt the relation-free stance of a spectator – then consequently nothing will remain from 'matter', and 'someone' will disappear from my world. And, secondly: to talk about things as about manifestations of a soul for a soul means to fall into that method of explaining the world that is typical for primitive peoples and children and who see in nature expressions of souls which, if not 'higher', then are at least equal to their own souls. This, however, represents a return to that form of anthropomorphism that drove modern-age enlightenment man to the opposite extreme, to the stance of a systematic spectator who seeks all reality in a view from outside, on the surface. This is why the approach that I am advocating is neither anthropomorphism, nor materialization, but rather *internalization*.

What I would perhaps most like to know now: What does a natural creative process consist of? How does it take place? And how can this internal event be understood? Do innumerable inner souls participate here, or some kind of unified inner soul?

As far as the first question is concerned – that is, a natural creative process – we know already that nature is not a technician and it is not a spectator. And, if we can use the testimony precisely of the technician and the scientist to our benefit, then we will certainly not spurn such a testimony: Who else could be freer of the suspicion of wanting to make our task easier?

In his book *The Technology of Life*, engineer Alexander Niklitschek writes: 'A living being is not processed from material by a process of division, but rather itself grows into a form intended for it and reaches its proper size without any wastage. And so it can be said that living beings arise in a quite different way than technical works do. ... Crystals also attain a shape assigned to them by their chemical character, without wastage. ... The natural path is founded on the operations of natural design engineers. However, these engineers are not sitting in some special office, as it may seem to the reader according to the picture that we often use. Not at all! These clever minds are present in every living being. Each living being is to a certain extent its own design engineer. And anyone who keeps a design office going in his inner being, according to our standard of measurement and also according to our designation, commits some kind of incredible carelessness. It is true that in the representation of nature he works as an artistic genius, but according to our civic standard this person is immensely careless. He is always willing to perform enthusiastically and excellently whatever happens to interest him at any given moment; but he completely fails to take care of everything else. In the end he does not even have a clean shirt and goes around with an unkempt beard. Someone like Michelangelo or Beethoven – certainly not the worst names – could serve as examples here for the natural genius principle of the concept of work. Modern human technology with all its capabilities attempts the precise opposite of this: it achieves products of incredible unity produced on a conveyor belt; it supports ever more thorough standardization; it requires all parts of machines to be identical to each other, and in the end thus for one machine to be the same as another. This process started with the bicycle and was then extended to the whole of technology. ... Nature absolutely hates any such thing. Precision and precise instructions, norms and adherence to these norms – these are things that go completely against nature.'

Here, then, a technician proposes to us a look into the workshop of nature through the prism of artistic creation, and directly discourages us from a technical way of viewing. By doing so, does he not also tell us that the opposition of nature and art as a part of culture is a deceptive opposition? But let us listen to another testimony. In his book *The Mysterious Universe* James Jeans writes: 'To my mind, the laws which nature obeys are less suggestive of those which a machine obeys in its motion than of those which a musician obeys in writing a fugue, or a poet in composing a sonnet. The motions of electrons and atoms do not resemble those of the parts of a locomotive so much as those of the dancers in a cotillion.'[56]

Similarly, biologist Jakob von Uexküll compares natural events with musical creation. Well, and what are the 'laws' that a composer uses as a guide when he composes a fugue, or which guide a poet when he writes a sonnet? Listen to this! 'The life of Michelangelo, for example, or of Beethoven, is an admirable symbol of this desperate pursuit which forbids man to halt in his path under pain of immediate decay and death, surrounded by ennui.' (Elie Faure)[57] – 'Artistic experience is painful and at the same time joyful, because it is acquired by experiences that always involve being and non-being. For the acquisition of experience an artist will go to the verge of death.' (Emil Filla in Kafka's book about artistic creativity) – 'The bourgeois do not even suspect that we serve them our hearts. The race of gladiators has not died: Every artist is one. He amuses the public with his afflictions.' (From the *Correspondence of Gustave Flaubert*) So, what, then, are the laws by which the artist is guided? No laws apart from the law against emptiness, nothingness, destruction; an incessant battle with the only thing that is given for the artist, just as in nature: nothing. The artist and also nature create their realities at the sharp edge of being and non-being. Such is the experience of an artist: nothing is given; if you want to conquer reality, then you must create like

56 Jeans, *The Mysterious Universe*, pp. 123–124.
57 Elie Faure, *History of Art: The Spirit of the Forms*, trans. by Walter Pach (New York and London: Harper, 1930), p. 470.

nature creates, create from nothing. It is impossible here not to recall the advice given by F. X. Šalda[58] to creative spirits: Your first law should be – forget! Forget what has already been done; otherwise you run the risk of being mere imitators, of merely repeating.

Nothing is given to nature, and that is why it has nothing to cognize; however, everything remains for it to create. And, insofar as we are also nature, then it also applies for us that we have nothing to cognize, but that everything remains for us to create. Because nature, which we are ourselves, does not have any reason to turn around in a circle and return through us to something that it already is in itself. Therefore, we can conclude that, insofar as we are also a part of nature, we enter into the world with an instrument for creating, and not for cognizing.

The natural scientist wants to have that 'which is' as given; religion wants to have 'what should be' as given. However, we have come to the conclusion that in the objective or absolute sense *nothing* is given; and, what must be emphasized: *not even this nothing*. Yes, the only inexhaustible, unredeemable power in the world is nothing; it is the greatest not because it is effort, but because it is not effort at all; it needs nothing: effort, work, creation, thoughts, victims, violence, absolutely nothing. If we try to ease up, to weaken, to allay our exertions, even a little, then it starts to eat away at us, to swallow us up, to annihilate us. This is something that is well known to 'illusionists', or rather to critics of illusionism. They well know that there are no final realities or eternal laws, that there is no objective reality, no reality 'of no one', no truth of 'no one'. However, they have fallen into a strange error: when in their expedition to reality they have ended up at nothing, out of the blue they pass off this *nothing* as an *objective* nothing. On the basis of this false notion they were then easily able to 'reveal' illusion-creating instruments in creative instruments.

---

[58]   Czech literary critic (1867–1937).

If they had not committed this error, then they would have understood that nothingness depends on a person's internal relation to the world, that an individual person's *inner soul* is absolutely the only single place in the world where *nothing* is given, felt or consciously aware, and that therefore the overcoming of this nothingness – that is, this reality – is a matter of internal creative forces, a task of the creative organs, not of the organs of perception; quite simply that reality or unreality is a question of an essential, living, and personal process, and not of a technical process, that it is a question of creation, not of cognition; quite simply that the reality of the world in which I live is closely connected with my own reality and that the world cannot be real until *Nothing* has been overcome in it. In the absolute sense cognition would mean: not being.

The thing that evidently takes you aback most, my dear friend, as a natural scientist, is the expression 'creation from nothing'. This probably immediately makes you think about religion, miracles, fairy tales. However, in one respect creativism, or creationism, is really not mistaken: that things are created from nothing. But this truth changes into a complete fallacy, if we view it in a technical way: if we look at nature as a technical work. A technician, as we know, cannot work without a given material and given laws. If, then, creationism is interpreted as the origin of things as created from nothing by a technician, then it must incline toward miracles, toward an all-powerful and unlimited technician. But, here begin fairy tales and arbitrariness. Science rightly resisted this, but instead of attacking creationism where its error begins – that is, in its technical point of view – it has taken on this way of viewing itself and crowned the error of creationism by deposing the miraculous technician and, failing to find a replacement, it has started to explain the world as a technical work without a technician.

First of all, I expressed the contention that natural science, on the one hand, is distancing itself from nature to the same degree as religion, on the other hand, has distanced itself from nature. Just as natural science has its eternal reality and all-powerful law, so religion has in God an all-powerful lawgiver and an eternal reality. This is why both for natural science and also for religion nothing fundamental happens in this world, and if it seems to us that something nevertheless does happen, then this is precisely merely a semblance. In the world of religious faith also, the world is the same from the beginning until the end. Nothing is realized, nothing is created, nothing is destroyed; we are simply waiting here, according to God's predetermination, for the 'true life' in the afterlife in heaven. This heaven, therefore, is not an ideal, not a goal of growth and striving for perfection; it is a ready-made reward for a person's proper and – *nota bene* – predetermined behaviour on Earth. The idea that a person does not become an angel in heaven unless he or she grows and matures to this on Earth – this faith is alien for a Christian, no matter how strange this seems. A Christian believes in miracles without any creative effort, while a scientist does not believe in miracles even at the cost of the most strenuous effort. Meanwhile, a scientist laughs at the idea that a person changes into an angel, but himself teaches us that a frog has changed into a human being. However, a scientist is capable of explaining how a tadpole changes into a scientist in just the same way that a Christian is capable of explaining his own transformation into an angel. Both of them, the scientist and the Christian, agree in the contention that what they actually are – that is, a person – is merely an appearance, a semblance. For a Christian 'final reality', is an angel, while for a scientist it is an element, an atom, an electron. And so we can say: religion distorts the world because for it reality is something that is not yet, something which will only be in the future (after death); while natural science distorts the world because for it reality is something that was already here since time began. However, the reality is that *reality is what is being created, what is created, something which must be created ceaselessly, otherwise it is not.*

If a human being is not a freak in this world, then – we have said – the character of truth and the conditions of salvation must be merely two different forms of the same thing. Now we can already express this somewhat more definitely. Everything that nature sends into the world has – it is possible to say – an indubitable mission here: to fight against nothingness, to make something real, to create from nothing. However, an all-powerful law or an all-powerful God promises us a paradisiacal reality in return merely for exemplary behaviour – this is what religion teaches us; or merely in return for exemplary observing – this is what science teaches us; or merely in return for exemplary imitating – this is what technology teaches us. Here we can already surmise why neither science and technology nor a dogmatic church can save a human being: *they assign him a lower mission than the one that nature itself assigns to him.*

But you are already certainly impatient to find out something more definite about this 'creation from nothing'. Even if perhaps your faith in the principle of the conservation of energy is not so rock-solid as it once was, you are nevertheless still very far from believing in the formation of something from nothing. But I am not even trying to persuade you to any such belief because I myself do not have this belief. Nevertheless, I do not appeal to the principle of the conservation of energy: if matter, or respectively energy, is merely a logical description, a necessary element of the technical explanation of the world, then what more can be sought in the principle of its conservation? This principle, which conserves merely a quantity, an amount, tells us absolutely nothing about the character of the substance that is conserved. It is like an assistant in the accounts department, someone who takes care that the figures add up, without having any idea about what is happening in the operations department. The comparison is imprecise because it is not the operation of nature that needs an accounts department, but rather only the technical interpretation of the operation of nature.

The principle of the conservation of energy, understood as the conservation of matter and energy, understood as an objective fact, turns a person's entire experience inside out. If the sum of energy as the final reality remains the same in the world, then this is only possible either in that maintaining the world in motion does not cost anything (perpetuum mobile 2nd order) and that this is therefore a case of merely apparent events, or in that the events of the world are real, but the consumption of energy is also factual, and for it to be maintained at its original level, it must be supplemented 'from nothing' (perpetuum mobile 1st order). If science is to avoid this contradiction, then it has no other option than to silently incline to the first case: to the conception of events as merely apparent, as a mere sequence of phenomena of an unchanging 'final reality'. However, a human being will never believe that his work and toil are mere appearances which in reality do not cost anything; he feels all too realistically that this costs him something. And, if we nevertheless assert to him that the fruits of his efforts, his lifelong gain, is merely appearance, merely a 'dream', then we will not want anything less from him than for him to accept that dreams must be paid in cash, while reality – as given for ever and always – is free of charge. Who is willing to believe such evident nonsense?

One thing, I think, is evident: if, when clarifying the origination of real things, we want to respect the principle of the impossibility of a perpetuum mobile, then we cannot understand this principle in a physical-mathematical way and base it on the principle of the conservation of matter and energy. Reality is not given; reality must be created. And the principle of the impossibility of a *perpetuum mobile* adds: and for natural science *it must be created from nothing*. Because the reality of nature is not paid in the currency of natural science, but rather in another currency. But in what currency? The answer to this question leads us once again to reality as a problem and a process that is vital and essential, not technical and observational, as it is presented by science and also by theology. The absurdity of 'creation from nothing' comes from the stance of a spectator, from a 'view from outside', from an objectification of negation, of nothingness, of 'nothing'. This is the source of Democritus's claim:

nothing arises from nothing, and what exists cannot pass away into nothing. Natural science, holding to this precept, consequently brought everything to extinction; searching for what 'cannot pass away into nothing', and for what therefore is the only thing that is, it found only things coming-into-being and passing-away, and thus it did not find among things this only thing that is. From this we should conclude that really nothing exists. Truly, objectively, from the external point of view, nothing exists; and it is necessary to add: primarily not even this nothing.

In his famous analysis of nothingness Henri Bergson deduces that the idea of 'Nothing' is a deceptive idea. 'A being unendowed with memory or prevision would not use the words "void" or "nought"; he would express only what is and what is perceived; now, what is, and what is perceived, is the *presence* of one thing or of another, never the *absence* of anything. There is absence only for a being capable of remembering and expecting.'[59] There is, then, no nothingness for nobody, but rather always for someone. However, is it true that nothingness is nothing more than a deceptive idea and nothing other than this? Of course, if we say with Bergson that the negation of some thing assumes the positive of this thing, and that negation is therefore more, not less, than the positive, that it is a 'affirmation of the second degree',[60] then not only 'nothing of no-one', but also 'nothing of someone' both change into a mere deception and the expression about 'creation from nothing' will be based on a deception. However, is this really the case? We should note that Bergson arrives at negation as an affirmation of the second degree through his critique of the *concept* of nothingness. He introduces his chapter on being and nothingness with the words: 'Let us then see what we are thinking about

---

59 Henri Bergson, *Creative Evolution*, trans. by Arthur Mitchell (New York: Henry Holt, 1911), p. 281. www.gutenberg.org/files/26163/26163-h/26163-h.htm.
60 Ibid., p. 304.

when we speak of "Nothing." To represent "Nothing," we must either imagine it or conceive it. Let us examine what this image or this idea may be.'[61] If there were no nothingness other than as something imagined or contained in a concept, then we would certainly have to give up on any chance of understanding nature as creation from nothing. However, Bergson himself tells us that this is not the case. 'All action aims at getting something that we feel the want of, or at creating something that does not yet exist. In this very special sense, it fills a void, and goes from the empty to the full, from an absence to a presence, from the unreal to the real.[62] ... The conviction persists that before things, or at least under things, there is "Nothing." *If we seek the reason of this fact, we shall find it precisely in the feeling, in the social and, so to speak, practical element, that gives its specific form to negation* [highlighted by author]. Now, it is unquestionable, as we remarked above, that every human action has its starting point in a dissatisfaction, and thereby in a feeling of absence. We are made in order to act as much as, and more than, in order to think.'[63]

It seems to me that we have no need of any better testimony. If the special domain of nothingness is the affective domain, and it is conceded that we are created more for action than for thinking, then nature itself stands behind us. Even if we say that the idea of nothingness is a pseudo-idea, then the feeling of nothingness will never be a pseudo-feeling.

If Bergson has proved that nothingness is a pseudo-idea, whose problematic arises in that 'the forms of human action relate to their own field', then he has shifted the unproblematic nothingness into the affective and free field, therefore precisely where it should not be if he wants to get to his anticipated aim: to an absolute that would act freely and that would endure in the true sense of the word. For

---

61 Ibid., p. 297.
62 Ibid., p. 273.
63 Ibid., p. 297.

Bergson's vital absolute it would be better if the concept or representation of nothingness was not a pseudo-idea, but if on the other hand the feeling of nothingness was a pseudo-feeling.

In a certain sense, Bergson represents an extreme case, an opposing extreme to the illusionists and nihilists. While they viewed being as an illusion and saw the absolute in nothingness, in contrast to this Bergson sees illusion in nothingness and the absolute in being. However, just as non-being, so also being, is 'for someone' and not 'for no one'. It seems that, like the illusionists, Bergson has also fallen into the trap of explanation.

It does not speak much in favour of Bergson's philosophical conscience, when he – having deduced that nothingness is a pseudo-idea – returns to the field of human activity in order there to conclude some kind of compromise and to allow nothingness to appear under the name of the 'absence of utility'. 'Our life is thus spent in filling voids, which our intellect conceives under the influence, by no means intellectual, of desire and of regret, under the pressure of vital necessities; and if we mean by void an absence of utility and not of things, we may say, in this quite relative sense, that we are constantly going from the void to the full: Such is the direction which our action takes.'[64] In response to this, it is necessary to say: If the 'filling of voids' takes place under the 'pressure of vital necessities', then in this 'quite relative sense' everything essential is expressed and there is no longer any place left here for an explanation in any other sense, for an absolute or objective explanation. It is evident that Bergson, for whom nothingness is an illusion and being an absolute, is at a loss about what to do with nothingness at the moment when it forces itself to his attention as an impulse to action, as a creative spine of life, quite simply as an internal, essential, vital state, and not as a mere pseudo-idea. This is why his creative evolution is not at all creative, and also why we do not find any reason why or

64 Ibid., p. 314.

how absolute being should or could be creative, when it is not even possible to well understand why it is evolving, or even why it needs to pursue utility and team up with it. If absolute being does not recognize nothingness, then evidently it does not lack anything, and therefore it does not even need to act, let alone create. Bergson's explication arouses the impression that he differentiates two different kind of activities, both of them similarly paradoxical: utilitarian human action, which is mere *action* even though it goes from the void to the full, and the free *creation* of absolute being, which is creation, even though it goes from the full to the full.

If, in this way, we have demonstrated the 'right of residence' of nothingness in the field of emotions and instincts, by this we have verified that creation – that is, the overcoming of this nothingness – is conditioned on participation. As such it is motivated neither by usefulness, nor by pleasure, nor by imitation. In fact it makes no great sense to speak about motives at all here: these could perhaps be the work of desire, of intent, but not however of instinct, which is – as we will show – of an entirely different character. It is not even appropriate to call this the 'instinct of self-preservation' because by this designation we assign to it something that is given and which it is sufficient to preserve; it would perhaps be better to call it the *instinct of being*, an instinct for which nothing is given and for which everything still remains to create. As such, it represents in us something which no one cannot not want. Because even a suicide does not want non-being; he also is fleeing from nothingness, and not fleeing to nothingness.

If for a spectator nothingness is a mere pseudo-idea, the entire meaning of which depends on preventing error, for a participant nothingness is a feeling 'of himself', a feeling of emptiness in life, and a falling of one's self into nothing, a loss of one's own reality. This is not a case here of a confrontation of the past or the future with the present as is the case of the spectator's negation; it is a case here of the present itself, because for the participant there is no other time dimension. The feeling of nothingness is an immediate 'living situation' – that is, a state of the inner soul, or in other words a state of the world; we have said that the world is real insofar as our soul is real, insofar as emptiness is overcome in the world.

It is perhaps clear that the phrase a 'living situation' here does not mean some biological or sociological situation, or some such similar type of situation. A person can fall into nothingness and non-being, even when he or she is in an optimal state biologically and economically. The feeling of nothingness – this is a feeling of a loss of the world, a loss of self, a loss of community with souls which are beyond 'bodies' and 'things'. To create means to preserve oneself, but also more: to realize oneself, to give a face to the soul, and by doing so also to the world; to multiply and intensify relations, to participate, to fulfil and enrich one's soul – this is to enrich and make real the world, the world of beings and things. Goethe, as is well known, says this in this way: 'Only what you do for yourself in the true sense of the word, you also do for the world.'

Well, then, is it now going to be less difficult for us to comprehend 'creation from nothing'? We are in Robert's workshop. Have a look around, my friend! Many things attract your attention and force your thoughts down unaccustomed paths. You are witness of changes that will not remain without response in your soul. For instance, you see a pile of clay and then a small figure made from this same pile of clay. Instead of a pile of clay you envisage an exact equation and you think about the process which would lead you to the equation of the small figure. But there is no exact path from the pile of clay to the sculpture; it is not possible to write a new equation. 'Nothing' has been added, 'nothing' has been taken away; a pile of clay has been rearranged into a pile of clay; the thing is the same; for a natural scientist nothing fundamental has happened. Are we supposed to conclude that only a pile of clay exists, but not however a sculpture? Yes, 'objectively' only a pile of clay exists. However, if we ask a natural scientist in what the objective existence of the clay consists, he will show us analogously that 'objectively' some kind of electrons and similar elements exist, but nothing however that we call clay. Not only 'artificial' things, but also 'natural' things are as such without objective existence. Concrete things which are immediately known to us, called sculptures, marble, songs, linden trees, bumble bees, planes, and so on, do not appear as such in the formulas of the exact sciences – that is, they are not of the 'physical' order; they are of another order. For natural science they have arisen from nothing, and in the final instance they are also nothing for it. And if after all for science – in some special sciences – they are nevertheless something, then only if, only insofar as – as we have shown – this particular special science does not push its objective cognizing to extremes.

Let us ask what differentiates a pile of clay from a sculpture made from this same pile of clay. Each of us more or less well knows this; the natural scientist also knows this, but as a spokesman for his science he forbids himself from paying attention to it. He sees a sculpture, but he says that the sculpture does not exist; there exists only a pile of clay, because it is not possible to write a 'new equation'. But, if it is not possible to write a new equation, what does this imply? This implies that the sculpture did not arise from some expenditure that is physical and countable. What arose from an expenditure that is physical and countable was only that a pile of clay was rearranged into another pile of clay. The sculpture arose from an expenditure of something else; it arose from an effort to overcome 'nothing', from an effort to give a face and an expression to the soul; it arose from an action of a soul balancing over emptiness and seeking and finding its stability, its living balance, its vital reality; it was paid for by suffering, exertion, angst, pain. Everyone more or less well knows this. Therefore – let us say this already now – to say that things are created from nothing means saying that *the equivalent of their creation is internal*, that it is necessary to search for their equivalent in the internal world, not in the external one; to search for it in the essential and living, not in the physical, the weighable, the measurable.

We are constantly led to the 'inside' or 'soul' as to a principle and a method of reality and events. If we want to extricate ourselves from the senseless notion that we must pay for dreams in cash, while we have reality free of charge, then the most obvious path to this is, I think, the notion that the world can be created and maintained only in that some 'consciousness', some 'feeling', some 'urge', quite simply – so that we do not speak only on behalf of human beings – some kind of 'inside' functions as a balance or scales of being and non-being, as an indicator of the living and the non-living, the substantial and the insubstantial, and this as itself being and non-being.

However, the question immediately arise here: For which itself? This electron, this atom, this molecule, crystal, amoeba, frog, warbler, Mr. X. or Mr. Y, or an electron 'as such', an amoeba 'as such', a person 'as such', or someone behind all this or above all this? Life with a capital L, Nature with a capital N, the Absolute, Spirit, God and so on? As is evident, the question that we have posed is directed at an individual; and, for someone who accepts the organic and inorganic world as an expression, not as an object, this question really has a fundamental significance. In the first order, therefore, it is necessary to talk about this individual.

What is an individual? In the sense of our hitherto deliberations an individual is that which is an expression of itself. Let us take as an example our friend Fred: Is this friend an individual, is he an expression of himself? For natural science, which is concerned with understanding things and beings from the outside, there is no inside, and thereby there is also no individual. However, an ignorance of the inner soul is regarded as an acknowledgement of some kind of realm of rational 'natural laws' that is above nature and above mankind. Natural science does not even try to refute the origin of these natural laws in human reason, and thereby from a human inside or soul. It well knows why it does not try to do so: it knows that by doing so it would become ensnared in a noetic and metaphysical labyrinth, all of whose exits end in solipsism, or – in the case that science makes some small concessions on its intellectual rigorousness – in the 'cosmic consciousness' of metaphysicians, or – if it makes some more concessions – in the gods of theologians.

Among the so-called spiritual sciences, which primarily come into consideration for the question of the individual, sociology contends that our friend Fred is created by 'society,' by his 'milieu', by the 'era', and in this way denies him as an individual. Society is something concrete, while an individual is something abstract. Psychology, if it does not go down the path of natural science, mostly takes the same point of view as sociology, only with the difference that, instead of viewing Fred as a product of a non-localized social and historical 'collective consciousness', it presents him as an expression of a 'collective unconscious', which it locates at the very bottom of his inside, his soul, where in some cases it makes way for genetics and physiology.

However, the psychologist and the sociologist have no small surprise in store for us, if we ask him to put forward guarantees that make his central concept – that is, collective consciousness, supra-consciousness and the subconscious, his libido and psychic energy – a substance *sui generis*; that is, that reality of which – among other things – our friend Fred is a phenomenon, respectively an expression. With amazement we hear that this reality, this concrete thing that changes our friend Fred into a mere appearance, into a mere abstraction, is nothing more than a mere 'hypothesis', a 'methodological' concept, a mere 'constructive aid', in short: a mere notion. This paradoxical inconsistency and many other discrepancies have forced the orthodox researcher to banish all together such concepts as 'inside', 'mind', 'soul', 'consciousness', 'spirit', and similar concepts, and he does not hesitate to declare that the human mind cannot be acknowledged as an instigator of 'manifest action'. He justifies this by saying, for instance, that 'the wish to eat can be followed by the action that a person goes into a restaurant or digs up a potato in a vegetable garden, or that he goes to work in a factory in order to get money for food, or he can sing for his supper in the theatre'. (Pitirim Alexandrovich Sorokin, *Contemporary Sociological Theories*)[65] – However, insofar that it is not possible to predict with certainty whether, from a desire to eat, a person will decide to dig up a potato or go to work in a factory, this impossibility of prediction apparently derives from the fact that the desire to eat is not at all an impulse for a person to do the one or the other. The consciousness of hunger should not be admitted as a concept at all in the chain of a person's action. If we ask what, then, initiates this 'trans-subjective' cycle of human behaviour and maintains it in motion, the reply that we receive – what a surprise! – is literally identical with the advice that mathematical conditionalism gave us for understanding natural events: in the equation of trans-subjective factors, we assume one of these factors as an independent variable! The same magic formula that helped us get natural events into motion is also supposed to bring to life human limbs and to explain our actions and the actions of our friends and family.

This is strange. When investigating physical and chemical phenomena, expressed in algebraic equations, we were incapable of envisaging these events as 'happening' until we posited the assumption of a non-physical actor who could not be absorbed into these equations and who was a 'prime mover' of events. However, this prime mover remained suspect to us all the while we did not know where to search for it and how to envisage it. Now, however, in the field of human and social action, which can also only be objectively – that is, technically – explained on the assumption of a prime mover-technician, when we finally find this technician in ourselves, in our inner being, we erase it and deny it. And what is

65 Pitirim Alexandrovič Sorokin, *Contemporary Sociological Theories* (New York: Harper, 1928).

more: when we are finally in a circle of events in which we are able to understand clearly and without difficulty, if someone says, for instance, that boredom made him go to the theatre, all of a sudden the sociologist steps up and claims to us that it cannot in any way be a feeling of boredom, a feeling of emptiness, that leads any person whatsoever to go to the theatre. And this is because out of boredom he could also go to a coffee house or to bed or God knows where else. Given that not all people in all circumstances, if they get bored, go without exception to the theatre, boredom cannot be an impulse for someone to go to the theatre. Because, if we designate boredom as A, the theatre as B, the coffee house as C, and bed as D, it cannot apply that A=B, A=C, A=D, because it evidently does not apply that B=C=D. An orthodox sociological researcher, investigating human behaviour and actions, does not think about people, but rather about physical and chemical rudiments. He does not pay any attention to the fact that on his experimental table he has the richest and most developed inner life; by hook or by crook and at all costs he wants to see through an optic of the most primitive, the dullest inner life. Sorokin asks: 'What kind of idea, desire, or wish as some kind of purely psychological experience could act on the sensory, conductive, and motor parts of the nervous system and of bodily movements together with such trans-subjective phenomena as war or a fall in the birth rate?' Really, I would also like to know how mere ideas, represented for instance by 'natural laws', can move dead things, things without an inner life. Sorokin asks how a 'desire' can grasp and direct a hand, as for instance a hand can grasp and direct a shovel. I, on the other hand, want to ask: How can a hand grasp and direct a shovel, when there is no desire, no inner life, behind this? If there is no such 'desire' which allows us to understand trans-subjective phenomena, such as war or a fall in the birth rate, then – I dare to claim – then there is nothing that would enable us to understand these phenomena better.

What is strange is that a person can study these sociological laws, which direct human and social events independently of any human inner life, 'for the purpose' of changing and directing social events with the help of these laws. Are these social changes, induced and directed by human knowledge and volition – that is, by the human inner life – also independent of human inner life? If yes, then what sense do knowledge and volition have here? What purpose is served by their teaming up with sociology and with the application of the laws of sociology in practice? One thing is evident: if a sociological researcher is to avoid drowning in absurdities, he can countenance a denial of the inner life only within a certain limit; and that limit is the researcher himself. Not only does a sociological explanation of social events not preclude an inner life; it even assumes such a life, albeit with the proviso that this is the inner life of the sociologist. However, this is not only his case; it is the same in the case of all other technical explicators. It is their own inner lives that enable them to explain everything by external factors, while denying an inner life to the things of nature. Let us recall what led the research- er to regard Beethoven as a chip of wood in the current of a river and to evaluate his creation as an activity 'which knows nothing of itself'. Beethoven created blindly, unconsciously, as a mere instru- ment of someone, because he was not aware of the laws of his crea- tion. Which kind of laws? Those laws which were discovered by the physicist, the biologist, the aesthetician, the sociologist, and so on. Beethoven acted like a mechanism, because he was not conscious of his own activity as a mechanical action. Quite simply, because he was not a 'spectator' and an explicator of himself. What, then, most prevents us from admitting an inner life to the things and beings of nature is the notion that this inner life cannot contain a con- sciousness of its own organic or inorganic behaviour. However, how do we conceive this consciousness? No other than as an awareness of physical, chemical, biological, and other precepts – that is, an awareness of oneself as a technical and rational process. A natural individual would have to become a physical, biological, psychological, etc. explicator of itself; the absurdity of this result is sufficient for us to deny consciousness and an inner life as such to everything that is not endowed with reason and accompanied by an explanation given by this reason. The greatest obstacle for us, therefore, is an anthropomorphic – that is, a rational, technical – conception of natural events. According to this conception, the only actions that are conscious and internal are those of a spectator, and no others. Yes, if the principle of natural events was rational and technical, it is possible that we would be conscious of ourselves just as we are described by the 'science of man' and the 'science of life'. However, since the principle of natural events is different, the description, for instance, of a tree as a chemical factory remains a mere explanation, in which we will search in vain for a technician and his head office in this factory, because this directing technician is merely the explainer's reason itself. This reason does not direct the event of the tree; it merely directs its explanation. The beings and the things of nature could, therefore, be represented to us in the technician's explanation as mechanisms and automatons, because they were described as technical works without a technician.

However, the originality and individuality of natural individuals is not concealed only by the rationalization of nature, by turning nature into a technological process. Sometimes, on the contrary, it is the very irrationality of instinct that serves as a mysterious tank which feeds an individual and changes it into a mere outer surface or peel filled with a collective liquid. For instance, we are challenged to consider this: we cut up an earthworm into four parts, and each of these four parts regenerate into four earthworms. Morgan even cut up a flatworm (turbellaria) into seventy-two parts, and each of these grew into a new individual. How should we understand this? Bavink puts forward this depiction: we should not look at an individual as an absolute unit separated from everything else, but rather as a more or less raised wave in the great stream of living events. Or: 'An individual

I has not so far appeared in the field of lower animals. ... A mental unity of multiplicity manifests itself here.' (Eugen Georg)[66]

This individual – this is, then, nothing more than a piece of foam borne on the water. If you divide it up into small pieces, then they will form into new clusters and float on downstream. The soul of such an individual – this is like foam streaming through water.

A piece going somewhere it does not want, will resist; but what is reacting here, what is resisting, is not a small piece of foam, but rather water, the river which is bearing the foam. Destroy the foam, and you have destroyed a trifling scrag; you have not touched the river.

Bavink's depiction will also serve in even more mysterious cases. What, for instance, should we think about the strange behaviour of myxomycetes (plasmodial slime-mould), when thousands of single-cell individuals, thus far living independently, all of a sudden aggregate together, as though in response to a command, in a body which forms a complicated plant, which behaves in its own way as a new 'higher' individual, quite different from its original parts? Or what to think about colonies of ants, termites or bees, which can apparently be more appropriately understand as a single living being, as Bavink advises us, or as 'one single idea in the state of an action, similarly distributed in a way as the various cells and filaments of a mammal brain instance', as Alfred Espinas, the author of *Animal Societies*, advises us. And before we start comforting ourselves that there is no place for human beings in this Alice's Wonderland, let us recall what Gustave Le Bon has written about us: 'The psychological crowd is a provisional being formed of heterogeneous elements, which for a moment are combined, exactly as the cells which constitute a living body form by their reunion a new being which displays characteristics very different from those possessed by each of the cells singly. ... An individual immersed for some length of time

---

[66] Eugen Georg, *The Adventure of Mankind* (New York: E. P. Dutton, 1931).

in a crowd in action soon finds himself ... in a special state, which much resembles the state of fascination in which the hypnotised individual finds himself in the hands of the hypnotiser. The conscious personality has entirely vanished; will and discernment are lost. All feelings and thoughts are bent in the direction determined by the hypnotiser. ... [An individual] is no longer himself, but has become an automaton who has ceased to be guided by his will.'[67]

The river is certainly full of eddies, rapids, gorges, and so it is no surprise when the floating blobs of foam all at once, 'as though in response to a command', speed up their course, cluster together and combine, here more freely and there more tightly (in a new 'body' or merely in a new 'colony'), and create a higher being. Of course this is no explanation, but it does reconcile us with the mystery. It tells us why a new and higher life form of a more organized individual was not predicable from the original individuals, and why it is not even deducible from the more complicated anatomy of the higher being: because this new life form, this new quality of being, derives directly from the living stream, from the mysterious and inscrutable flow of the river. The river is everything: individuals are mere floaters, making visible the river's course, the diversity of its currents, streamlines, depths and rapids, of its twists and turns. Why should we be surprised that hundreds of solitary myxomycetes join together all at once at a certain place and merge into a new being? Why should we be surprised when non-rational and non-deliberating small creatures create a perfectly organized colony of insects? And finally why should we be surprised when metallic filings form a line around something like a crowd of people around the podium of a public speaker or when a myriad of electrons creates a seamless marching file? It is sufficient to envisage the bottom of all this as a common current, as an underground river which bears them, as

67 Gustave Le Bon, *The Crowd: A Study of the Popular Mind*, (New York: Macmillan, 1896), pp. 6, 11–13.

Life with a capital L, as Truth with a capital T, the Absolute, and so on; or, for whomever it suits better, as a Cosmic Hypnotist.

Let us submit the personal details of this mysterious someone to at least the most essential check-up and try to deduce from this as much as we can. The 'hidden current' with its modifications and personifications has its origin in the circumstance that a living event, represented by any single individual, cannot be explained from this individual itself. The only things that can be attributed to the account of an individual are things of which the individual is conscious, the things which he knows – that is, only what can be transposed into the formulation: *I* feel, *I* think, *I* want, *I* do and similarly. However, alongside this conscious event, an individual's life is determined by far more extensive and diverse events, of which he is not conscious and which can be formulated in this way: *it* feels, *it* wants, thinks, does, or simply: *it* happens. Therefore, only a miniscule part of what I call *my* life, *my* existence, is *my* life; it is far more the life of something or someone else; it is the existence of dead or live matter – that is, physical, chemical, physiological, and so on, existence – but also psychological existence, including 'subconscious' or 'supra-conscious', or to put it another way: psychological, sociological, metaphysical existence. In short, I live an existence of something or someone else, and I am permitted to call only a miniscule splinter of this my own existence. And it is only these other existences that first explain my existence and give it meaning. Thus the reason and meaning of my life is the life and existence of someone and something else. I take my life from the arms of molecules, cells, tissue, instincts, collectives, and Gods. I must ask them, if I want to know why I am living, and why I live and act precisely in this way, and not in another way. They are my real life.

But we are not yet at the end. How can I find out about all these existences that I am living, but nevertheless not living? I have learned about them from science, philosophy, and theology – that is, *not through participation, but rather through particular methods of looking*. Therefore, I find my real life not by participating in it, but rather by observing it. And what is even more embarrassing: I cannot even participate in my own personal life, because only this *it* participates; I cannot do anything other than merely look on. If I say 'I feel', 'I think', 'I want', then this means that I become aware of, that I represent, that I objectify my feelings, my thinking, my wanting, that I perceive; however, 'a perceived feeling is not a feeling, but rather a perception'. In truth, then, I feel, I think, I want, when it is not *I* who feel, think, or want, but when this *it* feels, thinks, wants. When *I* experience something, therefore, I do not actually experience, but rather perceive, observe, explain; the process of experiencing is 'unconscious'; only observing and explaining are conscious. *I* am a spectator; this *it*, the 'river', is a participant. If I cease to look, to observe, I will change into this 'it', into the 'river', into a 'mass soul'. This 'it' is reality, and I am … what?

We already know that we can cease taking account of this 'it' if it is presented to us as a rational and technical process; as such it resides only in the explainer's mind. However, it is a different case if this 'it' is presented to us as something irrational, taking place as an unconscious process, or respectively a 'subconscious' one. And, moreover, how it is presented to us! As an object of observation, as a subject of science. Alongside the rational process, alongside observation and perception, we also know 'participation' as an irrational process. However, participation is neither unconscious and nor can it be a subject of science, because in the process of observing (or in the process of introspection – no other method comes into consideration) it disappears. If this 'it' is something irrational, and meanwhile it is not participation, what then is it? Could it offer us here some kind of other path to the inner life of beings and things, to the inner life of nature? We must investigate this possibility at least in its broadest outlines.

The branch of knowledge that has followed this path most thoroughly, and therefore what we are now going to consider, is the specialism of modern psychology classified under the term 'psychoanalysis'. It arose within the field of practical medicine, on the inalienable ground of extreme materialism, and the history of the revolution that gave rise to psychoanalysis here is appositely captured in the words of J. H. Woodger in his *Biological Principles*: 'The physical point of view has been, and still is, acting the part of a dead weight of prejudice against a psychological study of mental disease, both in practice and in the medical schools. The old metaphysical assumptions of materialism render men blind to the obvious fact that you can learn more about a man's mind by talking to him for ten minutes than by looking at sections of his brain for ten years, (not to mention the fact that whatever information may be obtained by the latter method will be of little avail for the treatment of the patient!).'[68]

For Sigmund Freud and C. G. Jung, the leading figures of psychoanalysis, the 'subconscious' is the actual psychological reality, while consciousness is a mere observer of this reality. This reality, called by Freud the 'id' and by Jung the 'objective psyche', has the same relation to consciousness as the 'external world' has to the sensory organs. Our consciousness observes our subconscious in much the same way as our sensory organs perceive the external world. The reality of the external world is the most difficult problem for the 'spectator'; the reality of the subconscious world will not be any easier problem for him.

Freud's interpreter Israel Levine comments: 'The analogy between [Freud's] standpoint and that of Kant is somewhat striking. What we perceive, according to Kant, is not to be identified with reality, or the thing in itself, but is "phenomenal," the product of mental forms and categories. So, according to Freud, conscious perception is not to be identified with the unconscious psychic process which is perceived. "The psychic," Freud writes,

---

[68] J. H. Woodger, *Biological Principles* (London: Kegan Paul, Trench, Trubner & Co., 1929), p. 58.

"need not, any more than the physical, be really as it appears to us." (Freud, *Complete Works: Vol. IV*)'.[69] The reference to Kant's 'thing-in-itself' not only does not lessen our doubts about unconscious psychological reality, but on the contrary intensifies these doubts. Just as Johann Gottlieb Fichte and Hegel entail an uncompromising completion of the thoughts of Kant's compromises, we can likewise regard the uncompromising completion represented by psychoanalytical thinking. And we can consider this charming narration by C. G. Jung: '"But why on Earth," you may ask, "should it be necessary for man to achieve, by hook or by crook, a higher level of consciousness?" This is truly the crucial question, and I do not find the answer easy. Instead of a real answer I can only make a confession of faith: I believe that, after thousands and millions of years, someone had to realize that this wonderful world of mountains and oceans, suns and moons, galaxies and nebulae, plants and animals, exists. From a low hill in the Athi plains of East Africa I once watched the vast herds of wild animals grazing in soundless stillness, as they had done from time immemorial, touched only by the breath of a primeval world. I felt then as if I were the first man, the first creature, to know that all this is. The entire world round me was still in its primeval state; it did not know that it was. And then, in that one moment in which I came to know, the world sprang into being; without that moment it would never have been. All Nature seeks this goal and finds it fulfilled in man, but only in the most highly developed and most fully conscious man.'[70]

Even the most dedicated Hegelian would sign this passage without hesitation. For the Hegelian also, the world only comes into being for the first time at the moment of the 'most highly developed'

69 Israel Levine, *The Unconscious; an Introduction to Freudian Psychology* (New York: Macmillan, 1923), pp. 134–135.
70 Carl Gustav Jung, 'Psychological Aspects of the Mother Archetype' (1939) in *Collected Works 8: The Structure and Dynamics of the Psyche*, p. 177.

consciousness – that is, conceptual consciousness. And if the psychoanalyst agrees with the Hegelian in claiming that the reality of the external world is a product of this consciousness, then where can a reason be found that the reality of the hidden world is not also a product of this consciousness? The psychoanalyst [Levine] claims that 'the Unconscious, on Freud's view, is the real psychic, which may or may not acquire the attribute conscious. Conscious, therefore, so far from being the universal or essential characteristic of mental processes, is merely a special function of a particular system of the mental apparatus.'[71] However, if you ask him for some guarantees or a confession of faith, then he slips away from you with the pronouncement that 'Freud nowhere claims that [the existence of unconscious mental processes] is more than a necessary hypothesis'.[72]

Psychoanalysts are fond of demonstrating that Robert's world, to which we are trying here in these pages to pave a way, is an expression of the unconscious, the irrational nature of which C. G. Jung never ceases to emphasize. 'Irrational creation,' he writes, 'which appears most significantly especially in art, in the final instance derides all kind of rational efforts.' But how then can I rationally explain an unconscious irrational process? If its reality consists in its irrationality, what am I doing when I explain it, or even when I explain it scientifically? I am doing this: I am replacing an irrational process with a rational process, and thereby inducing a quite new process, which has absolutely nothing in common with the previous one. Jung claims that 'the irrational as such can never be the subject of science',[73] but we should note that he posits in the irrational subconscious what he is seeking for there and what he then extracts from it: 'The forgotten, the suppressed, all kinds of things that are perceived, thought,

71 Levine, *The Unconcious*, pp. 82–83.
72 Ibid., pp. 96–97.
73 Carl Gustav Jung, *Collected Works 6: Psychological Types*, in chapter 'Definitions'.

and felt under the threshold of consciousness.' To an overwhelming extent, then, what was previously in consciousness, in the rational. Is not such an irrational merely a 'suppressed' rational? But so far we have been talking only about matters of the 'personal unconscious'. However, under this flows a 'collective unconscious'. The content of this collective unconscious are mostly so-called archetypes – that is, some kind of primordial images which reach back perhaps as far as the animal past of human beings. This cannot, of course, be a case of inherited images, since images are bound to a personal experience, but rather merely a case of an inherited faculty for images of a certain type, a faculty for breaking through ancient blocked-up watercourses, through which human thought once flowed; C. G. Jung calls these *Bahnungen* (channels).

That which is thought and felt in the unconscious – that is, outside of consciousness – does not permit the question of who thinks and feels these things. So, evidently only one possibility remains: what is thought 'of itself' and what is felt 'of itself'. The psychoanalytical 'id', or respectively the 'objective psyche' – this is the same as some kind of feeling of itself, thought of itself, and so on. The unconscious appears to us here as a mere requisite of the spectator, the explicator. In order to be able to replace an irrational process with a rational explanation, the explicator locates this explanation – that is, his consciousness – into the 'unconscious' of the person whose experiences he is explicating. As we have said that there are no spectators in nature, this also entails that there are no unconscious events there either. The 'underground river' is an invention of the spectator, necessary for localizing a rational explanation of an irrational process. Without a spectator there is no underground river and no unconscious. There are no other processes than conscious ones. A rational process is given by an explanation in the spectator's consciousness; an irrational process is given by an experience in the participant's consciousness. All the 'personal details' of an irrational process are given by the consciousness of the person experiencing this process, and there is nothing that could or should be connected to this. Psychoanalytical theory boasts of its successes in treatment similarly to the way in which science boasts of its techno- logical successes. A psychoanalyst treats his patient in the faith that he will rid him of something that is concealed in the subconscious of the ill person. I envisage a hungry person whom I would try to help cure his hunger by first examining whether his feeling of hunger was caused by the image of a baked goose or by an image of lamb cooked in garlic. I would describe a few different dishes to him, and would designate as the content of his unconscious the dish in the case of which his mouth dribbled when I described it to him. If we were to accept the treatment successes of psychoanalysis in the same sense that psychoanalysts give to them, then we would have to conclude that the irrational is nothing more than a suppressed or unconscious rational. In his book *The Psychology of the Unconscious* C. G. Jung goes so far in this rationalization of the unconscious that he deciphers the dream of one of his patients not as a symbol of her case, but rather directly as a symbol of psychoanalytical teaching and methods. The dominant features of her dream are a river, a ford across it, and a crayfish hidden in the water, which bites the patient in the legs when she attempts to cross. In Jung's interpretation, the ford represents the transfer from the unconscious to the conscious, the river an obstacle to this transfer, the water the unconscious, and the crayfish the content of the unconscious. In other words: the unconscious symbolizes itself as an explanation, as the rational. The unconscious is not a participant here; it is the spectator of itself.

What a small role deserves to be assigned to the 'content of the unconscious' in psychoanalytical treatment can be deduced from the thankless testimonies of psychoanalysts themselves. Freud, for instance, writes: 'If the treatment of neurosis is successful also in those institutions in which psychoanalysis is excluded; if it can be said that hysteria is not cured by a method, but rather by a doctor; if a blind devotion and a permanent bond is usually formed by the patient toward the doctor who has rid him of his symptom, then the scientific explanation for this must be sought in the transfers that a patient regularly creates toward a doctor. ... When this is not possible (that is, gentle and friendly transfers supporting treatment), then the patient disengages himself as quickly as possible, uninfluenced by a doctor whom he does not find "sympathetic".' – If the being who is the object of the suppressed idea can be replaced through 'transference' by another being, then it is evident that, rather than a suppressed idea, what really plays a fundamental role here is unsuppressed feeling. 'It would seem then', admits Levine, 'that the relation of repression to affect is of crucial significance. "Ideas are repressed," Freud writes in one place," only because they are connected with liberations of emotions, which are not to come to light." (Freud, *Delusion and Dream*, p. 179).'[74] 'Suppressed' feelings are not suppressed, because there is nowhere to suppress them; either they do not exist, or they are in the experience, in the consciousness, of the participant, who cannot or may not express them. They cannot be in the spectator's consciousness, because there lies only an explanation. There is no better way to demonstrate this than in Freud's own words: 'The patient cannot recall all of what lies repressed, perhaps not even the essential part of it, and so gains no conviction that the conclusion presented to him is correct. He is obliged rather to repeat as a current experience what is repressed, instead of, as the physician would prefer to see him do, recollecting it as a fragment of the past.'[75] If we so desire, a poet will provide us with a reliable key: 'Love is a need; whether we pour it into a golden vase, or into a clay vessel, it is necessary for it to be poured. Only chance will find recipients for us.' (Gustave Flaubert, *Correspondence*) – The thing that tortures the sick person is an unfulfilled need

74 Levine, *The Unconscious*, pp. 119–120.
75 Sigmund Freud, *Beyond the Pleasure Principle*, trans. by C. J. M. Hubback, revised by Ernest Jones (London and Vienna: International Psycho-Analytical Press, 1922), p. 13. www.libraryofsocialscience.com/assets/pdf/freud_beyond_the_pleasure_principle.pdf.

for participation; this is the source of the feeling of emptiness and nothingness. This notion, absolutely alien to Freud, is not alien to Albert Adler, and quite certainly not to Jung. Psychoanalysts, by reducing the essential thing – that is, emotion – to a mere 'accompanying phenomenon' of a (suppressed) idea, have thus conceded it a say only in adventures of pleasure and displeasure, and have thus obscured the fact that it should have a decisive say in the question of being and non-being.

In what does this illness consist? In that an idea or thought, undesirable for moral or other reasons, is erased, while the feeling that made this idea a living reality remains.

The thing that a psychoanalyst must treat in the case of an ill person is not, therefore, a suppressed idea, but rather an unsuppressed feeling. This treatment occurs either by 'satisfying' the feeling – that is, according to psychoanalysts by a 'transference' – or by its extermination, rationalization, in the speech of psychoanalysts: by its transfer from the unconscious to the conscious. This is actually a case here of a transformation of a participant into a spectator according to the direction: an objectivized, perceived feeling is not a feeling, but rather a perception, a cognition. The first path is more merciful. However, if the treatment is to end in success, then the doctor is here confronted with the task of 'displacement of the transference', that is, displacing his own person with another person. The second path is more dangerous. C. G. Jung recounts about one of his patients that 'the "poison" of cognition had to be administered carefully in small doses until the female patient gradually became more reasonable'.

The confrontation of psychoanalytical psychology with Hegelian idealism shows itself to be very fruitful for our fundamental question: for the relation of the explanation to the explained or, as is it is put more usually, the relation between reality and the explanation of reality. Psychoanalysts teach that reality is given independently of its explanation; the Hegelians, on the contrary, teach that reality is entirely dependent on explanation, on consciousness. They agree on limiting consciousness to reason – that is, in our sense, to explanation. This is why, for the psychoanalysts reality is exclusively irrational, while for the Hegelians it is exclusively rational. However, neither the one nor the other is able to make do with its extreme position. The psychoanalytical irrational – we have seen – is the 'suppressed' rational, its 'subconscious' and 'unconscious' is sublimated consciousness. Hegelians, on the other hand, for whom only the rational is real – that is, substantial – come to the unexpected confession that the *unreal also exists*. Their writings teem with strange assertions such as this: 'Nature is only feeling. As feeling is unreal, its reality consists in an idea.' Giovanni Gentile[76] concludes one of his books thus: 'Reality, the world, is an idea; however, Atlas, who bears this world – in which we live and in which to live is a joy – is a feeling.' Similarly, another Hegelian, Hermann Glockner,[77] distinguishes two worlds: the intellectually apprehended, objectivized world of subjects ('in the world' he calls this) and mere 'states' (*Zustand*) (designated as mere 'world'). Given that we know that for a Hegelian a subject is identical with a concept, and that this is the only reality, then we are certainly curious what this 'state' is. Glockner replies that this 'state' in fact does not exist at all. It can be asserted only of subjects that they 'are'; whatever, in contrast to this, cannot be called a subject, such a thing evidently belongs just as little under the category of being as it belongs under any other category. – Even Hegel distinguishes, in addition to real substance, 'factual substance', which he calls a phenomenon. Where do all these inconsistencies come from?

Let us take an example, let us say a song. A Hegelian will say that a song is not a song as long as the concept of song does not exist. Indeed, birdsong, for instance, is a song for us, who have the concept

---

76 Italian neo-Hegelian philosopher (1875–1944).
77 German philosopher (1896–1979).

of song, but not, however, for the singing bird, who does not have the concept of song. Is, then, a bird singing or is it not singing? If it is not singing, then what is it doing? After all, it is evident that it is doing something; otherwise we could not say that it is singing. And how about if I myself sing? If I sing while I am doing some work and think about my work while doing so, and not about singing – and not only do I not think about the concept of singing, but I do not think even about the words, the melody, the verse – then what am I in fact doing? Am I singing, or am I not singing? Am I singing only when I am actively conscious of the concept of singing? But I can also be conscious of the concept of singing, even when I am evidently not singing, and moreover even when I am not listening to someone else sing. In fact, we know that, if while singing, respectively while listening to a song, I concentrate my attention on the concept of singing, then I cease to sing, or respectively cease to hear the song. I have the concept of a song, but by this do I also have a song?

Psychoanalysts say that the reality of a song is present before the concept of a song, that I can sing already before reason gives this the designation of 'song', but then, however, irrational substance starts to reveal itself to us as rational substance. A Hegelian, in contrast, says that the reality of a song only first begins with the concept of song, but before the concept of song there is also something here, and moreover something fundamental: Gentile called this something an Atlas bearing the world of reality; H. Glockner called it a state; Hegel called it factual substance.

But from where do I gain knowledge about this irrational substance, according to the psychoanalysts the only real substance, according to the Hegelians an unreal one, and according to both camps something that does not have any place in consciousness? Do I not know about this from consciousness? Is it really unconsciousness when I experience, feel, desire, create? Listen how Benedetto Croce, a Hegelian, resists the idea that an artist creates unconsciously: 'Indeed, the activity of the artist, at the moment when he is really so, that is to say in what is called the moment of artistic creation, is not conscious of itself: It becomes conscious only afterwards, either in the mind of the critic or of the artist who becomes a critic of himself. And it has also often been said of the activity of the artist, that it is unconscious; that it is a natural force, or madness, fury, divine inspiration. *Est Deus in nobis*; and we only become conscious of the divinity that burns and agitates us when the agitation is ceasing and cooling begun. ... But this negation is founded on a false idea of consciousness: *spontaneous consciousness* [highlighted by author] is confused with reflex consciousness. ... But there is also consciousness in the act itself of him who reads or composes a poem, and he "is conscious" (there is no other expression) of its beauty and of its ugliness, of how the poem should and of how it should not be. This consciousness is not critical, but is not therefore less real and efficacious, and without it internal control would be wanting to the formative act of the poet.'[78] Let us leave to one side the fact that for Croce nature is nevertheless 'unconscious'. Those of us who do not have at our disposal the Hegelian 'Spirit' cannot assign the creative activity of nature to the care of anything other than nature itself.

One thing, I think, is clear: if the creative process as an irrational process is a conscious process, then it cannot be anything other than *participation*. To *explain* it means regarding it as rational and, because as rational it cannot be located in the consciousness of a participant – after all, the irrational is there – it is placed either in the subconscious, or in a supra-consciousness of this or that type, natural scientific or metaphysical, by which, however, the irrational consciousness of a participant becomes superfluous. However, what is more and moreover the main thing: if the participant's conscious-

---

78 Benedetto Croce, *The Philosophy of the Practical: Economic and Ethic*, trans. by Douglas Ainslie (London: Macmillan, 1913), pp. 13–14. www.gutenberg.org/files/54938/54938-h /54938-h.htm.

ness becomes superfluous, then the participant himself becomes superfluous – that is, the participant as an individual, as a separate being, as an internal life, or in one word, let us repeat, as consciousness. This is the source of the myth about creation that does not know about itself, about creation as an activity and expression of a 'mass soul', a 'collective soul', society, Spirit, God, and so on. This is the source of the notion of an individual as a mere outer peel filled with a collective liquid.

The unconscious and the supra-conscious – this is the same thing as the spectator's attempt at escaping from solipsism. If he is not to regard his explanation as a mere fiction of his own making, then he must find a location for it outside of his consciousness. The successful fulfilment of this role, which until recently human beings demanded from philosophy and theology, is today expected from science. And science resolves this task by subordinating those organisms which it regards as lacking any internal life to a non-localized realm of 'natural laws' derived from reason, and by locating the explanation of those organisms to which it concedes an inner life in the 'unconscious'. According to this account, then, the highest form of earthly existence today is a technician, because only in his case are the laws of natural events in his consciousness. The only problem is that they are only in his consciousness, but nowhere else, primarily not in natural events.

For a Hegelian, the real world is contained in concepts, but the pillar that holds up this world is 'feeling', 'state', 'spontaneous consciousness', 'factual substance'. If we note that Hegel called this factual substance a 'phenomenon', then it is clear to us that he already stood outside of the reality of a participant and was embroiled in the problematic of the spectator. Participation – that is the real world. However, the spectator approaches the world with the question: What is this thing? What other thing is this thing? – Why does he pose such a question? Precisely because he does not have a reality, he has a 'phenomenon'; he has a phenomenon and he seeks a reality behind this phenomenon, and he seeks it on the side of the phenomenon, not on the side of reality. He has left the bank of reality, the bank of the participant, and he has swum to the bank of the spectator, to the bank of the problematic of 'phenomenon' and 'essence'. However, he does not swim back, but goes further on the same ground, 'toward the phenomenon', further toward the notional. This is where metaphysics starts; this is the beginning of 'the thing-in-itself', of essence and final reality, and eventually it arrives at concept as reality.

To say that the reality of things consists in participation means saying that things are real insofar as they are in someone's being, or respectively that they are someone's being. Or to put it in another way: the reality of things is guaranteed by the fact that at the bottom of the inner life, of the soul, there lingers someone whom we have metaphorically called a weighbridge operator, but who is rather both a weighbridge operator and also a pair of scales combined in one, and who puts everything that requests entry onto the scales and distinguishes the real from the unreal, the living from the non-living, being from non-being, even including his own being and non-being. If we have called a spectator an explicator, we reserve for the weighbridge operator at the bottom of the soul the designation of a *guarantor*. This is the name of what is situated most deeply in us and about which we cannot even say that it is, or that it is not, because everything that is, or everything that is not, is and is not only through this someone; this is a name for what makes me myself, or for what makes you yourself. Participation, then, is *the providing of guarantees*, and by this we are not saying anything more, or anything less, than that it is through participation that existing things are, and non-existing things are not; that participation is what makes things real or unreal. It may be objected that in the wider sense this guarantor is not a moral concept or even a moral postulate. *The designation of guarantor is a simple expression of the fact that all our certainties are in the final instance psychologi-*

cal certainties, by which I mean: certainties of a participant, not of a psychologist. However, for a spectator psychological certainty is precisely solipsism, in the face of which he attempts to flee and save himself in notional existences.

A spectator turns an individual as an *expression* into a problem of an object and *its objective existence*; turns an individual as *participation* into a problem of the object as *something given*; turns an individual as a *reality* into a problem of *the thing-in-itself.* The mystery of the divided earthworm is, or at least for the spectator should be, merely a special case of a much broader mystery, which makes itself apparent for instance in the fact that it is only a question of participation, a question of the immediate concrete life situation, whether an individual is a leaf of a geranium, or its flower, or branch, or an entire flowerbed of geraniums, or a whole garden of them. Or a hair on my mother's hand, or this hand itself, or my mother, my family, my nation. Or a pebble, a boulder, a rock, a mountain peak made up of many rocks, such as Lomnica Peak,[79] or even an entire range of mountains, such as the Tatras.

On the one hand, as spectators we file things away in our memory as in a card index – that is, we place them in our memory just as we know them. However, on the other hand, as participants, we come into concrete contact with things – that is, things are individual expressions for us, while the extent of these expressions, ranging from the dullest to the richest, is not invariable or in any way at all firmly connected with the spectator's classification of objects. And because the reality of things depends on this concrete contact, not on this card index, it is evident that in the explanation of life and the world this circumstance must be granted an entirely different place than the one that it is usually assigned. If we reserve the terms 'subject' and 'object' for the card index, we can then assign to the world of participation the terms 'things' and 'beings' or in sum 'individuals'

---

79 Mountain peak in Slovakia.

in order to distinguish between duller expressions of inner life and the more lively and richer ones.

I would like to emphasize once again that to understand anything as an individual, as an expression of inner life, for me does not mean anything other than to accept this as an expression of itself – that is, not as an expression or a phenomenon of something or someone above it, below it, behind it, or alongside it; for me it simply means understanding the world in the most realistic way, in the least abstract and notional way. This question facing us – in my opinion the most important one – of the relationship of the explanation to the explained is approaching its final clarification. A few paragraphs earlier we stated that if I say 'I feel' or 'I think' or 'I want' then this means that I am objectifying my feeling, my thinking, my wanting, that I am perceiving, but that 'a perceived feeling is not a feeling, but rather a perception'. *I* am a spectator, while *it* is a participant. We consequently identified this 'it' as a participant; that is, as a guarantor, through whom existing things are and non-existing things are not. However, we should notice that, alongside 'I feel' and 'I desire', we also gave the example of 'I think' and we could naturally add to this 'I look', 'I observe', 'I explain' – in other words, this 'it' not only feels, desires, experiences, but also looks, observes, and explains, and if I say: I look, I expound, it applies just the same as it did in the first case with feeling, that I objectify looking and explaining, and that objectivized, perceived looking and explaining is not looking and explaining, but rather perceiving, recognizing. Well, where, then, is the difference between a participant and a spectator?

We can see that if looking is to be looking itself, and not an explanation of looking, then it must be participation; and if you like, we can go further still: if an explanation of looking is to be an explanation of looking, and not an explanation of an explanation of looking, then it too must be participation; and so on, ad infinitum. To put this in another way: logic is what it is, because it is a form of psychological, internal being, because it is a psyche, an 'experience', a participation of its kind, because it is reason – the kind of reason which G. B. Shaw says is nothing other than a form of passion.

This means: if *I* am a spectator and looking is a kind of participation, then this *I* itself cannot be captured exhaustively by mere observing. And we know well: *I* cannot dissect my own self, *I*, without witnessing this as my own self. Above the dissected, conceptualized *I* is leaning an I that is alive and active, an I that is dissecting and thinking, an I that is not dissected and cannot be dissected, an I that is providing evidence and guarantees. Hume's definition of *I*, the Self, as a mere 'bundle of different perceptions' assumes an I which considers or weighs this bundle. Just as reason cannot refute itself, so neither can *I* refute *I* myself; just as logic proves itself by refuting, so I prove myself by denying.

Here, as is well known, is the end of Descartes's doubting and the beginning of Cartesian certainties, albeit with the proviso that these – as we know today – are psychological certainties, not ontological ones. By this I have not proved myself as something 'in and of itself', as something objective, but I have halted in front of an I, in front of a spectator, an explicator, who asserts and negates objective being, and therefore is himself outside of all assertion and also negation. We can object to Hume's definition by saying that this *I*, this self which refutes this unity of my states, cannot do so without assuming this unitary *I* or self (but without however objectively proving this unity by this). Without this assumption, Hume would not even have been able to venture any such judgement, because he would not have had any (psychological) guarantees that the person who posits the premises is the same person who also deduces the conclusion – let alone the person who dares to build a philosophical system.

If we have now discovered that reason-spectator-expositor is a type of participation and guaranteeing, then we will certainly want to know what this guarantor is guaranteeing. We know already that he does not guarantee the reality of things: precisely on account of this we have distinguished him as a spectator and an expositor from a guarantor in the primary sense of the word – that is, from a guarantor of 'things', of individuals. We have seen that, even though he asserts and negates objective, 'material' being, substance, he guarantees this substance only logically; he posits it as a logical postulate of an explanation, but not as a guarantor of its reality.

What, then, is an expositor talking about, if he is not guaranteeing this as reality, but rather only as a necessary element of an explanation, as a 'logical axiom'? Quite simply: a mere explanation does not provide a guarantee for *what* is explained, but rather for the fact *that* an explanation is given. Applied to science this means: science as an 'explanation of reality' does not explain reality, but its explanation itself is reality. In short, *we participate in reality, and therefore we cannot explain it; however, the reality is that we do explain.*

The only thing that an expositor guarantees in an explanation is a 'logical prescription' – that is, the formal, logical correctness of the explanation. More than this, an expositor – that is, a spectator or reason – cannot guarantee. Logic – this is the extent of reason's participation in the events of the world and thereby also the extent of the reality of the world. Here also we see that the reality of the guarantor and the guaranteed is the same thing. For instance, the natural scientist, who has gradually denied and reduced his participation, has reduced his guarantees and finally condescended to guarantee only by his mathematical reason; he has transformed his world into bare mathematical events. However, let us not be fooled. Meanwhile he nevertheless lives like the majority of us – that is he spends eight working hours in his 'reality', but otherwise he sleeps, enjoys himself, gets married and has children, so let us not take him too very seriously when he speaks of his professional eight-hour reality as the only reality, as the final reality. What is actually in fact real in this 'final reality' is the precision of the logical construction, its mathematical consistency and indisputability; but his scientific reason cannot, and nor is it willing to, provide us with a guarantee for anything more than this. *All that science can and wants to guar-*

antee us is that its explanation of reality will not disputable within and of itself; what this has to do with reality itself is already beyond the limits of its guarantees, its competence.

We are witnesses of how science is starting to understand itself more and more clearly in such a way. Science no longer seeks – according to the model of Kant – some unified metaphysical or other basis as a guarantee of objective cognition of the 'external real world', but rather each of the specialized sciences, without taking much account of other specialized sciences, is trying to build up its own separate basis from a system of primary axioms, from which it requests primarily that they are mutually independent and not mutually contradictory. Rule-based laws, form, 'correctness' become everything; the question of the reality of things loses sense. 'Senseless questions from the standpoint of modern physics are, for instance: What is matter and force? And also whether the external world really exists and whether we can perceive its true essence.' (Dratvová) Of course, for mathematics, respectively geometry, as pure imaginary laws and relations, it is easy to start with a few evidential proofs given by reason and to build the entire science in question on the basis of these proofs. However, other sciences, burdened by 'material', are in a more difficult situation. We know that the *raison d'être* of their particular existence lies in recognizing and accepting certain sensory facts, certain experiences, and that this is therefore at the expense of the perfection of cognition, at the expense of scientific exactitude. Therefore, it seems that experiment and sensory data will continue to be more important for these sciences than some kind of axiomatic basis, which in my opinion will be virtually impossible to provide in practice, especially as an analogy of mathematical axioms.

The extreme of metaphysical pan-mathematics, into which philosophizing researchers of the type like James Jeans drag natural science, causes many people to give more respect once again to sensory experience. Thus Pascual Jordan writes in his *Illustrative*

Quantum Theory: 'The creation of scientific concepts and theories does not represent any kind of acknowledgement by scientific research of the existence – over and above sense experience – of natural phenomena, but rather merely a construction thought up by us as an aid, one useful for registering and arranging our sensory experiences, analogous perhaps to geographical latitude and longitude. Blue light is not *in reality a wave motion*, but rather to accompany our sensory experience of 'blue' we also *imagine* a notion of waves in order to clarify the various sensory experiences that we can expect when we cause this light to impact on certain physical instruments.'[80] Jordan does not favour sensory experience at the expense of mathematics; he himself seeks a new basis for biology in integral calculus. He rescues formulas and also experience – and all kinds of other things too, for instance teleology in biology – by a decisive operation: sacrificing reality. For this purpose, he revises the noetics of natural sciences, arrives at a 'positivist' concept and defends this concept even against 'positivists': for instance, he criticizes [physicist] Ernst Mach by saying that his basic building blocks – sensory perceptions – are mere analytical abstractions, and he accuses [physicist] Philipp Frank of materialism. I regard as the most serious of Jordan's arguments for our purposes those arguments that concern reality. Jordan writes: 'The grammatical division of possible questions into problems making sense and problems that are merely apparent corresponds to the division of possible *answers* into meaningful ones that make sense and nonsensical ones that do not. *Only meaningful answers* are *correct or false*; contrarily, an answer is meaningful only when it is either correct or false, and when it can be understood as a problem (not necessarily immediately, but in any case fundamentally) whose solution would decide between alternatives. ... A very widely held misunderstanding is that the positivist theory of perception denies the existence of

80 Pascual Jordan, *Anschauliche Quantentheorie* [Illustrative Quantum Theory], 1936.

a *real external world*. However, the denial of a senseless answer is once again a senseless answer; an assertion of the non-existence of the 'external real world' makes no more sense than an assertion of its existence. *The one, like the other, is neither correct nor false*, but rather senseless, until it – as a symbolic answer – has been given *an agreed sense, through definitions and assessments inserted in it.* Therefore, it is not possible to say: according to a positivist conception (as meant here), the whole world is merely my notion which does not correspond to any objective reality. However, according to the positivist conception, it is necessary to say: no experiment *can be envisaged* that could prove or disprove such an answer; *that is why it necessary to exclude such answers from a scientific system as senseless.'*

We have spoken of solipsism as a curse of the spectator; but now we are being told that a spectator, if he does not absolutely renounce science, does not even have the certainties or uncertainties of solipsism, because the dilemma of a world as merely his notions or as an external reality does not have either a correct solution or an incorrect solution for him, because it represents a senseless question. Science as an explanation of the world does not give reality or unreality; it gives only the indisputability of an explanation. Here a researcher has realized that he is standing on the verge of the problematic of 'appearance' and 'reality' – that is, metaphysical, conceptual reality. He guesses that there is another bank, the bank of reality, to which he is not allowed to cross over if he wishes to remain a scientist. And so, while rejecting metaphysical, notional reality, he is aware that on 'this bank' the question of reality is for him 'senseless'.

When considering Kant, Engels, and Smuts we have noted that they remain silent about how they make their notional substance dependent on 'experience'. Now we see that the reference to experience is nothing other than a piece of advice to swim over to the other bank, to the bank of reality. In order for us really to reach this other bank, we have no other option than – during the crossing – to throw out all fixed predetermined categories, whether idealist or materialist, in short all metaphysical categories. Or simply: to change from spectators into participants.

For cognition, for an explanation – as we have said – reason prescribes three elements: prime mover, laws, and material. Reason requires materials for its explanation, but (as we now know) it does not guarantee the actual reality of this material; therefore gradually (when reason really comes to rely on itself alone) the question of reality becomes 'senseless' for it. Reason creates laws as a form of self-realization; it guarantees them through itself. Reason fails to find a prime mover as an 'object', and therefore it denies its existence, but in order for an explanation to be possible, it then smuggles this prime mover back in within the concept of cause, which comprises a prime mover plus laws, or in the concept of all-powerful laws, which amounts to the same thing. Why does reason not find a prime mover? It does not find one because reason itself, as a creator of laws, is itself cause; reason itself is the prime mover of explanation. This is also the reason why no mathematical, chemical, or logical formula, or indeed any formula whatsoever, can ever in itself apprehend reason – that is, a formula can neither prove nor disprove reason, because the formula needs reason as a witness and guarantor of its correctness.

What enables natural science to be universal is – as we have said – the circumstance that in theory the prime mover can be concealed, while in practice it 'is always in place'. The denial of a prime mover is, therefore, without any great significance, as long as science remains an instruction for a technician. However, it is a different matter as soon as science attempts to extricate itself from this supporting role and to put itself forward as an authority on 'cognition' – that is to say: as an arbiter of reality. Here this is no longer a case of a prime mover-technician, but rather of a guarantor. The question of reality is a question for a guarantor. The guarantor of science is always the intellect. And this intellect – like every guarantor – cannot give as a guarantee anything else than its own participation, its creation, and in the case of the intellect this is logic, or respectively mathematics. The intellect, therefore, does not guarantee for science anything more than the logical and mathematical correctness of its formulas. It is evident that a mere concealment of the prime mover would not be sufficient for the universalism of science; science must pay much more dearly for this: by a loss of reality. If the reality of things is bound with an individual life situation, with a vital process, it is evident that a universalism that is not permitted to pay attention to such 'localities' and 'immediacies' renounces, along with these, reality itself. To get rid of reality and become pure rule-governed laws – this is the ideal of scientific effort. An ideal which modern exact science has already almost achieved. We can already understand why this science – and it is the ideal of all sciences – prefers to speak to us in plain equations without commentary.

The circumstance that a 'spectator' does not guarantee for reality, but only for the formal indisputability of an explanation, allows him to regard the most varied and strange explanations as reality. However, if for instance a chemist says that love is nothing more than a promenade of molecules, then he is simply prattling, because he is mistaking the thing for which he is giving a guarantee (a chemical formula) with something that he does not guarantee (love which he does not experience). Or, if he says that life (that is, primarily he himself as a living being) is nothing more than a conglomerate of physical-chemical reactions, then once again he is talking nonsense, because, as a spectator (that is, as one who does not guarantee life) he wants to disprove his own life, which as a participant he does guarantee.

Rule-based laws – these are the only things which a spectator guarantees, which he creates. However, he does not defend himself so vehemently against any charge as against a charge of creation. He tries to objectify everything that he begets. Why does he try to do this? In order to escape solipsism. The certainty of reason, the spectator's certainty, is not weighed on the scales of the real and the unreal, of the living and the dead, of being and non-being. A spectator's guarantees are not sufficient for this. His certainty is only logical, mathematical, and if he does not have a source of this certainty externally, then the main pillar of the spectator's self-assurance collapses. That is why he is willing to look askance with both eyes and 'derive his approach from his successes' – that is, from technology. However, just as the living and the non-living is given in me by whether I am living or am not living, so for instance the certainty that 2+2=4 cannot exist as an 'equation', as a balanced structure, other than as an integral form of the existence of reason: it is in reason, it is reason; it is not outside of reason.

Finally let us touch at least briefly on *the relationship between science and truth*. In order for a certain answer to be true, it must be guaranteed both formally and materially, practically. Science represents an explanation in which the reality of 'material' is not guaranteed, because science does not produce *truth*, but rather only *precepts*. An explanation given by science is neither truthful nor untruthful, but rather either correct or incorrect. In order for an explanation to become truthful or untruthful, a participant from outside the sphere of reason, a guarantor of things and reality, must become involved. This is why, for instance, it is possible to separate the life of a scientist from his science, but not however that of a philosopher from his philosophy. Of course, the case is actually much more complicated; confusion is introduced by the fact that almost every specialized science is not 'pure' – that is, unburdened by concrete things and not contingent on an irrational participant. This leads to science being conceived as a producer, or a seeker, of truth even in places where the material is not guaranteed as a reality, but rather merely as an 'object', as a formal element of an explanation. The 'truth' of an explanation is not in the explanation, but rather in the life of the expositor – that is, in his participation, provision of guarantees, experience, in his being. This also applies to the case of an explanation in the narrowest sense, in the case of a concept.

If a philosophy is to be truthful, and not merely correct, it cannot be universal; it cannot, therefore, be science. A philosophical work can be judged scientifically only from the point of view of its formal correctness and logical coherence. This is a double-edged irony, which disposes of philosophical works as 'explainable' by the philosopher's 'temperament' and his 'way of life'. Philosophy cannot be criticized by a scientist from the point of view of truth, because it is either accepted by a person, or rejected – that is, guaranteed or not guaranteed. To put this in another way: science demonstrates, but philosophy appeals to witnesses; it calls for witnesses and guarantors.

Pascual Jordan has made a simply essential step, taking science out of a dishonourable situation. On the one hand, science defended itself against accusations of metaphysics by the contention that its theses and principles are mere surmises and hypotheses, methodological aids and constructions, and so on; however, on the other hand, its spokesmen have presented themselves as the only competent interpreters of truth and a proper serious world view. However, *truth is a certitude, and not a hypothesis*. Therefore it may perhaps be possible to 'interpret' a precept or a rule, but not truth. This certitude comes from the guarantees that science is not willing to give; it is, therefore, a gesture of honour when science declares its unfitness in matters of reality and truth, and remains a methodological search for rules and precepts.

It seems to me appropriate to add here a remark on the relation of our deliberations to so-called pragmatism, insofar as by this word is meant a noetic, epistemological criterion of truth. According to this criterion – to put this in a popular way – truth is what proves to be successful and effective. The difference between our view and pragmatism will be evident from this: according to our account, truth is constituted by the person *who provides proof for it* (as a guarantor), whereas according to pragmatism, truth is constituted by the person *for whom it proves to be useful and effective.* In the first case truth is 'being', while in the second case it is an 'instrument' for achieving something; this is where the 'instrumental' theory of truth comes from. As we can see, a pragmatic criterion is not a measure of truth, but rather a measure of precepts. It is a technical criterion, not a vital, living one, and pragmatism has also to a predominant extent become a philosophy of technicians.

In its way it is admirable how much effort natural science has invested in trying to persuade us that the world arises and proceeds as a rational event, but is not however itself a fruit of reason. Both the organic and the inorganic world. The actions of many animals are supremely reasonable, but where is the reason that guides them? 'A female bird, which when confronted by a pest drags one of its wings along as though injured, does not deliberately imitate injury, but rather mere performs an innate reaction.' 'A leaf insect does not say to itself: let me be more similar to a leaf every day.' 'It is the sharp eyes of birds that cause a bug to look like an ant, and not the bug's will or intelligence.' According to Hegel, everything real is rational; but was it reason which made them real? If I make my way across a log thrown across an abyss, then I really do not say: 'I am performing an innate reaction' rather than 'at every moment let the vertical of my centre of gravity pass over the axis of the log'. Nevertheless, it is my inner life, my *feeling* – not knowledge – of balance and imbalance, my feeling of stability and emptiness that decides how I proceed and whether I succeed in crossing or not. If I fail to cross, then a spectator on the bank will say: 'He proceeded carelessly.' If I cross successfully, then he will say: 'He proceeded reasonably.' However, in truth whether you cross or fail to cross, you have proceeded in the same way. What is certain is that you were not led by reason and the laws of mechanics, that you did not direct yourself, nor were you directed, by some lessons of statics and dynamics, just as Beethoven was not guided by mathematics when he composed his works. The only thing that actually decided and determined whether you crossed or did not was your feeling of balance, of life and of potential downfall, just as the feeling of being and non-being was decisive in the works of Beethoven.

Whoever wins in any kinds of fights or battles, this person is credited with 'seeing ahead', with acting 'far-sightedly and realistically', he acted with reason; whoever lost, on the other hand, was blind, was a fantasist, a bungler. However, in essence both sides usually act in the same way. It is only the battle itself that brings this differentiation into dreamers and realists, into the blind and the far-sighted.

The spectators looking on from the bank at those who cross reckon that what has happened could not have happened other than deliberately and in accordance with laws. And they ask themselves: Where are these governing laws, powers, and aims? In those who are crossing? Evidently not, because they are not aware of any laws. The governing laws, therefore, must be outside of them, above them, in front of them – that is, they must exist independently of them. In truth, they do indeed exist independently of them. However, the question of whether they also exist independently of the spectator is a different question; as is the question of whether they are not an exclusive matter of the spectator, but not however of the participant.

Really, if these governing laws and Gods were to exist somewhere above us, then life would be an easy matter, a reasonable and rational matter, a technical matter, such as H. G. Wells, for instance, envisages it, or as a young catechist does. But no such thing pushes the world forward along a string. Nature is in a worse situation. It is possible to believe that nature would love with all its soul to be reasonable; unfortunately, there is no one who is able to tell it *before an act* what is reasonable and what is not, what will prove itself successful and what will not do so. Therefore, every single step forward is a piece of madness, a step into the dark.

For reason and for the technician, the world is a pyramid of problems, which have to be solved before it is possible to go forward; it needs to resolve these problems in advance and only then proceed. A person as a direct participant of events usually has to go forward before he has resolved problems. He may even have to go forward – as Bergson says – in order to resolve them. However, since Bergson is a dubious authority for Wells, we shall rather call Wells himself as a witness in support of our case. In his *Short History of the World* he writes: 'It is always some real danger, some practical need, which gives birth to an action; and it is only after the action, only when the act has ruptured the old bonds and given birth to a new state and a new confusion, that theory comes to have a say.' Such is the situation of nature and also our situation: the text with the conditions of being is not known and it is not even written anywhere; there is no place where it would be possible to read and recognize it. It is only our participation – our life, acts, suffering and joy – that first writes this text: it is these things that fulfil the conditions of being. Because there are no all-powerful Gods and laws that are capable of writing or dictating to us the inscribed tablets of the agreement.

Acts carried out 'from the needs of the heart' are equivalent to the personal risk that they contain within themselves; 'reasonable' acts request general consent in advance – that is, they do not demonstrate a willingness to guarantee personally for the result. If the result is detrimental in the first case, then the blame and the punishment fall on the head of the originator; if the result is detrimental in the second case, then the *vis major* is guilty. A reasonable creature never puts himself at stake; he transfers responsibility for his actions from himself onto the whole. What is somewhat grotesque is that most of those things that are considered reasonable have been achieved by everything other than by reason: by enthusiasm, conscience, anger, self-sacrifice – in one word by the 'heart' – and have also been paid for in accordance with this. A wise person retains reasonable things, but he neither creates them, nor pays for them.

'The best thing that we can say about wisdom is that it retains what has already been secured for us,' says William James. An example is a typical lawyer or bureaucrat. Since time immemorial, human rights have always had to be struggled for at the cost of the greatest sacrifices against tyranny of all types, against unreasonable laws and soulless decrees, against the letter of the law, in short against *injustice*. However, a lawyer is always in favour of the law: in heaven for heavenly law, and in hell for the devil's law. And therefore the lawyer – or simply the bureaucrat – is a being who decides about everything, but does not fight for anything. He is a creature who is reasonable through and through.

However, the nature of things is such that, even if there were no other beings in the world than reasonable ones, the world would soon be at its wit's end with reason. Nature, which does not behave reasonably, which risks everything, eventually creates reasonable things. A reasonable person risks as little as possible, and this is also why he does not want to live from his own inner resources, but rather from what is given; he makes use of the 'reasonable', but he does not give birth to it. People, societies, and nations in a state of reasonableness, wisdom, and creative impotence exist in a state of bare existence; they merely live out their lives to their end. An extremely critical and analytical spirit is a sign of breakdown. The critic comes after the creator; science comes after nature. A critic discovers a law where the creator has already finished his work or moved on to something else. In whatever a law is discovered, in whatever is defined, formulated, discovered by reason, for a creator this is something that is worn out, lifeless, exhausted, infertile, forsaken. If a scientist finds rule-based laws in a work of nature and in a work of art, all the better for the artist, and all the better for nature; but neither an artist, nor nature, has anything to do with these laws; they go their way without them. These laws are a conclusion, in the way that an archive or a museum is a conclusion, and as a graveyard is a conclusion. Wisdom is a fruit of retirement. A person is wise at the price that he no longer attempts anything. The greatest amount of wisdom about life has been pronounced over graves.

It is possible to believe that life would be glad to entrust itself to reason; however, so far the wisest advice that reason can give life – the man on the high-wire – is that as far as possible he should not move on the tightrope, that he should stand silently and not balance from one side to the other side, so long as he remains alive, if he is to avoid a certain fall, rather than to act so 'unreasonably' as he has so far.

We all know: whatever is real, whatever is capable of life and life-giving, cannot be unreasonable. Why, then, is reason not sufficient? It is not sufficient because it is impossible to calculate already today what will be living, animate, life-giving tomorrow. It is not sufficient because there are no all-powerful laws, Gods, or guarantors that are capable, with their eternal perpetual prescriptions, of making life into a technical problem, into a problem of calculation and reason.

You will perhaps conclude, my dear friend, that what I am trying here to explicate in a long-winded way could be stated in one sentence of William James: 'Instinct leads, intelligence does but follow' and it would thus be immediately clear into which waters I am steering my ship. However, I would say that precisely the fact that this statement is accepted as quite clear and evident is in fact the source of much unclarity. If I say that instinct leads, then I must understand this leading in a different way from that in which it is usually understood. If we envisage leading as knowing – that is, we combine the usual notion of leading with reason, and if we say: instinct leads, then we mean: instinct knows as reason knows, and if instinct is leading reason, then it perhaps knows more than reason, which in turn means for us: it knows the future. We err – as we usually do in similar cases – by rationalizing the irrational.

However, instinct knows precisely just as little about what is ahead of it as reason does. Apart from that, we know that there is not even anything to know here, because what is cloaked in secrecy ahead of us is only that which is waiting to be created. Instinct does not lead us; instinct drags us, neither knowing nor caring whither. Life is like the man on the high-wire. Instinct tells him – if he wants to be preserved – to hurry forward and balance from one side to the other, even when there is a danger than he will put a foot wrong or will lean too much to this or that side. He does not care about where he is going to; he walks not in order to get somewhere, but in order to maintain balance now at this moment and not plunge down. If, then, we say that instinct leads us, we do not envisage that it is aiming at some tomorrow, at some future life; in truth it does not have any other aim than the most essential: to maintain us alive today. For instinct there is no other time than present time; past time and future time are requisites of reason. Reason, which wants to know ahead where it is going, why it is going there, how it will get there, usually avoids a sudden fall, but it heads inevitably towards such a fall by slowing its step and subduing the swinging of its limbs to complete immobility. Balance is a condition. However, if there is no firm point outside, then balance as a state of rest, as a 'static' balance, is not possible; externally, outside, there is nothing firm, nothing given, on which this balance could support itself, remain at rest, repose. The only possible balance is a 'dynamic' balance, a balance of flight, motion, action. If there were external supports, then internal supports would not be necessary – that is, no *inner life* would be necessary at all. In its way it is logical that someone who wants to prove objective substance has denied the existence of an inner life, of a soul. If something is guaranteed by its being given – that is, as 'something of itself' – then there is really no need for an inner life, for a guarantor. For a materialist, a 'soul' is a superfluous complication for his explanation. However, even for a theologian, who reckons with an 'external' (transcendental) all-powerful guarantor, the existence of a human soul in this world loses all sense.

It is popularly said that instinct is blind. In reality, if the main thing for the man on the high-wire is to maintain himself above the void, and not to get somewhere, then he does not have any need of eyes; in fact, he will even step much more surely, because he has his organ of balance in his interior. He does not have to observe, to listen, to measure and calculate; it is enough that his state is in his consciousness, and this state is not even one in relation to 'his surroundings', to the external world, because this is not actually a case of awareness of his state with regard to the external world, but rather of a complete immersion in himself, in his inner life, because the void is not seen from outside, but rather felt from inside. The question of balance here is an utterly internal question. It only becomes a question of a relation to the external world for a spectator who is watching the 'sleepwalker'.

Reason, which in order to proceed, to take a step forward, needs to know where it is going, as well as why it is going there and how it will get there, sets out tasks and aims for us for tomorrow, but the actual task and aim of tomorrow's tasks and aims is today's proceeding, not tomorrow's aim. Tomorrow will catch us in a different relationship toward today's aims, or possibly will replace these aims with quite different aims. Reason is not a guarantor of reality, and therefore the close connection between reality and the present is lost to it; because reason does not have a present as a reality, it locates the real in an imaginary time dimension and therefore it understands the present through a prism of supposed past or future reality.

With respect to the past and the future, it is a matter of complete indifference what we place in the past, or respectively in the future; all this is decisive only for the present. In the past, just as in the future, nothing happens; a happening, an event, is the present. There was no act yesterday that would have secured reality for our soul today; there is no act today that would secure reality for our soul tomorrow. To halt, to stop, and remain alive is not possible. For the man above the void the current movement of his limbs does not secure his balance for the next moments. Everything that he does, he does from the need and the necessity to preserve himself now, in the present moment. The void is a feeling, the present state of inner life; there is no act that would be sufficient to overcome anything more than the present void; there is no act today that would fill the emptiness of the soul tomorrow.

5
THE TIGHTROPE WALKER'S SAFETY ROPES

AS YOU CAN SEE, my dear Melin, Robert is not going to be such an easy nut to crack as it seemed to us. Even before we have finished chewing him up, we find ourselves also in the jaws of the nutcracker and our gilded nutshell threatens to crack. Uniforms and distinctions do not mean anything here; the only thing that we can rely on is what we are inside, in our souls. All of us, one like the other, are placed on the high-wire and we have to show what we are made of. At stake is life. Each person will be paid that quantum of life that he succeeds in vindicating. Let us leave Robert until last. Let each one of us of the people around him be already holding his share at the moment when we will inquire into Robert's share. You, my dear friend, in the role of researcher, and I in the role of technician, are first in line.

The duo of scientist and technician symbolize and at the same time attempt to solve the problem that has troubled the human mind since time immemorial: the problem of the 'relationship between cognition and action'. It is – I think – from the time of Socrates, who taught that to know well means to act well, that dates the postulate, intensified by the modern intellectual into an imperative: knowledge should precede action! Two tendencies – we have stated – struggle for ascendency within a human being: the spectator and the participant. A participant, free of any faith in the 'given', of any faith in a firm ground on which he can stand, directs his orientational sense in the direction of his inner life, his soul, and seeks stability in the dynamics of constant movement. In contrast, the spectator, looking outwards, feels that he is in danger from this 'sleepwalking' behaviour and he looks for some support that would enable him to slow down his step, to stop and catch his breath, which would offer him a stability less risky and wearying. He maintains the conviction that, outside of himself, there exists something firm, something 'given', which it is possible to seek out, feel, 'cognize', and in which the certitude of his existence is anchored. However, if reason is to perceive and cognize, it must understand, and it can only understand something which itself is in some way reasonable, and therefore: the 'given' objective world must be rational; and therefore a participant is an unreliable leader for the reason alone that he is 'blind' – that is, incognizant of the rational conditions of stability. And if these conditions are 'objectively' valid, then the behaviour of a participant can only be understood as expressions of 'moodiness'.

Socrates, born more than two thousand years before the birth of modern science and technology, could not have had any idea what a deceptive notion was concealed in his imperative. His command – Acquire knowledge! – was not intended to be a guide for the technician. Precisely the opposite: it was meant to be a guide for the participant; it was supposed to safely lead a person to goodness, morality, beauty. Many of us understand his command in this way still today. We can shine a light on the absurdity of the misinterpretation involved here, if we translate Socrates's request that action be determined by knowledge into our terminology: let participation be determined by an explanation! This does not merely mean that an explanation is supposed to engender participation and be *replaced* by it – by this a spectator would once again merely give up the helm to 'blind instinct' – but rather that an explanation should also *accompany* participation. So, in sum, it is necessary to say here: participation should remain an explanation, action should remain observation, movement should continue to be stopping – in short, the irrational should remain the rational.

Of course, as we have shown, for a spectator the irrational is merely a sublimated rational. So, in these circumstances we can easily understand the postulate knowledge before participation – that is, the rational before the irrational – when the irrational here is actually the rational masquerading under the guise of the irrational.

The requirement for 'knowledge before action', then, is comprised, on the one side, of action from rational grounds under the guise of the unconscious, or respectively the supraconscious (including the realm of 'natural laws'). If, then, the rational is primarily an explanation, and not participation, then it is evident that the requirement for knowing *before* action is nothing other than a requirement for knowing *instead of* action. Then the sense and aim of cognition is not action, but rather the exact opposite: non-action. To know – this means: not to have to act; to have certitude in clinging, in resting, and not, therefore, to have to move, to risk, to enthuse. Have we not attributed all-knowingness to our Gods so that we can free them of the burden of action, the necessity of acting, the risk of participation? Such is the ideal of the spectator, the heaven toward which he is aiming.

If nature and the natural were rational, then natural science would engender nature, ethics moral behaviour, aesthetics art, theology piousness, and so on. However, for the meanwhile natural science has led to technology, ethics to social morality (that is, to good appearance), aesthetics to imitation (that is, to artistic trade and industry), and theology to ceremoniousness – in short, *knowledge precedes only technology*. What is technology? The mediating component between cognition and non-action. We look to technology as to an instrument that relieves us of the burden of action, of the necessity of acting, of the risk of participation. Why is this mediating element between cognition and non-action necessary? Because the world is not rational, and therefore cannot be perceived and cognized by reason, rationally, but rather can only be irrationally created. Cognition, therefore, is not cognition in the true sense of the word; it is merely knowledge of precepts. And precisely because cognition is nothing more than a knowledge of precepts it does not lead to anything other than to technology. The existence of technology is sufficient evidence that the world is not rational. If the world was rational, then mere knowledge would be sufficient, such as for instance Jeans's 'thinking of the mathematical thinker' who in a wide variety of guises – metaphysical, theological, and natural scientific (laws of nature) – figures as a self-sufficient principle of the world's existence. If the world were rational, then a spectator would not have any need of technology, because cognition would not be mere knowledge of precepts, but rather ownership of truth and reality. However, since the world is not rational, a spectator cannot get by in it with mere knowledge, with a mere knowledge of precepts, but rather either he has to resort to technology, to 'praxis' (and here praxis, technology, must be understood in the widest possible sense, ranging from applications of natural science to moral, legal, religious, and economic organizations and societies – and praxis as a profession in general), or he must attach himself to someone who is closer to the irrational principle of the world, and thereby also to the 'conditions' of truth. This someone is a participant.

We have already noticed how in a spectator's explanation of things and events, comprising three elements (prime mover, laws, material), the last element 'material' refers to the spectator's dependence on another guarantor, on the participant. That is: without reference to a participant, 'material' remains a mere logical postulate of an explanation and the entire explanation an abstract notion, in the best case a precept. Truth, however, requires material as reality; the guarantor of this reality is a participant. However, this process of guaranteeing fundamentally changes the material; we can say that it makes the material real: instead of imaginary 'final realities' or 'things in themselves', concrete real things are formed. Reality, and thereby also truth, is conditioned on participation; this, however, means that it is bound to the 'here' and 'now'. Truth is not universal; it is only precepts that are universal and these – we have seen – have paid for the universality by a loss precisely of reality, truth. Because the world is not rational there is no universal truth. Truth with a capital T. Truth cannot be mere knowledge; a person's thirst for truth can never been slaked by mere observation. There is no truth without a *unity* of spectator and participant, of 'reason' and 'heart'. I repeat: a *unity*, not a mere symbiosis, which is rarely friendly. Truth is not a compromise between reason and heart, half of this and half of that; truth is that rare, miraculous moment when reason and heart feel as one and unified: as a person.

There is a difference – we have already mentioned – between an announcer of precepts and an announcer of truth, for instance between a (positivist) scientist and a philosopher. The first offers us an explanation that is correct, while the second offers us one that is truthful. This is why we do not bind the first to participation – that is, to guaranteeing reality – and also why we ourselves do not feel encouraged to such participation. However, it is different in the case of the second: he appeals to our testimony for the reality of his world; he calls for our participation, and therefore we also assume and request his participation. The scientist as a person is a matter of indifference to us with respect to his science, since the reality of the world is indifferent toward his precepts. However, the person of a philosopher is not a matter of indifference to us with respect to his philosophy, because his philosophy is, or respectively should be, his participation in the reality of the world. Let us recall: if the world was rational and given, it would be sufficient to know it and observe it, for it to be truthful – that is, real. However, since it is not rational and given, knowledge is not sufficient for its reality, and this is simply because there is nothing to know here; everything, on the contrary, must be created. Because, then, the world is not rational and given, in order for it to be truthful participation in its reality must be guaranteed, created. If, then, someone presents his world to us as truthful, then we receive this truthfulness not as a mere knowing and observing the world, but rather as a will to the world's realization.

Truth is the will to make the world real – to be more specific, the internal world; it is the will to transform human souls, inner lives, to give them a rebirth, to make them into participants and guarantors. Each truth appeals to our participation and to our provision of guarantees, and according to how our inner life, our 'feeling of being and non-being', reacts, we either accept this truth in the depth of our soul, or we do not accept it, and we do so a long time before we realize our reasons for doing so.

A spectator, attempting to achieve a static stability, builds – we have said – on *knowledge* of the world, not on his participation in it. If natural events took place as a rational process, the spectator would have achieved his aim; there would be no difference between knowledge of the world and the reality of the world. If this is not the case, then it is necessary to give a reply to the question concerning the source of the certitude and objectivity of cognition and knowledge – that is, the source of the *givenness* of the world and the *universal validity* of the laws of its events.

We have already given a partial reply to this, when we deduced material and the rule-based laws of nature as a 'logical prescription' – that is, as a creation of reason, as a method of its participation, its being, as the conditionality of its existence. For a spectator, who is not a guarantor of reality, every concrete thing becomes a mere phenomenon, whose essence – that is, true reality – he seeks. The main attribute of a participant's reality, and thereby also of a spectator's phenomenon, is the 'here' and 'now'. An attribute of 'true reality', therefore, is evidently going to be that it is bound neither to 'here' nor to 'now'; it is 'always' and 'everywhere': in short, it is 'given'. A concrete thing or event, unleashed from 'here' and 'now', becomes material and rule-based law. Material, 'matter', for instance, is 'everywhere' – that is, it is neither here, nor there; everywhere and nowhere is the same thing. It is everywhere because it is a material and a law of *everything,* and as such it is a postulate of cognition, of knowledge, *of all* knowledge, universal knowledge; or, in one word: science.

The birth of logic from the spectator's inner life, from his position on the 'high-wire', seems, therefore, to be clarified. However, if this logic is a kind of internal individual experience, then this merely makes even more serious the question of whence the same validity of logic for all spectators – that is, for all rational beings. We will try to illuminate this question together both for logic and also for mathematics, in the case of which it is even more pressing. However, an explanation of the origin of logic does not yet tell us anything about the origin of mathematics, and so we have no other choice than to consider the tough nut of mathematics in advance. This is made all the more necessary by the fact that mathematics remains today the only and final certitude that the exact scientist offers to a spectator as an external support. Exact science has reduced the question of the spectator's fate to the question of the origin of mathematics. If human reason is capable of developing mathematics on its own (that is, without any kind of experience of the 'external world') then it will never be possible with certainty to demonstrate that the external world is really external (that is, independent of human beings) and the spectator will never attain the certitude that his scaffolding, the external support on which he bases his existence, is anything more than a mere unstable fibre of his dreams.

It is worth noting that, while James Jeans in his earlier books – evidently still unaware of the whole fatefulness of this question – toys with the notion of mathematics as something that 'our mathematicians have formulated in their studies directly from their inner life, without any kind of regard for experience of the external world', in contrast to this in his book *Physics and Philosophy* he declares his allegiance to the tradition of the English empiricists, rejects the *a priori* stance of Kant and Arthur Eddington and gives his backing to an empirical origin of mathematics. However, his argumentation is pretty strange. As evidence for the empirical nature of mathematics, he uses, for example, the fact that only experience teaches us that, if we put together two apples and two apples, then we have four apples, but if we do the same thing with drops of water, then the result will be only one single drop of water. I have substantial doubts as to whether such a dual experience could have given rise to something so evident as mathematics is. The empirical origin of mathematics really depends on whether objects 'retain their identity in the course of physical counting', and if, therefore, objects exist that do not have this property, then it is difficult to deduce an empirical origin of mathematics. 'To retain one's identity' in time – that is, one's reality and individuality – here assumes a participant as a guarantor of reality. This participant, however, does not guarantee reality in time, because he does not know a time dimension; he guarantees it only 'here' and 'now'. A spectator, on the other hand, who is a guarantor of 'material' and 'laws' in time, cannot guarantee the reality of things in time, because he does not have a reality of things. The experience of a participant, therefore, does not in any way participate in the foundation of mathematics, and by this the question concerning the empirical origin of mathematics (that is, an origin from the world of concrete and sensory things) is actually answered: negatively of course.

Some people attempt simply to deduce mathematics from logic. For instance, for Bertrand Russell and A. N. Whitehead logic is some kind of universal mathematics, to whose formulas they attribute the character of universals – that is, validity also for the 'world of itself'. The transfer does not succeed without remainder, and other writers in contrast point to some kind of 'extra' irrationality of mathematics compared to logic. Idealists (for instance, the neo-Kantian Heinrich Rickert), of course, interpret this irrational in their own way – that is, as a supraconscious (in reality, therefore: sublimated) rational.

We have ascertained a certain irrational 'something extra' in logic (in explanation), to the account of which must be attributed not *what* is explained, but the fact *that* it is explained. (Of course, we have also noticed yet another 'extra' irrational in an explanation: in the logical element of 'material'; and following the trail of this 'extra irrational' we arrived at the symbiosis of the spectator and the participant.) I would say that this irrational 'something extra' in mathematics must be understood in the same way: this shows that the origin of mathematics is not in logic – that is, in a rational explanation; that mathematics is not merely something that is explained, but rather something that has arisen autonomously alongside logic, as a certain kind of (a spectator's) participation and experience, simply as one of the forms of the self-realization of reason. After all, the logical principle of identity does not have anything in common with the mathematical principle, which is actually a pluralist principle, and moreover some kind of special case of it; this is a case here of *equality* – not identity – a case of the interchangeability of elements without qualities: numbers. (In metaphysics the logical principle of identity leads to monism, while the mathematical principle leads to pluralism: remember Leibniz!)

According to Poincaré, we are supposed to understand calculations and measurements as an agreement, a convention. So be it. However, at most this agreement established which or what kind of geometry we are going to use. No agreement could have assigned reason the task of thinking up geometry if it had not itself so far thought up any. Or in other words: if it had not yet created this as a realization of itself, as an essential necessity of its own being. This is also why we could not force reason by any convention or anything else to acknowledge and use a geometry and a mathematics which it did not itself engender. However, it is not necessary to defend a conventionalism limited in this way from the accusation of arbitrariness and run for help to experience, as Poincaré does. If we can speak of any experience here, then only of the experience of 'pure' reason – that is, independent of reality; this is a case here of an evidential record, 'experiences', of the psyche, of the creative process of reason. An unmistakable sign of such an origin is that 'whoever is born in such a way' is not a herald of *truth*, but rather of pure *correctness*. Modern, so-called formalist mathematics not only concedes this about itself, but even itself claims this status and poses this as a condition.

Now that we have elucidated in this way the direct intellectual certitude of logic and mathematics (the evidential record for this), it still remains for us to clarify their objectivity, their validity 'always' and 'everywhere' for all rational beings.

As is already known, logic and mathematics do not guarantee reality and truth; they guarantee only precepts. What, therefore, are accessible to reason in the form of logical and mathematical cognition are precepts. In precepts a spectator does not recognize the reality of the world, but rather the conditions of his security in the world, or to put it more precisely: the conditions of his consciousness of security, his knowledge of security. However, as there is nothing to cognize, and the cognized (the perceived) means the created, neither in mathematics nor in logic can it be a case of cognition of something 'given', but rather of a certain type of participation and guaranteeing, but of an entirely different nature than is the participation and guaranteeing of a participant. While guaranteeing on the part of a participant creates a world of reality and truth, an 'internal' world, guaranteeing on the part of a spectator creates a quite different world, a world of precepts, an 'external' world, or – I am not sure whether this is an entirely appropriate designation of mine – *a world of security and insecurity*. In the first of these worlds (that of the participant) experience is never the same; doubtless because it is bound to the 'here' and 'now'. If, then, for the second world (that of the spectator) we are to allow the possibility of the same experience (and only in this way can I understand the 'objective validity' of anything), then it is necessary to conclude that this is a case of experience that is not bound to the 'here' and 'now'. However, such experience – we have shown – cannot take place as a specific lived experience, but rather merely as *knowing*. It is not possible to have the same lived experience, but it is possible to know the same thing. Realities cannot be the same, but precepts can be the same. A precept must be objective – that is, it must apply 'always' and 'everywhere' for all people. To apply 'always' means applying independently of 'now', of the present – that is, applying at any time in the past and also in the future. The loss of present reality is reflected in a putative past and future reality, 'eternal' reality. A spectator's 'material' and 'law' – this is a chain stretched from what is out of view to what is beyond view; and his present stability and load-bearing capacity – this is the same as his anchorages in some place beyond view. For a spectator it is enough for him to catch hold of the chain, to hold on to the 'ropes', in order to proceed with a consciousness of security through the world of phenomena, through the appearances of 'here' and 'now'. But – we have seen – all reality of the past and future is present knowledge of the past and the future. 'To apply always', then, is a present state of knowledge. 'Always' – that is past and future, or to put it better: knowledge of the past and the future. This is one of the methods of objectivisation by which a spectator makes his creations, which he needs for the construction of his 'safety ropes', his 'scaffolding', his 'external' world, putatively independent of himself – that is, independent of 'now'. We already know that this scaffolding does not give him certitude because it is given independently of him and he merely finds it, but that it does give him certitude when and insofar as it is *created* by him and for as long as it is created by him. It is symptomatic for reason that it objectifies its creations. It has a greater ambition to be a discoverer than a creator. It is like those expert fraudsters who bury their manuscripts and sculptures so that they can then 'discover' them as works of eternity. This stubborn anonymity – this is like an act of a lack of trust in oneself, scepticism, doubtfulness, a gnawing feeling that reason is not capable of creation in the true sense of the word – that is, the creation of reality. The world of reality is closed to it; led by its doubts it creates its own world, a world of 'scaffolding', a world of security and insecurity.

However, knowledge 'always' as knowledge of the past and the future has nothing whatever to do with a knowledge of history, which is a series of specific places and particular immediate moments; it means a simple evidential register of reason that the teaching that two and two is four, which applies now, applied at any and all times previously and will also apply at any later time. This is the precise opposite of history: it is a discarding of all particular localizations, of all specific times and places; it is ever-present in time; it is 'always'; it is independent of time, independent of 'now' today, of 'now' yesterday, of 'now' tomorrow. It is knowledge of the past without knowledge of history; it is knowledge of the future without any magical clairvoyance; in one word: all-knowingness. Or more simply: it is science. It is knowledge of the world, independent of what has actually happened in it, moreover independent even of whether this world exists and when it existed or not. Knowledge of the world does not require the world. It is sufficient in and of itself; it creates its own world, independent of the world of specific realities and specific locations. It is an ideal scaffolding for the man on the rope who refuses to walk, so that he is not left at the mercy of blind instinct. This man does not need to walk, because he can survey the whole world with one look; he knows everything without having experienced anything; he acquires knowledge of everything without even shifting from where he is. He partakes of the tree of knowledge and plans to establish on the throne – on which he previously first placed his all-knowing Gods only later to overthrow them – a mere idealization of his own needs and desires.

The extreme point that this godlike effort has attained bears the name of a four-dimensional, or sometimes a multidimensional, continuum. This continuum is so divested of concrete things that the only interpreter between it and mortals of this world has become mathematics. The world of the four-dimensional continuum could bear the sign: 'Always and everywhere.' In this continuum everything that has been and will be, *is*, and everything that is here and there, no matter where it is, *is here*. If we consider that the continuum is contained in knowledge, then this knowledge represents temporal ever-presence; it represents all-knowingness. The spectator has reached his aim; he does not have to move forward, because he is everywhere and always; he does not have to experience the world and make it real, because he knows the world. He is ever-present and all-knowing; he is like God.

How is the walker, the participant, going to appear to the spectator viewing events from this Olympian tower? Let us hear what words the spectator's puts in the participant's mouth: 'Events do not happen; they are just there, and we come across them. "The formality of taking place" is merely the indication that the observer has on his voyage of exploration passed into the absolute future of the event in question; and it has no important significance.'[81] – What is the participant here? Nothing more than a needle that moves across a gramophone record on which everything has been recorded previously and who convinces himself that he is composing what is reproduced there.

But let us consider: a gramophone record with a moving needle – this is the same as a spectator's knowledge of a participant and his world. Let us ask: How does the record sound to the participant who runs around it, and how does it sound for the spectator, who looks on? For instance, a participant falls in love, he 'encounters' love. A spectator looks on and perceives the participant's momentary passing 'promenade of molecules'. Or: a participant 'encounters' an apple and ravenously starts eating it; a spectator looks on at how he stuffs his mouth with a gravel of atoms. A young woman is struck by the feeling of motherhood; but the spectator perceives only what percentage of a certain chemical in her body changes. However, with all this we also place great demands on the spectator's participation. In order to perceive all this, he cannot stand entirely immobile; he must also move a little. And if he stops almost for good, then he will perceive all the events that encounter the moving participant as purely algebraic and numerical operations according to the schemata: $a+b=c$, $2+2=4$.

---

[81] Paul Eddington, *Space, Time and Gravitation: An Outline of the General Relativity Theory* (Cambridge: Cambridge University Press, 1920), p. 46.

There is a blindingly obvious question here: What is *really* recorded on the 'gramophone record'? The participant's melody, or the spectator's schemata? I know only one possible reply: there is nothing recorded on the record. The record sounds today just as the person listening to it himself infuses sound into it. It reproduces such a reality as whoever himself inscribes into it. The guarantor of reality of things and events is not in a multidimensional continuum, not in a multiplied surface, but in the inner life, in the soul.

At first sight it is strange that precisely the theory of relativity, which placed such emphasis on local time, speaks in favour of a static character of the space-time continuum. According to this theory, 'here' and 'now' are inextricably connected to each other, and so the present makes sense only in connection with some 'here'; from this it follows that some such thing as 'ever-presence' is an absurdity. However, here it tells us: a continuum *is*; it does not happen, it does not move, it is. The contemporaneity of two present moments is just as absurd as the identity of two various 'heres'; but in the continuum there is a sum of 'nows' and a sum of 'heres', which cannot be understood in any other way than that 'here and now' is.

However, if the sum of all 'heres' and all 'nows' is a gramophone record, a space-time continuum that is 'here' and is 'now' and that allows us to say that the gramophone record *is*, that the space-time continuum *is*, then this is evidently a case here of the 'here' and 'now' of a spectator's consciousness. This consciousness in the interest of the spectator's maintenance of himself above the void needs to be 'cognition' – that is, knowing 'always' and 'everywhere'. Ever-presence is necessary for the spectator, because he does not shift from his place; all-knowingness is necessary for him, because he does not have any reality. What he seeks is not reality, but a 'map'.

For instance, a participant's landscape is dependent on 'here' and 'now'. You stand and look out at the plain in front of you, at the river, the village, the range of mountains in the distance; these are individual things. However, a real landscape is not composed of individual things; it is not a sum of parts, it is 'one singular thing', it is an individual single thing. It is entirely 'here' and 'now'; it is not composed of a river one kilometre away, a village two kilometres away and some mountains five kilometres away – that is, it does not contain the river that you will reach in a quarter of an hour; it does not contain the village that you can reach in half an hour; it does not contain that mountain ridge to which you can climb up before midday. Between the 'current' river and the river to which you can walk in a quarter of an hour, there is an event; the two rivers are neither a contemporaneous 'now', nor an identical 'here'.

In order for the two rivers to become identical – and similarly, in order for the broadest variety of villages, mountains, and so on, to become the same village, the same mountains, the landscape must change into a map, and a participant must change into a spectator; the landscape must be transformed from an experience into a concept, into knowledge. A map is neither truthful, nor untruthful; it is correct or incorrect. A map is not reality; it is a precept, knowledge. In order for a map to be knowledge 'always' and 'everywhere' for a spectator, it must absolutely detach itself from the participant; or, in other words, it must become a pure geometrical picture. The space-time continuum is such a picture; in it, all the world's problems are transformed into measurable tasks. It represents perfect knowledge, knowledge 'always' and 'everywhere'; it represents universalism, ever-presence, and all-knowingness, but with the proviso: at the cost of reality.

This brings us to a conclusion which is at the least noteworthy: *a sum of realities can never be a reality*. If this statement is to make sense, then it is necessary to conclude that realities lose their reality through 'addition', through 'aggregation'. In truth, a spectator, counting and aggregating a participant's 'events' in the continuum, no longer had anything to do with the participant's realities; these realities fell through a net by which the spectator collected them, and what in the end remained as a 'sum' of reality was nothing more than the spectator's net. To count, to aggregate, to 'unify', means to rationalize, by which is meant: to get rid of reality, to replace it with a explanation, a map. A space-time continuum constitutes the reality of the world in precisely the same way as a geometrical map constitutes the reality of landscape.

The constituent element of the new physics is neither one-, two-, or three-dimensional, nor merely temporal, but rather space-time, or in other words: it is an event. The ambiguity of this word allows the space-time continuum to present itself as something that it is not. In the theory of relativity, an 'event' is a concept that relates purely to measurement and as such it can be inserted into a 'map'; because in this sense it does not mean anything more than a geometrical point, determined by four coordinates. However, the fact that these notional lines are designated by the terms 'space' and 'time' and that the notional intersection of these lines is designated by the term 'event', creates the impression that this is a case of a real event, an event bound to the 'here' and 'now' in the world of the participant. However, a real event does not have its guarantor in coordinates; it has it in the inner life of the participant. After all, precisely because of this no other 'here' and 'now' are accessible for you than your own ones; precisely because of this you cannot 'prove' any other inner life, because in the present you cannot exchange your own 'now' for another 'now', nor can you identify your 'here' with another 'here'. Neither can you succeed in such an exchange between your own 'here' and 'now' today and your own 'here' and 'now' tomorrow, because what leads from the one to the other is precisely an event, a reality, and until this event takes place, your 'here' and 'now' tomorrow is a mere notion, a piece of knowledge, or precisely your presence today. There is no other 'here' and 'now' than your own ones, and other inner lives have no access to you other than through an event – that is, through your own 'here' and 'now'.

However, the theory of relativity understands an event 'objectively' – that is, in this case 'here' and 'now' are not connected to someone, to an inner life, but rather they are sufficient without any connection to anyone; this is a case of 'here' and 'now' for no one. (Of course, in truth for no one means for a spectator, for his knowledge.) Even though one of the most important requisites for a relativist explanation is an 'observer' – that is, a living being who can take up a specified place in order to be able to follow his impressions; or in other words, his *events* 'here' and now' – physics nevertheless does not cease to emphasize that an observer merely takes on the role of an instrument of measurement, which if it was to be placed in the position of the observer would record on its scales precisely the same as the observer relates. The machine with its numbers is here used as an aid to show the event's independence from an inner life, to demonstrate its objectivity, its being 'of itself', its 'givenness'. Let us allow a machine instead of a person, but let us also immediately draw the consequences: firstly, an event will lose its reality; secondly, if it is supposed to be something at all, then it must be at least knowledge – that is, there must be a 'spectator' here who reads the machine's data and gives them sense with respect to his current need for perception, cognition, knowledge. As such, these events can be aggregated, categorized, united, mapped. A map, then, represents the sum of 'heres' and 'nows', but it does not have anything in common with the reality of 'here' and 'now'. A map as a sum of all 'heres' and 'nows' *is* – that is, it has the *same* time and the *same* place: the ever-presence of the spectator's knowledge.

If an event is reality, then a map does not have reality; if a map does not have reality, it is a world without events; if it is without events, it is without real dimensions. *In the real world, events determine distance and time.* This is why, for instance, the principle of least action (principle of stationary action), which is once again becoming significant in the most modern natural science, does not concern the real world. In a world in which an event is the only real – and thereby the only possible – link between two 'heres' and 'nows', it does not make sense to speak about least action. This principle only first gains sense in a map, where two various 'heres' and 'nows' are given at the same time (in knowledge), which allows us to notionally posit more possible connections between them and to compare these connections with each other. It is a similar case with the principle of probability. A real event is not subject to probability. Probability does not direct the actions of an individual; it directs the behaviour of 'elements' of a whole entity, of a map. For instance, I might observe ants emerging from a hole in the ground and hurrying off in all different directions. Each ant represents a real event, whose justification is in its inner life and which has nothing to do with probability. Let us say that the terrain around the hole is divided up in some way, and that my relationship to various parts of this terrain is not the same. For instance, I would like to know whether there is some rule that would allow me to predict how many ants visit a certain part and how often. In order to ascertain this, I divide up the area around the hole into sectors – let us say, roughly into northern, southern, eastern, and western – and I set out to observe, record, and count. What conclusion will I come to? I conclude that in the case of an individual ant that comes out of the hole to the Earth's surface, I can never predict with certitude which direction it will set out in, but I can however say that it will certainly be one of four directions heading toward the individual sectors (excluding of course the possibility that the ant turns around and goes back or halts). I will even be able to state the degree of probability that it will go to one sector rather than another. This degree of probability will be equal to the percentage of ants that fall into the sector in question, but this percentage is determined primarily by how I have divided up the circle into sectors and into how many sectors. The laws of probability, therefore, is not a law of individuals; it does not say anything about their real world. It merely gives a method for me to map the individuals for my own purposes. The law of probability is a law of the elements of a map. Once upon a time, some people (Laplace, Poisson, Pearson) wanted to use probability calculation to refute Hume's scepticism and achieve a means of mathematical fore-seeing *ante rem*; today we are more modest and we are satisfied with statistics, with calculating probabilities *post rem*. Statistical laws, or the statistical nature of events, is derived from a narrowing down of the endless variety of reality to a few cases determined and limited by some interest, need, or point of view. Probability has validity in a map. The principle of the preservation of energy and matter is also a principle of a map, and not of reality. It is a principle of an ever-present spectator. A participant does not know its benefaction – as we have shown earlier. It is evident that the same thing could be said about a majority of the principles of science, or to put it better: of knowledge.

If an event is reality, then the sum of events is not reality. The universe, the world – as an *entirety* of real events – does not have any reality. It can be real only as an event connected to 'here' and 'now'. For instance, a map of the celestial skies is not a map in the true sense of the world, because it has been drawn 'here' and 'now' by earthly beings. 'To map' the stars – that is, to make a model pre-senting where the stars 'really' are at this moment, and not merely where the stars *seemingly are*, would be a senseless task. Every such map would be bound to some point of the universe, to some 'here' and 'now'. Try transferring the requirement of ever-presence to the universe! It is only first in these dimensions that it becomes clear how absurd the concept of *the same time*, which is an essential prin-ciple of every map, actually is. If the concept of a same time (uncon-nected to any spectator or participant) applied to this world, then mathematical-geometrical dimensions would be the real dimensions of the universe. The distance between two places at a certain mo-ment would be an absolute concept; it would be distance 'of itself'. However, if the same time does not apply for the universe, then this means that real dimensions are events, by which we say that *real dis-tance* cannot be notionally measured and counted, but rather *it must be realized, made real*. A space in which nothing happens – or to put it better: in which there is no happening – does not exist. Perhaps if we could understand light, or to state this more precisely in terms of physics an 'electromagnetic wave', as something which *does not pass through* dimensions, but which *creates* dimensions, then the mystery of the constant speed of light and the mystery of the vacuum would lose something of their mystery for us.

The theory of relativity teaches that 'the same time' does not apply in its world, but nevertheless it conceives its dimensions as measurable and countable, or to put it another way: determinable for *the same time* (the spectator's of course). The dimensions of the space-time continuum are 'world lines' as the 'geometrical places' of events. If an event is a reality that is dependent on one 'here' and 'now' (the participant's), then the sum of these events – that is, the world line – as dependent on another 'here' and 'now' (the spectator's) cannot be the reality of the events. Even though the points of the world line are dependent on non-identical 'nows' and non-identical 'heres', the theory of relativity manipulates them, orders and arranges them, compares them, and in the process of measuring them relativizes them to this one single 'here' and this one single 'now'. However, this is only possible in a map fabricated according to the principle of ever-presence.

Because truth is conditional on reality, the same thing that we have said about reality also applies to truth: *a sum of truths can never be true*. In view of the fact that truths lose reality in the process of being aggregated, their sum is not truth; in the best case, it is a precept; however, most often it is not possible to carry out such an aggregration. This is why I am sceptical toward the doctrine that offers us absolute truth as a sum of 'partial' (subjective, individual, 'perspective') truths. A 'perspective' is a reality; a sum of perspectives is a map without reality. A sum of truths can in the best case be correct, but never true. If it is true, then it is no longer a sum, it is no longer a 'whole of parts'; it is 'here' and 'now', it is a 'perspective'.

This further clarifies for us much of what we have already considered earlier. For instance, it is clearer for us why concepts like 'whole' or 'entirety', 'holism', 'organism', and similar concepts do not explain anything. It is clearer to us why, for instance, the concept of development is self-contradictory. If I define, let us say, an individual as a 'whole of parts', it is evident that I am combining two quite different things here: 'individual' and 'whole'. A whole is a map, while an individual is a reality: two things absolutely incompatible. One belongs to the inventory of a spectator; the other to that of a participant. When in the main work of the founder of holism (Smuts) I searched eagerly for a magical bridge leading from the one to the other, I did not learn anything more about this matter, which is absolutely key for holism, than that the whole is an appropriate foundation for an individual. This is the same as an ignoramus.

Let us say that cells are realities, individuals. However, if I say further that the sum of cells, 'the whole of the parts', is my friend Fred, then I am stating evident nonsense. In the moment when my friend Fred exists for me, then the cells ('of which he is the sum') do not exist for me. And if a *sum* of cells exists for me, then this 'whole' does not have any reality, because if it is a *whole* for me, then it cannot at the same time be an *individual* for me, my friend Fred; it is then only a mere map.

Perhaps it will also now become clearer to us why, for instance, we get from a stone as an individual to a rock as an individual, and further to a mountain, a range of mountains, and so on (and similarly also in the other examples mentioned) only by a 'leap' – that is, we gain the reality of the second when we lose the reality of the first, when we abandon the first. It is similar in the case of myxogastria (plasmodial slime moulds), cut-up earthworms, or turbellaria (flatworms) and other creatures.

Psychology has no small share in the lack of clarity hitherto reigning in these matters, albeit not entirely through its own fault. The concept of 'whole' that has been introduced by modern psychology is too historically burdened. It bears within it a protest against an earlier psychology, an atomizing, poetic psychology. It emphasizes correctly that 'it is no longer founded on fictive elements, but rather on the wholeness that is characteristic for our experiences'. However, instead of placing emphasis on the elementariness of this 'wholeness' it has elevated (on account of its opposition to the old psychology) not the individuality of this wholeness, but rather literally its wholeness – that is, its composite nature. Or, in other words, it has retained as a 'whole of parts' something which is actually not any whole of parts, because it is an individual. Gestalt psychology 'sees in this complex compound the primary psychological reality with its own laws, which have their origin in the whole and can only be interpreted from the whole'. (Ferdinand Kratina)[82] There is nothing to be done: either reality or a map; either an individual or a complex compound; either my friend Fred or an entirety of separate parts. There is no bridge. If there were a bridge, then the evolutionists would long ago have crossed over it. However, as there is no bridge, the science of development does not have its own laws, not to speak of its own subject. What it does have are all kinds of incantations like holism, synthesis, emergence, organism, dialectical leaps, and so on, which are offered to the spectator as a key to cementing together its partial maps, its specialist sciences. But there are no 'partial' maps in the plural; to take one means throwing out all the others. All of these keywords put together do not say as much about the true character of the problem as the solid old Darwinist 'chance'.

If we are to seek some kind of way out at all, then I do not know of any other than this: *an individual represents an absolute beginning.* Let us imagine (only as a suitable example, because this is a case of an imaginary world) free protons and electrons as individuals – that is, we should understand them as expressions of themselves. Or to put it another way, let us grant them an inner life – that is, in human speech: some form of 'affective' consciousness. If these individuals combine together, then an 'entirety of parts' arises. Is this entirety an

---

82 Czech psychologist (1885–1944).

'atom'? In order for us not to operate within the confines of the map, but rather in reality, let us cease to be spectators and become at least figurative participants. Let us identify ourselves notionally with one of the individuals. If I combine together with other individuals in an 'entirety', then either I retain my consciousness and this 'entirety' is at most my notion or a feeling of a connection with other individuals; or I do not retain my consciousness and then we can put an end to the entire matter. One way or another, in no case is there a bridge from me to an 'atom', to a 'higher' individual that would be a whole of 'lower' individuals. I cannot even say whether I would understand this entirety of electrons and protons as 'my body', because this already assumes a symbiosis of the participant-spectator duo – that is, in addition to a guarantor of reality, also a designer of the map. But let us nevertheless assume that as an electron I would have a consciousness of both my spiritual and also my bodily nature. It is evident that in this case an 'atom' could not be something bodily, something material for me. An 'atom' in my consciousness would be only a feeling of new relations to other concrete individuals, a feeling of a certain affinity, community. If we are going to view an atom as a creation of electrons, then the only reality of this creation will be the creation of new connections between individuals. This is, then, a case of a purely spiritual creation, and if we ask about reasons, about the 'cause' of this creation, then we arrive at an internal, psychological equivalent, at 'creation from nothing', at a feeling of being and non-being, life and emptiness, reality and nothingness.

This anthropomorphization is primarily supposed to show us just how much influence a symbiosis of participant and spectator has on the psychological and spiritual equivalent of creation, of the creation of new things, and how it is pointless to try to capture in words the character of extra-human creation in which a spectator is not present and in which, therefore, there is not a dualism of body and soul, of spirit and matter, of internal and external, of reality and maps, of an individual and a whole.

I think that the conclusions we have so far drawn are sufficient for us to demonstrate the arbitrariness and illusory nature of the concept development. 'Development' is not even a decent map, let alone reality. A general explanation of development usually proceeds by defining a certain individual as a certain whole entity of parts, then procuring new individuals in another whole of parts, and finally – instead of the term 'whole of parts' – starting without any good reason to use the name of another individual, and then continuing on in the same way. What this general theory of development is really doing here is jumping from a map to an individual, from an individual to a new map, and so on, and in this way it is sinning against your good will that you are going to make these mental loops along with it. However, if we are to remain in the real world, it is evident that we cannot thread individuals to some kind of causal cord, attach them to some causal chain. To understand anything as an individual means understanding it as an expression of itself, and not as an expression of anything behind this, above this, or alongside this. And to understand an individual as an expression of itself means understanding it from its inside, its internal nature, understanding it as a beginning.

Causality is a postulate of the spectator's explanation, a postulate of knowledge, a safety handrail that keeps him safe above the abyss. It is a strange error to contend that causality is a source of things. The truth is precisely the opposite: causality means getting rid of things. Recall the 'crayfish march'! Causality is a spectator's method for liquidating the participant's world. Causality is a net through which a spectator collects things and shakes them through a sieve for as long as it takes until there is nothing else left as the 'sum of things' than the sieve itself. Such is the aim of the spectator's efforts: he needs to prove that his world is the true one, while the participant's world is illusory.

Things are created from 'nothing'. This paradox is actually a confrontation between the world of the participant and the world of the spectator. This statement recounts that the reality of things depends on 'here' and 'now' – that is, on the participant's inner life; the process of the origination and extinction of things is substantive, animate, irrational, not technical and rational. A causal explanation is a rationalizing process, dividing the world of reality into appearance and essence, eliminating the 'here' and 'now' and introducing the misleading principle of ever-presence and a design map. 'The postulate of causality,' writes A. Dratvová, 'is derived from the principle of identity in that all variable phenomena have their cause in invariable phenomena, which are permanently identical (in time). ... The causality principle, underlaid by the principle of identity, has led to an attempt in science to eliminate time and unify matter.'

This attempt to unify matter ('material') begins with the well-known question: Which other thing is this thing? And it ends with the finding that there are not things, but that there are only laws, the sieve of things.

The formation of things from 'inside' makes it clear to us why things that are sorted and attributed to each other as cause and effect must be guaranteed in their reality each separately and independently, and why all system-builders and lawgivers, if they do not want to part company with the real world, restrict the validity of their laws to 'experience'. No kind of real thing can demonstrate any other reality than its own reality, or to put it more accurately: every thing is what it is, because we guarantee it as such, and, if it does not have such a reality, then we will not reach any such reality through the reality of some other thing.

'Nothing of that which is our mental experience,' says Bertrand Russell, 'is a question for us.' What is an experience is a fact. Reason is the capability of making problems out of facts. Causal and teleological causality resolve these problems. The problem is actually resolved; we have a result. What is being sought for here is a solution, a means of solving it – that is, a rational path to the result. As we have seen in the 'crayfish march', the solution is always a step back from 'the resolved'. The difference between causality and teleology lies only in the fact that teleology takes the result as already existing at the start, whereas the causality theorist considers that the result does not yet exist. The 'resolved' is in the present, but the solution – as an explanation, rationalization, knowledge – has at its disposal the past and the future.

We have used the picture of a spectator looking on from the bank at those balancing over the abyss. It is only the efforts of those who have crossed to the other side and who pass by the position of the spectator that are granted mercy. However, the spectator's bank has been shown to be mere scaffolding over the abyss, scaffolding that collapses if it is not built and secured again and again. The spectator contends that his 'bank', his scaffolding, is the aim of those trying to cross. However, the person crossing is at his aim with every step, because he has no other aim than to maintain himself above the void. The bank is a problem for the spectator, and the person crossing is supposed to be the solution. Each of his steps is a partial solution. The 'sum' of the steps, the causal chain, is the entire solution. But for the person crossing, no step is a 'partial' step; it does not depend either on the previous step or on the following step; it depends only the state of *the inner life* of the person crossing, on his feeling of balance. Therefore, what is a reality for the person crossing, is for the spectator a mere segment, an addend. Causality imprints on every event the character of external necessity, because it is composed of mere steps, without capturing the internal process of which the steps are an expression.

According to a causal explanation, which sees in every step only the effect of the previous step, a person moving across our hypothetical bridge over the abyss whose consciousness suddenly died would actually continue to move uninterruptedly.

We compile the causal chain from a sequence of manifestations, as though one manifestation were a cause and another manifestation an effect. However, the source of every manifestation is in the inner life. Each step by a person crossing is an expression of his internal battle for his very being or non-being, life and the void, reality and nothingness. Causality knows only about being, but it knows absolutely nothing about the fact that being is actually made real on a pair of scales, with being on one side and non-being on the other, and that this pair of scales is constituted by the inner life of being and of things. Causality links up in a chain something which in fact evades all linking into a chain: absolute beginnings. In other words: it seeks the sum of all 'heres' and 'nows'; it draws a map. Causality is based on the principle of identity, both temporal and locational, on the principle of ever-presence. In the process of the summation of a participant's 'heres' and 'nows', the reality of things is lost; alongside an 'essence' things are mere 'phenomena' – that is, fictions. Whose fictions? There is only one reply: fictions of the spectator. A spectator, a denier of the inner life, must make use of fictions, creations of the inner life.

Well, since we have analysed here the concepts of 'always' and 'everywhere' – perhaps a little broadly – let us further look at the question on account of which we have examined these concepts: the question of the universal validity of logic and mathematics.

'Always' and 'everywhere' – this is the principle of ever-presence, the principle of a map, a condition of knowledge, cognition, a condition of the spectator's certainties. 'Always' and 'everywhere' – this is, therefore, the 'here' and 'now' of the spectator's consciousness of security. A map is a sum of all 'heres' and 'nows' of a participant. The participant's 'here' and 'now' guaranteed reality; but the spectator's map does not have any reality. There must be a fundamental difference between a participant's 'here' and now' and a spectator's 'here' and now'. What is this difference?

A fundamental feature of a participant's 'heres' and 'nows' is their non-identicalness. This is a non-identicalness of realities, a non-identicalness of beginnings; it is the impossibility of causal linking in a chain. It is participation. In short, it is what we have metaphorically expressed as 'walking', 'crossing', 'stepping forward'. This depiction permits us the notion that the principle of non-identicalness wanes along with a slowing down of movement. If this movement was to stop for good, it is impossible to see what could continue to maintain different 'heres' and 'nows' as non-identical, given that without movement there are not actually any experiences and there is no reality. How can we characterize the identity of 'here' and 'now'? So far, we have encountered only the sum of 'heres' and 'nows' – this is a map; this is the 'always' and 'everywhere' of the spectator's knowledge. However, the spectator's 'here' and 'now' was nothing more than the spectator's *consciousness* of 'here' and 'now'. This consciousness is – as we already know – an irrational fact, and therefore unique, because it is linked to the 'here' and 'now'. Only its content is rational; this is *knowledge* 'always' and 'everywhere', or simply a map of 'here' and 'now'. However, the *identity* of 'here' and 'now' is not a sum, a map, of the spectator's 'heres' and 'nows'; it is the identity also of these 'heres' and 'nows'. It is not, therefore, a case of 'always' and 'everywhere' of mere *knowledge* as a unique act of consciousness, but rather a case of the 'always' and 'everywhere' of *consciousness* itself – that is, it is a case of the identity of consciousnesses, of the ever-presence of consciousnesses, and not, as so far in the case of a map, a case of the ever-presence of knowledge. It is, then, a case of consciousness 'always' and 'everywhere', of a consciousness that is not bound to any 'here' and 'now' – that is, it is not bound to any concrete thought, to any concrete individual. Here we arrive at some kind of 'consciousness as such', reason as such, to a cosmic 'transcendentalism'; in short, to the 'supraconsciousness' of the metaphysicians as a source and guarantee of the universal validity and objectivity of human thought and cognition. The identity of consciousnesses has guaranteed the identity of knowledge; and the identity of knowledge – this, of course, is absolute knowledge. Here we should recall that supraconsciousness is nothing more than sublimated consciousness. Supraconsciousness represents an attempt to make reason into the principle of the world, the consciousness of the world. It represents a knowledge that is so perfectly independent of any kind of 'here' and 'now' that it is identical with what we have called absolute cognition. However, to cognize in the absolute sense – we have said – would mean not being. We could pay no regard to 'supraconsciousness' as a pure absurdity. However, the circumstance that all thorough rationalist metaphysicians have arrived at supraconsciousness in some form or another indicates that this is rather a certain extreme case: evidently an extreme case of what we have called a 'spectator' and depicted as a man situated above a void in a motionless, petrified position. In contrast to this extreme case, we could undoubtedly also outline an opposite extreme case, the extreme of a 'participant' accelerating his pace toward the abyss, which at its limit would lead us to the current moment and the identity of all the participant's 'heres' and 'nows' – that is, once again *ad absurdum*. This is why it is not without significance to clarify that the 'spectator' and the 'participant' are actually mere personifications of opposing tendencies of a person's soul, tendencies which make sense insofar as we understand them as directions and tendencies, but without sense as soon as we follow them in their direction to consequences as far as their ideal form.

Supraconsciousness as an identity of consciousnesses does not, therefore, provide the key to the objectivity of logic and mathematics, because this ideal spectator in his immobility is not even capable of that experience represented by logic and mathematics. Like every experience, experience of logic and mathematics is also conditioned on the irrational; it is bound to the 'here' and 'now'; it is dependent on concrete consciousness. Therefore, insofar as logic and mathematics are not bound to the 'here' and 'now', it is not possible to attribute this universal validity of theirs to an independence of consciousness. Consciousness is irrational – that is, a uniqueness that is uncountable and non-equatable, a unique event that cannot be multiplied or repeated and for which there is no other event that is identical to it. However, equating and counting take place in consciousness, and this activity is performed in consciousness as *knowledge*, as the rational.

The counting and equating of consciousnesses, which is a condition of this counting and equating, must lead to *ad absurdum*, to some kind of absurd map. This is why the 'always' and 'everywhere' of logic and mathematics is knowledge in consciousness, bound to the 'here' and 'now'.

It is not possible to deduce the universal validity of logic and mathematics from 'supraconsciousness', from an identicalness of consciousness, but neither is this necessary. An identicalness of consciousness is not necessary; an 'identicalness' of knowledge is sufficient; or to put it more adequately: a sameness – that is, an interchangeableness of knowledge. The metaphysicians arrived at 'supraconsciousness', because for them the sameness of knowledge was the same as the identicalness of consciousness. Knowledge is not equatable, because it is bound to a concrete, unique consciousness; however, it can be the same, interchangeable, by which we are saying: *transmissible*. The sameness and interchangeability of knowledge increases with a decrease in reality; reality is non-transmissible, but a map is transmissible and interchangeable. And the more perfectly a map is detached from a participant, from a guarantor of reality, the more interchangeable and transmissible it becomes – that is, the more universal validity it has. A map, in being merely correct or incorrect, and not truthful or untruthful, is transmissible, repeatable – that is, it can be 'the same' subject of different consciousnesses-knowledges. All regular teaching and schooling is based on this.

So, logic and mathematics represent maps of simple reality, so to speak – that is, reality with a higher level of universal validity, interchangeability, repeatability, transmissibility. The fact of interchangeability points to the fact that *the world of a map can become a common world of spectators*. And this immediately gives rise to the question as to whether what we have just called a fact, does not rather deserve (in view of its true nature) to be called a condition, a condition of a spectator's cognizing – that is, his *creation* of the world. This world is the world of scaffolding and handrails, of safety and danger, and it is blindingly clear that, if this scaffolding is to serve the spectator as a safe prop, then this prop cannot reside in reality, for the simple reason that scaffolding as a mere map does not have any reality. Scaffolding, lacking reality, bases its load-bearing capacity on a collective. The thing that seemed to lend firmness and load-bearing capacity to the handrails, to the tightrope's cord – its anchoring in an unlimited view forwards and backwards – is nothing more than a beneficial fixed idea; in truth all the firmness and load-bearing capacity of the cord derives from the fact that this goes through the hands of a collective. This, however, is a not a convention, an agreement, because it is not possible to designate as a convention something that is a condition of existence, and here this is really a case of the spectator's existence. The collective of the spectator's world consists in the sameness, the 'interchangeability' of existential 'safety' conditions. In our depiction of the man above the void, this sameness encourages a tendency toward immobility.

The spectator's movement tends toward inaction; his 'here' and 'now' loses particularity and variation, and it is possible to surmise that in the state of inaction there will no longer be anything that would differentiate the 'heres' and 'nows' of different spectators and which would not make them the same, equal and interchangeable.

However, total immobility is an extreme case; *de facto* 'here' and 'now' are never absolutely the same and interchangeable, and the universal validity of logic and mathematics is, therefore, far from being as ideal as it seems to metaphysicians and *a priori* theorists, and also to logicians and mathematicians. Kant compromised on this universal validity, even if not explicitly, at least sufficiently to limit this to reasonable beings. However, it is necessary to make even greater concessions and limit the universal validity of logic and mathematics to a factual universal validity – that is, to limit the 'always' and 'everywhere' to the 'here' and 'now' of the spectator's consciousness-knowledge.

The mystery that we see in the fact that mathematics, even though it is thought up by a mathematician in an ivory tower without any kind of experience of the 'external world', has the same validity and binding nature for 'all people' – or in other words, it has 'proved itself' in the 'external world' – has, therefore, a quite simple solution here. It is merely necessary to clarify some concepts. For instance, the external world in the expression 'experience of the external world' usually means the world of reality, the world of participants, while in the expression 'proves itself in the external world' the external world means the world of spectators, the collective world of scaffolding. Therefore, a mathematician can get by very well without experience of the participant's world, because mathematics as devoid of all reality does not have anything in common with this world. And it proves itself very well in the collective world of scaffolding, because precisely on account of its absolute deficiency of reality it has the highest degree of transmissibility, and thus actually represents a condition of the construction of a collective world. In fact, it is even possible to say that it directly creates the skeleton of this scaffolding, which this collective world is.

In response to the possible objection that in an ivory tower it is possible to think up all kinds of things which, even though they are devoid of all reality, nevertheless still do not have any great amount of transmissibility and are thereby totally unsuited to the construction of scaffolding, we can recall that we have already rejected this objection by pointing to what actually serves as a condition of a spectator's existence and not as some mere pastime of his: precepts, the principle of correctness, the degree of transmissibility, the extent of rationality. In short, science – this is not some kind of arbitrariness; it is not even an agreement; it is the text of the conditions of the spectator's existence, conditions that are specified and codified by a cautious and prudent man in a precarious position over the void.

We have already noticed that the internal world, the world of reality, also depends on the creation of a community; this, however, is a case of a community of an entirely different nature than the collective of the external world, the world of security and insecurity. Reality, which is non-transmissible, non-interchangeable, and unteachable, creates a community of the internal world in a fundamentally different way than is the case of the collective world of the external world, built on the principle of a map. In the first world the inside is everything, while in the second world the surface is everything. The internal world is inhabited by individuals; the external world by objects and uniforms. This is understandable: your being and non-being depend on what you are; your security and insecurity depend on what you appear to be. Therefore, the external world is the same as the world of social moralities and of technologies in the widest sense of the world. The reality of the internal world does not allow us to categorize individuals as mere numbers to be counted up; it does not allow us to 'map' them. The unreality of the external world not only allows the categorization of individuals as 'parts of a whole', but directly requires this. Scaffolding will not provide you with support other than on the condition that you become an element of its construction. And since, as a human being, you are not only an element of the scaffolding but also an individual of the internal world, and since these two worlds place different requirements on you, and usually entirely contradictory ones, it is one of the most difficult tasks of a human being to reconcile within himself the enmity and incompatibility of these two worlds. For instance, in the internal world, which is founded on reality, truth is placed above collective discipline; in the world of scaffolding, which is not founded on reality, external obedience is above truth. The security of the outer world requires from you as its price the being of your internal world. But the internal world has scales that weigh up living and non-living, real and unreal; it weighs every 'here' and 'now' on these scales reliably and independently of all other 'heres' and 'nows'. The external world does not have such scales; it cognizes life only as a map, a plan, and builds it as a rational construction. The principle of a map, a construction, scaffolding is 'always' and 'everywhere'. If you are once mapped, assigned, and categorized, then this means that all the richness and variety of your internal world, all the reality of our 'here' and 'now' is aggregated, unified, and plotted on a map as a mathematical-geometrical element, as a mechanical element incorporated as a cog in a machine, *and this as an element 'always' and 'everywhere'*. Deprived of the individuality that lies in the unceasing process of creation and extinction, you become for 'always' and 'everywhere' the same point on a map, the same part of a whole, the same cog in a machine. You are deprived of the inexhaustibly changing and constantly renewing world of things, realities, qualities, individuals; you are deprived of life that is incessantly burning out and being reborn, and you are fixed as a serially moulded rivet and lost forever in the entrails of a monstrous machine, about which you know neither its beginning or its end, neither its sense or its aim.

According to Auguste Comte, we are entering the third phase of human development, the 'positivist' phase, whose motto is: *to know, in order to foresee; to foresee, in order to make secure*. However, the more we make our lives secure, the more by doing so we have to renounce. At the moment when this security is finally perfect, there will no longer be anything left to secure.

What if, my dear Melin, the whole difference between us and Robert is in the fact that, while we have made ourselves empty and sterile in order to make life secure, he has not renounced life? We have branded on his forehead the seal of an enemy of life, but what if we, the ensurers of life, do not have any right to do this?

Making life secure has captivated us to the extent that we no longer talk about theory and technology other than as about the 'living form' of the oncoming era. However, mere theory and technology will never be sufficient to create a new form of human life, and this is simply because they themselves are without any life at all. They possess no scales balancing the living and the non-living, or the human and the non-human; they only have scales balancing the correct and the incorrect, or the secure and the insecure. They have no measure of truth; they only have a measure of precepts. The confusion of these two different measures is truly one of the fundamental signs of our spiritual crisis. We leave school with our heads stuffed full of precepts and with the conviction that these precepts, which do not bind a person's conscience, are truths. Or, to put it another way, truth is something which does not personally bind a person, something which is not guaranteed by an individual person but rather by 'science', 'nature', 'objective laws', or, to use our terminology, by safety ropes, scaffolding, a map – *de facto*, by a collective. In this way, the majority always possesses the truth and the only path to reality is through collective obedience.

Precepts are certainly beneficial for our security and comfort. This is all too evident to us, as long as we do not want bridges to collapse under us, insects to threaten our crops, or goldsmiths to sell us brass as gold. However, these precepts have no implications for our consciences, for our personal relationship to the world, to people, to the ultimate matters of a human being. It is a matter of total indifference for a precept whether we are brave or cowardly, honest or deceitful, good or bad, or indeed whether we are, or are not, at all. Moreover, and what is worse, if in the final instance it is indifferent as to whether I am brave or cowardly, then for a precept, bravery is madness and cowardliness is wisdom, and honesty is stupidity, while deceitfulness is reasonableness. In reality, such are the living maximums in the world of security.

To fight and die for a technical utopia – what a misunderstanding! After all, the old society must fade away not because it was not capable of bringing science and technology to their culmination, but rather because it was capable of doing this, but without giving them a human and living mission. If what is confirmed by the sacrifice of life is the truth, then on the contrary a precept is what is refuted by a loss of life; and, therefore, no one will lay down their life for a precept. The thing that people are really prepared to fight and die for is not, therefore, a faith in theory and technology, but rather a faith in a new human being.

Is it not precisely doctrine and technology in the broadest sense of the word that are causing human institutions and societies to languish? Do we not see a symptom of their agony in the fact that, instead of internal reality and actuality, they rather delight in traditional explanations, in dogmas and ceremonies, in a mere compliance with regulations, in collective social morality, in mere external discipline, in mere 'behaviour', or in one word: in technology? Such is the paradox of the contemporary era: a person who is most alive, internally most true, engages in a struggle under the slogan of mere theory and technology with those who, under the emblem of life and truth, are in fact wasting away as a result of mere moralizing and a technical approach to life.

Prophets proclaiming the onset of a 'new form of life' – of theory and technology – overlook what a massive and intensive ethos accompanies this theory and machinery. This ethos makes technology into some kind of new romanticism, and this is what imparts to this 'new form of life' the life of which it does not itself have even the smallest shred. The entire question of science and technology as the fate and living realization of a new human society lies completely in the question of how long and in what force this ethos will last. With the loss of this ethos, this 'new form of life' will immediately lose its scales of the living and the dead, the measure of the human and the inhuman, and what will then occur, you can figure out very well for yourself, if your imagination is sufficient for this.

6
THE TIGHTROPE WALKER GETS VERTIGO

ALL OF US, my dear Melin, are balancing in our own way above the void and we are inclined to regard other ways as bad, unhealthy, reckless, dangerous to life. We would like to force the way in which we maintain ourselves above the void on everyone else as the only method appropriate. We criticize those whose collective safety railing is painted a different colour from ours, and we feel ourselves especially threatened by those who do not hold on to any railing at all. Moralists and people who, rightly or wrongly, call themselves religious had no small share in creating Robert's lot in life. Many of these people were very close to Robert, and even those of them who otherwise adopt a moral pose only rarely and diffidently, in the case of a relative adopted no other pose than such a moral pose, and what is more they did so with all severity and intransigence. It is evidently this circumstance that in the case of a person of Robert's type gives burning intensity to the old experience that in practice we have less in common with our legally recognized relatives than with some Zulu tribesmen. While we are provided with a father and blood brothers, as a rule we have to find soul brothers and a spiritual father ourselves. In this fundamental respect, the continuity of life is hopelessly muddled up; the official organizers, time and space, are of no use here. It was the moral yardstick that was the most significant factor in forming Robert's behaviour and external character, and in making his internal nature so bitter. This is why we must also subject this moral measuring stick for judgement to the man on the tightrope.

A spectator receives even a *moral expression* as a moral *phenomenon*, whose essence he is seeking. A fact becomes a problem; the solution of this problem lies in searching for a rational path to moral virtue. For biologist, for instance, moral virtue is a biological phenomenon, for a chemist a chemical one, for a sociologist a sociological one, for a theologian a godly one, and so on. Each of them submits, or respectively would like to submit, moral virtue to the general laws of his own field. However, in the case of moral virtue, something which has so far remained in the background comes to the forefront; something which has caused people to postulate an essential difference between natural science and the science of moral virtue: this something is the provision of a guarantee, a guarantor. In ethics, this is most often called obligation. In this sense, ethics is talked about as a normative science in contrast to natural science as a causative science. It is claimed that moral cognition, in contrast to natural scientific cognition, obliges a person to act as he has cognized. However, in truth natural scientific cognition obliges a person in the same way as moral cognition; or rather, ethics does not impose any more obligation on a person than natural science does: both the one and the other oblige him technically, not morally. In this sense there are no other sciences than normative ones: the laws of any science whatsoever are merely a prescription for a technician instructing him as to what he should do to achieve by a rational path what a participant achieves by an irrational path, by 'sleepwalking'.

If the course of nature was rational, there would not be any normative sciences – that is, sciences technically binding human action; there would not be any difference between knowledge and reality, and action would therefore be superfluous. Precisely such a thing is – we have shown – the spectator's ideal. However, since the process of nature does not proceed rationally, knowledge is not a guarantee of reality, and the spectator must embody these processes in a technician in order to attain at least a consciousness of security. The erroneous differentiation of ethics as a normative science from natural science as a causative science arises from overlooking the fact that technical obligation is one and the same for all sciences without difference, and that an obligation is asked of ethics that it cannot possibly give: an obligation to conscience, an obligation for the participant. The failure of a science of moral virtue is then explained by reasons that are – if we use the words of H. Poincaré – 'purely grammatical'. It is said that, since the explanations put forward by every science take place in the indicative voice, the conclusions of any science cannot of themselves issue in the imperative voice. Or to put it in another way: from a determination of *what is*, it is not possible to deduce *what should be*. However, we know that nothing is given and everything remains to be created, and so neither for natural science is anything 'given' – that is, something that is rather than something that should be. In this case, this something that should be is something that should be in order for the spectator to attain a safe support in his precarious position over the void.

The need for security obliges a spectator to act in accordance with rational formulas; the urgent nature of being obliges a participant to act according to his conscience. So, the thing that every teaching of moral virtue comes to grief upon is the absurd effort to invest formulas and teachings with the same binding character that conscience has. No teaching about moral virtue wants anything less than that a person should act in the interest of security in the same way that he acts in the interest of being: for him to guarantee as a spectator something that he is only capable of guaranteeing as a participant. We have said that the principle of the spectator's world is disproved by a loss of life, while the principle of the participant's world is confirmed by a sacrifice of life. A science of moral virtue is confronted with the impossible task of placing an equation sign between something that is disproved by a loss of life and something that is confirmed by a sacrifice of life. This is the source of the effort by most teachings about moral virtue to transform moral virtue into a more or less evident or concealed form of egoism and security. However, a science of moral virtue is not the only science that we confront with the task of placing an equation sign between the conditions of a world of security and the conditions of a world of being. Rather we confront every science from which we expect truth instead of mere instructions with the task of placing such an equation. If the absurdity of this equation sign was not so evident in the case of the natural sciences, this was because it was not difficult for natural science to conceal the guarantor. It was all the easier for natural science to do this, the better it was able to present itself as a non-evaluative science, in contrast to ethics, aesthetics, and other sciences that regard themselves as evaluative sciences or at least as sciences about values. For a participant, who receives everything as an *expression*, there is no difference between reality and a value: both of these are an indivisible and integral expression of the participant's 'here' and 'now'. Science, which aims toward universality, through the process of adding together 'heres' and 'nows', deprives the participant's world of its reality, and thereby also deprives it of its value. Natural science has attained an extreme degree of this absence of reality and absence of value in the concept of material or matter. Technical values are neither truthful nor untruthful, neither good nor bad, neither beautiful nor ugly; they are correct or incorrect – that is, they are worthful or worthless for a map, for a construction of scaffolding, for the world of security or insecurity, for the 'here' and 'now' of the spectator. Durkheim knows very well what is necessary for ethics to become a true science, a universal science untied and disengaged from the 'here' and 'now' of the participant, from his values, when he proposes that a science of ethics understand a 'moral phenomenon' in the way that the natural sciences understand phenomena – that is, as an object, as a value-free 'thing', and not as *an expression, a manifestation.* The easier it is for natural science to conceal the difference between reality and a map, the more the triumph of technology is able to obscure from us the fact that natural scientific discoveries do not lead to the reality of nature. However, the science of moral virtue has practically no such triumph to its name that might conceal to us the fact that a knowledge of its teachings does not give rise to conscience. The personal, individual guarantor steps forward here too alive, too concrete, too immediate for it to be concealed, as required by a universal science. This is the reason why every attempt to transform a moral commitment into a knowledge of precepts, a knowledge of laws, makes such a grotesque impression. These attempts make this grotesque impression precisely because they posit an equation sign between the correctness of a precept and the necessity of conscience. To put this concretely and exaggeratedly: because two and two are four, you are morally obliged to jump into the water to save a drowning person. Already earlier we showed that a formula does not even have the power to give you an image, for instance, of the apple that it is supposed to represent, if up until that moment you have never seen and tasted an apple. Formulas are of no use, unless a participant, a guarantor, precedes them. If formulas precede the participant, then that is the end of reality; only formulas are left.

Nevertheless, a scientist-moralist addresses us in this way: 'Moral norms cannot be established in any other way than by deducing them from a law – that is, if they are to have a scientific authority, and by doing so arouse in the inner life of a human being the consciousness of a duty to obey them. ... The authority of ethical norms flows from their scientific nature; it is given by the right of science.' (František Krejčí, *Positivist Ethics*)[83] This leads to extremely strange results, for instance: 'Something which a norm prescribes, occurs only if I or someone else wants this to occur. A law is above desire; it is actualized, whether I want, or do not want. ... If the dispute between the notion of a norm and that of a law is to be resolved, then a norm must be regarded as indisputable imperative expressed by a law. When, and insofar as, I know what will happen, because it must happen, I can communicate imperatively to someone else, as prophets and seers did, whose words were received as an expression of the will directing world events, which is nothing other than the law-based necessity of world events.' This mention of the Old Testament prophets is not here by chance. This merely shows that 'moral teaching on a natural basis' – the subtitle of Krejčí's *Positivist Ethics* – does not differ in principle from a morality on a supernatural basis.

All-powerful natural laws, or the all-powerful will of God – in essence, these are really the same. To oblige us not to act against the first is just as senseless as obliging us not to act against the second; we

---

83 František Krejčí, *Positivní ethika* [Positivist Ethics] (Praha: Jan Laichter, 1922).

have absolutely no power to do anything against either the one or the other. The moral obligation that is placed on us here is equal to the command: act so as not to oppose the rotation of the Earth.

The rationalization of reality gives rise to a map. By a rationalization of moral reality Kant arrived at his categorical imperative: act so that a maximum of your actions can become a general law! Kant treats conscience in the same way as knowledge: he regards conscience as the same for all consciousnesses. The moral law is 'always' and 'everywhere'; the moral law is a sum of participants' 'heres' and nows'. This is why the categorical does not have any reality, or as it is more usually stated: it does not have any content, it is a mere form. However, the categorical imperative does not have any content, because *de facto* it has nothing other than 'content'. The actual categorical imperative – that is, conscience – is a unique, concrete experience bound to a participant's 'here' and 'now'; it intervenes from case to case, individually. It can only be aggregated, rationalized, objectivized by a loss of its reality, of its internal binding nature.

To concede an irrational character to moral virtue means understanding it as a natural process. However, opponents of such a conception object that moral virtue is evidently limited exclusively to human beings and that therefore its roots are located in reason rather than in nature. These objections take on a strange taste when they are raised by those who regard natural events as rational. The circumstance that human beings are the only creatures in the whole of nature who possess reason evidently does not bother them enough to prevent them from declaring the course of the whole of nature as rational; however, this circumstance evidently bothers them so much as to prevent them from conceding that moral virtue, founded on reason, is a natural event, even though according to them nature is a rational process. They argue that, though nature is governed by rational laws, an individual natural being is governed by instinct, not by reason. A marsh-marigold, a centipede or a dog, therefore, are not nature; nature is something above and behind them, it is the rational supra-consciousness or subconsciousness of the irrational consciousness of a marsh-marigold, a centipede, or a dog. However, both rational laws and instinct are supposed to be amoral: instinct simply because it is not rational, 'aware', while rational laws, on the other hand, because they are 'natural' – that is, objective, independent of human beings as reasonable creatures – and therefore in the last instance because they are also not 'aware'. It is only in a human being that these rational laws become aware for the first time; only a human being *knows* them, and it is precisely this knowledge that is supposed to give a person this consciousness of freedom, of the possibility of choice and decision-making, without which there is no moral action.

If we pose the question of freedom of will in this way, this means that we are asking whether an *explanation* accompanies our actions, or respectively precedes our actions. Or to put it another way: in order for our actions to be free, we must figure in them as spectators, and not as participants. According to this, a technician acts freely, because he knows what he does, while for instance an artist acts unfreely, because he does not know what he is doing. According to this, there cannot be successful action without correct cognition. According to this, perfect moral virtue depends on perfect theory. And since the technicians have the most perfect theory, technicians are closest to perfect moral virtue. Well, this is where the chain of deductions snaps perfectly. If there is one thing that is sure in this world at all, then it is that the technician is furthest from morality. He knows no other obligation than a technical one – that is, the obligation of the correctness of his precepts. However, even 'respect' toward the fact that two and two are four cannot impel anyone to sacrifice himself for another.

Anyone who wants to base moral reality on freedom, cannot go to a technician for teaching about freedom. The freedom of a technician applies only in a map; perhaps something like the principle of least effort or the law of probability. A map is a sum of fictive events, and therefore also possible events. It is possible to freely and indeed quite arbitrarily choose in a map. *Conscience does not choose; conscience actualizes itself, makes itself real.*

Only a spectator could give birth to the whole problematic of moral virtue and freedom of the will. Even consciousness is apparently determined; chemically, physiologically, climatically, and so and so on... Of course! We will no longer return to these technical explanations and spectators' maps. However, there are other arguments here. Every action, including morally virtuous action, is supposed to be conditioned on character and motive. The position with regard to character is like that with laws of nature. The scientist – we have said – has become accustomed to speak about laws of nature that determine the behaviour of things, even though the only thing that his research gives him the right to assert is this: the behaviour of things creates laws of nature. In the same way we have become accustomed to say that action is conditioned on character, even though at the very most we are entitled to say that character is created by actions. Just as there are no laws of nature without things of nature, so there is no human character before human actions. Precisely like a law of nature, character is a summation of concrete actions, events; as such, character is the 'always' and 'everywhere' of a spectator's knowledge, but thereby only a mere 'here' and 'now' of his consciousness.

A spectator bent over a map of human nature is overcome with horror at the thought that a human action should flow from the 'here' and 'now', and not from 'character' given 'always' and 'everywhere'. But the world of reality is not the world of a map. And the fact of being bound to the 'here' and 'now' does not turn a participant into a piece of paper flying in the wind, but rather precisely the opposite: the fact that this turns him into a *personality* – that is, a guarantor – is shown by no one less than F. X. Šalda in his 'confession' made in his book *Battles About Tomorrow*.[84] Let us cite at least

---

[84] František Xaver Šalda, *Boje o zítřek* [Battles About Tomorrow] (Praha: Volné směry, 1905).

this: 'A lot of theoretical twaddle about method has unfortunately smothered the only postulate that makes sense; they have *diverted* attention from *unum necessarium*: from the question concerning a *critical personality*, concerning *his character legitimacy*. They have convinced educated idiots that everything depends on method, and that method creates criticism. Meanwhile the truth is the opposite: a critical personality creates his method, and not only one method, but a range of them from case to case, according to the momentary commands of his sentiments, his aims, his moods, his pathos, and possibly even his whims.'

Character, attributes, innate qualities, motives – all these are an expression of our attempt to attain for a human being the certainty and precision of a map at the cost of reality. As a map a person is predestined; the sum of his actions is given in advance, but as such he is not a reality, he is knowledge, and from this – we have said – comes the paradox of a map: knowledge of determinism and a consciousness of freedom; the possibility of choice, albeit in an explanation only a motivated, determined choice. Action as an element of a map is not real, it is possible. However, at the same time it is given in advance – that is, determined, and the paradoxical combination of determination and possibility expresses itself precisely as a knowledge of necessity even during an awareness of freedom, of the possibility of choice. This is the origin of the determinist's command: cognition – that is, a knowledge of the necessary laws of events – is necessary for us to be able to guide ourselves freely in accordance with them.

However, action as a real event cannot be a choice, because it is not a possibility, but neither is it determined, because it is not given in advance. A real event simply actualizes itself, makes itself real, by which is stated that it is neither determined, nor undetermined; indetermination is contained within determination and, along with it, creates the schema of a map. If we do not want to operate within a map, but rather in the real world, it is necessary to understand that a real, natural process, a process of nature, is 'justified', 'motivated' in and of itself – that is, it is an expression of the inner life. It is neither a consequence, nor a cause of another process, but – if we really want to talk about cause here – it contains within itself its beginning and its end; it contains within itself its immediate cause, or according to our terminology: its *guarantor*. However, in reality this is merely a concession to speech and its grammar, a concession to this interpreter to whom – because we have no other – we have entrusted the interpretation of the irrational world. It is only because of language that we must differentiate 'guarantor', 'guarantee', and 'guaranteed', which are all various words for something which in its reality is one single elementary thing. To provide a guarantee is not a characteristic or a quality of a guarantor. In its reality – that is, in the act of participation – the provision of a guarantee is a guarantor, and a guarantor is the provision of a guarantee. The question of whether the guarantor is determined in its provision of a guarantee, or undetermined, does not make any sense here. From your own experience it is after all sufficiently known that what you perform 'naturally', you do not feel either as free action or as unfree action; but this is because in the act of participation, action and actor are merely two different terms for the same thing and because there does not remain any space between them in which freedom and unfreedom could be placed. After all, the word 'natural' itself means usual behaviour, which is not justified from outside, but on the contrary spontaneously. It is only reason that first brings necessity and possibility, choice and reasons, freedom and motives, into an event. It is for the needs of reason and for the satisfaction of reason, and in opposition to reason's external causes, justifications, and motives, that – in order to designate in some way the world of reality in contrast to the world of scaffolding – we have had to resort to internal causes, justifications, and motives, to all the things that we have tried to encapsulate in the 'feeling of being and non-being'. If we now have in mind moral reality, conscience, it is evident that for these themselves, the question of freedom or unfreedom does not make any sense. Freedom and unfreedom of conscience only acquires sense in relation to reason, in relation to the collective world of scaffolding; to put it roughly and on an interim basis: in relation to society.

We will digress here to one more matter. A mention of characteristics and innate qualities may give rise to the question of their relationship to an internal, psychological equivalent, which – as we already know – is for us an equivalent of the origin of things. To put it simply: if nothing is given and everything remains to be created, how can it be that one person achieves with a minimum of effort what another person cannot achieve no matter how hard he tries, to the disadvantage of the person who tries harder? What can we say about this psychological equivalent when as an equivalent of the 'same' thing in the case of a talented person it approaches zero, while in the case of someone dull it reaches a sky-high value? Can we explain anything at all by this? By the notion of a psychological equivalent we wanted to say that no one receives anything for nothing; that the inherited means nothing, while personal effort and endeavour means everything. But does not the existence of talented and untalented people prove precisely the opposite?

However, the entire misunderstanding vanishes when we clarify that a psychological equivalent exclusively concerns the real world, while in the world of scaffolding it makes no sense. The very concept of a characteristic, of an innate quality, is abstracted from the world of scaffolding and is also aimed at this world of scaffolding. For instance, today's so-called psycho-technics does not recognize any other notion of characteristics and innate qualities. When it speaks about innate qualities, about talent, as a rule it is thinking about the capability to be successful in society, in a career and professions of all types, about the ability to be materially successful; in short, the capability of achieving what is generally called happiness and what is measured by a person's place on the social ladder, by the ownership of material goods, by cleverness and health, by a minimum of effort in achieving the maximum of profit, and so on. In this collective world, it is really possible to use the expression 'the same thing' as a designation of what everyone is aiming for, and with regard to this, innate qualities really mean a very unequal and unjust division of basic capital among individuals. However, in the real world, in the world of being and non-being, all of this makes no sense. Here everyone starts at nothing; here nothing is inherited or not inherited. Here talent does not mean easier earnings, but rather primarily the command: work, try hard, toil! Talent – this means a bigger task, greater responsibility, a heavier load. So, it has to be said that the greater the talent, the greater the load of 'nothing' nature allots to someone, the more effort and creation it requires of him. Creative talent – this actually means a greater feeling for emptiness and the void; this is a gift of 'metaphysical unease', of pain from the void. A creator does not actualize some innate qualities, but rather in his way he confronts emptiness, nothingness, non-being. He feels his 'innate qualities' only as a necessity of extreme effort to achieve what an average being would achieve with considerably lesser effort: simply being, living. He feels his 'innate qualities' as his fate, which is harder, more painful, crueller in comparison with the fate of other people. And we can also possibly say that, in comparison with a 'normal' person, a genius feels his innate qualities as a deficiency of innate qualities for a normal and happy life on the well-beaten track.

I perhaps do not need to stress that effort should not be understood here as a technical process – that is, a deliberate, planned, programmed process; the aim of effort as a vital process is not tomorrow, nor is it progress, nor 'creation', nor 'growth', nor 'attaining perfection', nor 'ascent'. Let us learn from an artist. An artist does not say incessantly: I want to grow, to rise, to create. An artist does not create, an artist lives. We, in observing how he lives, see that he is creating. And any one of us who wants to imitate him and resolves that he is going to create like this artist, will merely languish in emptiness; whoever does not live, does not create. Life is creating. However, a deliberate attempt at creating is mere languishing, mere wasting away. If we are not creators in what we breathe, in the very depths of our entire being, we are not going to be creators in anything else. Nature itself does not command us: grow, rise, develop, create! It merely challenges us: do not dissemble, do not desert, live!

This creation from nothing, this psychological equivalent as an equivalent of the real world, this vital process as a creative process – all this tells us that nothing is given to us for free, that everything has to be paid for. But how to pay for it, in what currency? By one's participation, by oneself, by one's life. Life is a currency for which we do not gain anything as long as we save it and store it in a safe trunk, but which is capable of giving us everything if we pay with it. And since this currency wears out and loses its purchasing power, whether we save and store it, or we pay with it, I judge that we have it for payment and not for storing away. And now let us return to where we left off.

If we are to say that morality is located in the irrational, and not in reason, you are going to ask how I explain that it is limited to human beings – as rational beings. In truth, it seems certain that animals do not act either morally or immorally, that they are absolutely outside of good and evil. A human being also, when for instance he is driven by hunger to 'despair' (however, in reality this will hardly ever be a case of total despair) and steals bread from a shop, does not act either morally or immorally. Similarly, however, when – let us say – without thinking twice he jumps into the water to save a drowning person. However, by this we are not saying that his actions do not appear moral or immoral to others who are observing and evaluating him. However, his actions would not appear moral, or respectively immoral, if the observers were aware of his despair. They would not then appear any more moral or immoral than if, instead of a human being as actor, there was for instance a dog.

Moral emotions only and first appear in the case of action accompanied, or – as the case may be – directed, by reason. If I steal bread or jump to save a drowning person after a mature deliberation, or if I later reflect on this action, then a moral emotion emerges that clearly designates the act to me as bad, or respectively as good. In short, the conclusion is this: a moral emotion appears as though to say that it must intervene or at least be on its guard, as soon as reason becomes involved in action – or to put it another way, as soon as this is a case of deliberate, motivated action, when a person 'knows what he is doing', when he does not simply act as a participant, but rather as a technician.

But what kind of intervention are we concerned with here? What exactly is supposed to be on its guard and against what? Evidently this is a case of an intervention by a participant against a technician, a case of the one who possesses the scales of the living and the non-living being on its guard with respect to one who does not have such scales. In this *first clarification, a moral emotion appears as a vital reaction of nature against the mechanism of reason.* A moral emotion – this is what a rational being must have additionally in comparison with an animal in order not to threaten life more than an animal itself does. We should note that a moral emotion is not provoked if a technician becomes a pure theoretician who wants only to know and who breaks off absolutely any active relationship of his knowledge to the world. In this extreme case this would lead to that absolute knowledge which would exclude any kind of participation, and by doing so also exclude any relation to the concrete world; it would be as though he would not exist for this world, and therefore a moral emotion would not have any reason to arise or anything to stand up against. This explains to us the high degree of amorality in so-called pure science. For instance, pure mathematics is so far cut off from nature, so far outside life, outside the concrete world, that its formulas are free of any kind of morality.

We have already mentioned that an ethics that makes an appeal to reason always leads to some evident or concealed form of egoism. Such ethical systems take upon themselves the task of positing an equation between what is confirmed through the sacrifice of life, and what is refuted by the loss of life. The absurdity of this task confirms that – if we can put this in such a way – the principle of moral virtue and the principle of rationality (a technician) are diametrically opposed, that moral virtue cannot defend rationality (a technician), and that on the contrary it makes its appearance in order to defend life against the technician. Since a technician does not appear in 'lower' nature, since it is provoked into existence only first by reason, and moreover by a reason possessing an active relationship to the world, then we must conclude that the existence of a technician requires a certain intervention in life – and what is more, such an intervention that life would be destroyed by it, if a moral emotion did not (so to speak) restore life back to its original state. And since both conscience and also reason each in their way impose themselves on a person as essential for his preservation (one in the feeling of being and non-being, the other in the consciousness of security and insecurity), by this a human being acquires a notion of some kind of dual conditionality of life: rational, egoistic, parasitic, on the one side, and moral, altruistic, self-sacrificing, on the other. In this *second clarification, a moral emotion appears as a prescient agitator against the parasitic conditionality of life.*

If we are searching for a point of contact between the world of reality and the world of scaffolding, for the only place that reason could make its intervention in life, we will find this in the concept of matter, material. As has already been mentioned, the explanatory element 'material' refers to the spectator's dependence on another guarantor; here is that point of contact on which reason-as-a-technician relies for its existence and preserves itself at someone else's expense as a foreign body. Of course, this reason-as-a-technician does not call this theft; it calls it 'givenness'. What is in fact taken away is here simply 'given'. Creation is not necessary for the given; a mechanism is sufficient. Where there is no creation, neither are individuals necessary. Matter, material, is enough. For something that is given, matter and mechanism are sufficient for it to exist. Contrary to that, a moral emotion leads to an act of self-sacrifice not for an 'object', nor for matter, nor for a mechanism, but for a concrete living individual. In this *third clarification, a moral emotion appears as a rehabilitation of an individual degraded by technology to a mere mechanism and matter.*

Our first measure of moral virtue is very similar to that reached by Bergson in his *The Two Sources of Morality and Religion*. Unfortunately, this similarity is more lexical than in accordance with any sense or content and does not therefore bring such support for our conclusions as it might seem to promise at first sight. In the book mentioned, among other things, religion – as a 'defensive reaction of nature against the dissolvent power of intelligence'[85] – has the main task, while moral virtue merely hangs onto religion's coat-tails in some way. In addition, Bergson uses the term 'nature' in a completely different way than we do. For him, nature is one of the sources of moral virtue, and the living elan is the second source. Bergson says the following about the difference between these two things: 'There is a static morality, which exists, as a fact, at a given moment in society; it has become ingrained in the customs, the ideas, the institutions; its obligatory character is to be traced to nature's demand for a life in common. There is, on the other hand, a dynamic morality which is impetus, and which is related to life in general, creative of nature which created the social demand. The first obligation, insofar as it is a pressure, is infrarational. The second, insofar as it is aspiration, is suprarational.'[86] In essence, therefore, this is a case here of

---

85 Henri Bergson, *The Two Sources of Morality and Religion*, trans. by R. Ashley Audra and Cloudesley Brereton (London: Macmillan, 1935), p. 101.
86 Ibid., p. 232.

the difference between social morality – that is, technology – and moral virtue. The author of social morality is reason-as-a-technician, and, if it is here called 'nature', then this nature simply represents reason, and not something *below* reason or *above* it. This is why Bergson has no other option than to rationalize his 'nature' and in fact he does say that 'nature is utilitarian ... and that those instincts which we might call intellectual are defensive reactions against the exaggeratedly and above all the prematurely intelligent element in intelligence.'[87] Instinct is here, as we see, in order to command reason for the period of its immaturity – that is, until it has developed into science and technology. Then – that is, at the time when life is in greatest danger from reason-as-a-technician, Bergson relieves the guardian of his service and allows him to go wherever he likes. Religion and moral virtue, therefore, continue to exist during the maturity of reason, but they go their own ways independently of reason. Bergson's 'defensive reaction of nature' against reason has, therefore, to be understood in this way. If we turn nature inside out, then we must also do the same with natural behaviour. So: 'Whereas natural obligation is a pressure or a propulsive force, complete and perfect morality has the effect of an appeal.'[88] For Durkheim, pressure is a sign of a social phenomenon – that is, of something that is imposed on an individual from outside, something that is not innate, natural to him. We also have really shown that what is natural cannot be felt as pressure; what is natural is neither determined nor undetermined. Bergson, if he is to be thorough and consequent, has no other option than to introduce social morality also into nature: 'Moral obligation may extend its scope in societies that are becoming open, but it was made for the closed society. ... The obligation we find in the depths of our consciousness and which, as the etymology of the word implies, binds us to the other members of society, is

87 Ibid., p. 135.
88 Ibid., pp. 23–24.

a link of the same nature as that which unites the ants in the ant-hill or the cells of an organism.'[89]

Of one thing there is no reason to doubt: that neither open moral virtue nor closed moral virtue (social morality) is a tie of the same kind that mutually connects ants or cells together; and this is so simply because both personal moral virtue and also social morality assume the existence of reason, and we do not concede the existence of this reason to ants, cells or 'lower' nature in general. An ant-hill, or respectively an organism of connected cells, cannot be compared to a human society, whether closed or open. Moreover, an open society, held together by moral virtue, has only an ideal existence for Bergson, and not a positivist and historical existence: 'But the great moral figures that have made their mark on history join hands across the centuries, above our human cities; they unite into a divine city which they bid us enter. ... From the real society in which we live we betake ourselves in thought to this ideal society.'[90] What he is really saying by this is that moral virtue knows only individuals, and not society, and that therefore it is not possible to say that 'generally the verdict of conscience is the verdict which would be given by the social self.'[91]

Conscience cannot be a social phenomenon, because moral reality is immutable and non-transmissible – that is, it cannot be knowledge 'always' and 'everywhere'. In order for such knowledge 'always' and 'everywhere' to occur, it must be aggregated, rationalized, objectivized in a map, in a technical instruction for building a collective world; in short, it must be objectivized in an order, a rule-book, in a prescription for human behaviour, in one word in a social morality. The existence of society is not conditional on moral virtue, but rather on social morality. To preserve oneself in the world of reality,

---

89 Ibid., pp. 28–67.
90 Ibid., pp. 53–54.
91 Ibid., p. 8.

in the world of individuals, depends on what and who you are, while to preserve oneself in the world of security and insecurity, in the collective world, depends on how you appear, on how or what you seem to be. Conscience is something to which people resort of their own accord, at their own risk, on their own responsibility; obedience to morality, however, obviates a person in society's eyes from all responsibility, all risk, and all personal guarantees.

What is the import of good appearance here? Where does this emphasis on external behaviour come from? What exactly is meant here by good appearance? What exactly is supposed to appear, or respectively what is this good appearance supposed to cover up and why? We have shown how the intervention of reason in life brings a division into a dual conditionality for life: into a parasitical one and a morally virtuous one. If nothing is given and everything must be created, then 'to find the given' means us taking without giving. In theory, as we know, this principle will eventually lead us to 'nothing'. In practice we would have ended up in the same way, if it had not been for nature here, which is not governed by this one-sided principle. Thanks to the creative work of nature, we are able to make do with this 'given', but such a 'given' is not given, but rather purloined, misappropriated. And, since the misappropriator, rationality (a technician), is the builder of the collective world of scaffolding, ownership is the basis on which this world stands, and thereby also the basis of the consciousness of security on the part of its members. The question of private or common ownership is on the whole a subsidiary one. The process of collectivization is not an intervention against ownership; on the contrary, ownership here achieves its full function, which is to serve as a support for the consciousness of security. Private ownership dissipates this function and makes the consciousness of security – both material and immaterial – illusory. Society as a mere protector of private ownership is not, therefore, yet a true society – that is, one providing a consciousness of security. It is only collective ownership that provides a group with this unified and rectified material force and power, on which an individual can find a support for his consciousness of security. However, in return for this, society must demand from an individual that which forms the basis of its unified and rectified power: unconditional obedience. This is why obedience to an external power today is becoming the surest path to a consciousness of security for individuals.

In this sense, therefore, it is possible to say that the principle on which the existence of a society is grounded, is an egoistic principle, a parasitical one. However, society cannot declare, cannot openly admit, such a principle as a condition of its existence. This is a principle that is devastating with regard to life and reality, and putting this principle into effect thoroughly and consequentially would mean extermination. The existence of society is conditioned on a principle that destroys existence. In an effort to evade its own destructive foundations, the destructive conditions of its own existence, society prescribes for its members as a rule of behaviour the precise opposite. It prescribes for its members behaviour that, if it was not mere technique, mere good appearance, would make social organization superfluous; however, such behaviour requires the provision of a maximum guarantee, and this is exactly what society was supposed to free us from. We find a way out of this, then, in the fact that externally, *de jure*, we behave according to the rules and we take care to ensure that everyone complies with them, but inside, *de facto*, we live according to our egoistic needs; we console ourselves with the belief that the others are better than us, and we are inclined to accept as fact what is in fact only good appearance. Bergson describes this appositely: 'Even in those cases where moral precepts implied in judgments of values are not observed, we contrive that they should appear so. Just as we do not notice disease when walking along the street, so we do not gauge the degree of possible immorality behind the exterior which humanity presents to the world. ... The evil is so well screened, the secret so universally kept, that in this case each individual is the dupe of all: however severely we may profess to judge other men, at bottom we think them better than ourselves. On this happy illusion much of our social life is grounded. It is natural that society should do everything to encourage this idea.'[92]

However, morality as good appearance 'does not satiate' a human being; it is an empty sack which must be filled with something real. If it is filled with a moral reality, it ceases to be social morality; it becomes moral virtue. It is not, therefore, tailored for moral virtue; it is tailored for a misappropriator, for an egoist, for someone depraved. For social morality, pillage and depravity are not pillage and depravity, as long as they remain hidden pillage and depravity. Social morality demands a clean shield; it does not look behind this shield. However, life as reality is decided behind this shield, not on the shield. And if there is evil behind the shield, then this remains evil, even if we were to paint the entire shield with saintly scenes.

Put simply: social morality cannot compensate for the destructive one-sidedness of egoism and parasitism; only real moral virtue and creation can compensate for these.

The intervention of reason in life manifested itself in a dual conditionality for life. While human societies set out in the direction of one conditionality, a virtuous individual embodies the other, opposite, conditionality. A morally virtuous individual as a maximal guarantor represents a natural living counterweight to a socially moral creature as a minimal guarantor. In this way, a morally virtuous individual stands up against society as its conscience. This opposition, consisting in a complementarity of vital life conditions, must however lead to tension and conflict. A virtuous individual, whether he likes it or not, feels with his conscience placed above society, but society does not concede to any individual any other place than as an element of itself, society. How could society concede a human individual as an authority and guarantor of virtue, when it preaches and prescribes this virtue in its own social morality, written and un-

92 Ibid., p. 4.

written? How could it not see its greatest saboteur in a person who accuses it of hypocrisy and insincerity?

During human history, both sides have appealed to all kinds of authorities, starting with religion and ending with science. However, in reality there have not been any other authorities than individual conscience and collective morality. And while even today conscience still does not dare to place itself on the scales without an additional makeweight – Bergson, for instance, considers it necessary to note in his book about moral virtue that he has not said anything 'that could not in time be confirmed by the tests of biology'[93] – on the other side, society has found science, to which it has found fit to assign the role of a sovereign authority: 'If we do not reckon with the intervention of supernatural beings, then we cannot find inside a human being or above him any other source of authority than society or rather the sum of those societies of which he is a member.' (Antonín Uhlíř)[94] If society is the guarantor of moral virtue, then of course an individual is not a guarantor of moral virtue, and then even in the moral point of view an individual is a mere 'abstractum', a mere abstract concept, alongside a 'concrete' society.

Let us take a certain and well-known event in human history: Golgotha. Even if not everyone agrees that one of those crucified was a saint and one of the greatest moral personalities that has ever graced the Earth, nevertheless there is hardly any human conscience that would classify him together with the scoundrels along with whom he was executed. A human conscience asks itself: How is this possible? According to what moral measure did society make an evaluation and come to a judgement here? From where have they taken the competence to do this? To these questions there is no more adequate reply than this: the moral competence of a society is given by the fact that this society exists. If we then ask what a crime is ac-

93 Ibid., p. 219.
94 Antonín Uhlíř, *Sociologická idea* [The Sociological Idea] (Praha: Otakar Janáček, 1932).

cording to this moral competence, society cannot give us any other reply than this: 'We observe that certain actions exist which all possess the one external characteristic that, once they have taken place, provoke on the part of society that special reaction known as punishment. We constitute them as a group *sui generis* and classify them under a single heading: any action that is punished is termed a crime and we make crime, so defined, the subject matter of a special science of criminology.' (Emile Durkheim)[95] In order that there is no doubt about the character of this criminality, Durkheim explains: 'Those actions condemned as crimes by primitive societies, but which have since lost that label, are really criminal in relation to those societies just as much as those we continue to repress today.'[96]

By this the following is stated: Christ was a criminal because society executed him. Yes, that is right: the moral authority of a society lies in the fact that a society is. Imagine, then, that society is something concrete and an individual is something abstract, that a crime is a 'social fact' and that 'the determining cause of a social fact must be sought among antecedent social facts and not among the states of the individual consciousness',[97] and ask yourself why an individual, an abstract thing, is punished, and not society, a concrete thing? Why is responsibility borne by the product, and not by the producer? Why does society even regard it as a special mark of its cultural and moral maturity, when it excludes the concept of collective guilt from its legal code? In social theory, a crime is a social phenomenon; in social praxis a crime is an individual phenomenon. Why is this? It is because a society's actual measure of moral virtue is this: whatever is not collective is against society; individuality is a crime. Individuality is a crime in society, a crime in the conditions that it posits for

95 Emile Durkheim, *The Rules of the Sociological Method*, trans. by W.D. Halls (New York: The Free Press, 1982), p. 75. monoskop.org/images/1/1e/Durkheim_Emile_The_Rules_of_Sociological _Method_1982.pdf.
96 Ibid., p. 79.
97 Ibid., p. 134.

society to exist, in the conditions for what a society is. If there are to be differences among individuals, then society itself dictates these in the name of its own interests and designates these differences with distinctions, uniforms, status, professions, and so on. However, 'self-appointed' individuality – that is, substantiated internally and not recognizing any higher authority than its own conscience – threatens the existence of society. Why does it threaten society?

Society has always attempted, and evidently is always going to attempt, to qualify this threat primarily as a moral one. If society issues moral prescriptions, then it can after all regard itself as a morally virtuous person, a morally virtuous entity. Well, it is true that it issues them, but why? If its existence were conditioned on virtue, then it would necessarily have to actualize virtue. By this, however, the following is being stated: society would have to individualize virtue in human consciences – that is, society would have to transform a minimal guarantor into a maximal guarantor; however, this would of course mean that society itself became superfluous. However, for the meanwhile it does not have to fear such an extinction even in the slightest, because it does not pursue the actualization of virtue and neither does it have to pursue such an actualization; its existence does not depend on it. However, what its existence does depend on is the tightest possible degree of obedience, discipline, and submission on the part of its members. Why this tight degree of obedience? Bergson replies: 'Our social duties aim at social cohesion; whether we will or no they compose for us an attitude which is that of discipline in the face of the enemy.'[98] Who is our enemy? Any person who threatens our consciousness of security. Any person who has what we do not have and which we need, or any person who does not have what we have and who needs this. An enemy in this sense – as seen – is a very broad concept and comprises not only people, but also 'living and non-living nature'. A concrete society is

98 Bergson, *The Two Sources of Morality and Religion*, p. 21.

never 'everything', a universe, or even the whole of humankind. A society is always a more or less numerous group which is engaged in a competitive, and often direct, battle with other groups of the same or a different type. In this battle, it is always a case of expanding or maintaining ownership – that is, ownership of the appropriated, of 'the given'. Ownership of 'the given' permits – as we already know – good appearance to exist in place of (internal) reality. In this way, society makes do with mere obedience, outward discipline, with prescribed behaviour. Why, then, does it prescribe moral virtue, instead of plain obedience? It does this only insofar as it expects from this a tightening of discipline. The force of an active willingness to make sacrifices, which is the mark of moral conscience, is very attractive and desirable for the discipline of a group and for its offensive and defensive strength. However, there is an enormous risk contained here in the individuality of moral conscience. This is why society prefers to prescribe conscience to a person rather than to appeal to this conscience. But the fact that moral virtue and truth are secondary matters for a society and that discipline is the main thing is a fact that is all too well known. Who, for instance, does not know that if a sense of moral virtue, or respectively truth, induces an individual to renounce obedience, then moral virtue and truth immediately recede into the background and an individual's actions are then qualified exclusively according to the degree of obedience? Many powerful institutions – military and clerical, for instance – often do not even make the effort to conceal the bare requirement of discipline under the coating of moral virtue and truth. Incomprehensible dogma and senseless commands often then comprise the 'sense' of the disciplinary order. History piles up examples demonstrating that the least advantageous and suitable path leading to power and a more certain existence for social groups has been the path of virtue and truth. It is also worth noticing that all moral commands change into precisely opposite commands towards members of an enemy group or toward 'renegades' of one's own group. Neither is it possible to overlook the fact that a morally virtuous agitator is much more problematic for society than some robber, because the robber does not refuse to maintain a good appearance, and he is not far from the truth if he feels himself punished for not having succeeded sufficiently in maintaining appearances. A robber is not an individual – that is, a maximal guarantor, a creator; he wants to live from the 'given', the owned, the stolen, precisely just as society does; he gets into conflict with it only because he exaggerates to an extreme what should remain hidden, and by doing so he violates good appearance and sins against social morality. After all, the legal and also the moral order of society provide enough possibilities for people to mutually swindle one another quite legally, 'honestly' and 'honourably'. The lawyers demonstrate that moral virtue has nothing to do with the legal concept of crime, when they say that 'the metaphysical question of whether a person has, or does not have, free will does not have anything whatsoever to do with criminal law. If we view crime and punishment as an event taking place in time and space, we can only – as in the case of every other event – join the individual elements of this event into a chain of causes and effects; we must also presume here that every expression of human will must have its causes. However, if we view criminal law as a collection of norms, attesting something that should be, then we already presume the possibility also of other behaviour; that is, we presume that a person has the possibility either to act in accordance with the norms, or not to act according to them. ... These unfruitful disputes between the classic approach and the modern approach, therefore, were a result of confusing sociological research with legal and political research.'[99]

If 'sociological research' was to think through to its conclusion its thesis that the very existence of society provides a basis for its authority, then it would easily agree with 'legal and political research' on the fact that society prescribes, judges, and punishes simply be-

---

[99] Jaroslav Kallab, *Trestní právo hmotné* [Criminal Law] (Praha: Melantrich, 1935).

cause 'society is'; legal science – which is normative not in being legal, but already in the very fact that it is a science – represents rational instructions for a technician. It represents a set of norms that prescribes for people, and binds them to, a certain kind of behaviour which is required for a society to exist – that is, required for the technician to accomplish a consciousness of security. The science of sociology is distinguished by the fact that the elements that are counted, the elements of its map, are people. While other sciences have generally speaking rationalized 'nature', sociology directly rationalizes human beings. The scientist was not able to assign consciousness to the natural element, and so to enable him rather to place in this natural element interchangeable and transmissible knowledge – that is, his laws as rules of behaviour – he circumvented this difficulty by placing these rules of behaviour into an imaginary empire of natural laws, into a supra-consciousness which was in fact merely his own consciousness inserted. However, the sociologist is concerned with individuals of his own kind, with rational creatures, to whom he can concede a consciousness similar to his own. Nothing prevents him from locating the main condition of every science – that is, an 'identical', or to put it more precisely an interchangeable and transmissible knowledge of laws – in human consciousness. However, if he overlooks the cardinal difference between interchangeable knowledge and incompatible concrete consciousnesses, it can easily happen to him that, instead of 'identical' knowledge, he starts talking about identical consciousness, and arrives, for instance, at the metaphysical concept of 'collective consciousness' as a source and a cause of individual consciousnesses. This is precisely what happened to Durkheim. The approach by which he arrives at 'collective consciousness' is typical for its summation of individuals, for its amalgamation of realities into one whole, into a map. However, the result is not a new individual, but rather an aggregation of elements, a map. The substance *sui generis*, the 'ultimate reality' of sociological science, is not, then, society, but rather 'individual souls', human consciousnesses, just as the 'ultimate reality', the substance *sui generis*, of physics is not lightning, but rather electrons, protons, photons, and so on; just as the ultimate reality of chemistry is not water or ammoniac, but rather atoms and molecules; just as the ultimate reality of biology is not the body of an animal, but rather cells and possibly elements even lower than cells; just as the ultimate reality of psychology is not the soul, but rather certain psychological capacities, such as sense perceptions, feelings, reason, will, drives, instincts, and so. The difference is only in the fact that society is not an originally irrational 'phenomenon' such as lightning or water and so on, but rather is already a rational structure.

Social science, if it is to squeeze people into this structure, cannot do anything else than the other sciences do. It, too, is primarily concerned to make its elements countable and unifiable in a map. For this purpose it is necessary to divest them of anything that they possess which cannot be counted or unified, of anything that is not identical with some other things – that is, to divest them precisely of reality, quality, individuality. In order for people to be sociologically mappable, they must be mutually interchangeable. What was self-evident, a matter of course, in the case of electrons, in the case of people would be a pure impossibility, if there was not already a collective world of scaffolding here in which people are prescribed a uniformity of behaviour, norms of behaviour that are binding for all and which people are able to comply with thanks to their particular capability – and a capability that is *particular to them alone* – to be one thing while seeming to be something else. Moreover, in truth it must be said that it was evidently this capability that gave rise to organized human society, to the world of security and insecurity, to the world of a minimal guarantor, to the world of good appearances, ownership, and material power. Thanks, therefore, to standard behaviour and good appearances sociological science finds in society, instead of non-interchangeable individuals, rather already countable elements, a ready-made type, a 'species' – that is, that notion which other sciences find it so difficult to attain. It is understandable that a sociologist – rather than 'going out and about among people' and making contact with living individuals – thus soon finds it more productive for his science to count and compare statistical records and legal and moral codes of law, to compile all kinds of questionnaires, and generally to investigate everything where he can find already categorized types and kinds, ready-made elements of a map.

The human being of the social sciences is an inhabitant of the world of good appearances. In contrast, the natural sciences at least have the advantage that their elements, albeit that they are also mere 'phenomena', mere appearances, at any rate are not *good* appearances – that is, they dissemble and dissimulate. Therefore, a technician can take their behaviour, their 'appearance', at face value; he can rely on them, they 'prove their worth' for him. A sociologist, whose ambition is for his science to resemble the natural sciences, knows only a person with a mask, but regards him as a person without a mask; he takes a sanctimonious person as a saint, and when a change of environment shows up the supposed saint as merely someone sanctimonious, he declares people to be sanctimonious hypocrites, and declares piety, virtue, honesty, self-sacrifice, and so on as 'purely acquired behaviour', as an outer coating, concealing a predator. He thinks that he has is dealing with society as nature, but meanwhile he is actually dealing with social morality. The map of social morality applies best to the behaviour of socially moral people – that is, to those who are most easily adapt their behaviour in accordance with changes in circumstances and external pressures. However, this map fails totally in the case of people who are morally virtuous and creative. The reason, therefore, why the natural scientific method works well in nature, but fails in human affairs, is that society has morality, while nature does not have any morality.

This is the reason why a sociological ethics will always get caught up at the level of social morality, and why moral virtue is bound to elude it forever. And, if it nevertheless attempts to identify an individual morally virtuous act with its socially moral map, it commits – measured in human terms – the grossest error and perversion. It will qualify virtue as a crime, or at least as a pathological phenomenon. In the sociological sense, everything that does not correspond to the norms – that is, to social morality, to good appearance – is pathological. Therefore, for sociology it is precisely individuality – whatever resists being mapped, or in short, whatever resists everything that is interchangeable, social – that is pathological. And because in this way the entire real world of human beings becomes pathological and criminal for sociology, and because sociology has not been able to differentiate this world from the world of scaffolding and maps, or even to erase this world from its soul, it is no surprise that it has allocated it arbitrarily to the collective world, and has thus come to the paradoxical conclusion that that crime is a necessary, '(socially) moral' phenomenon in society, which in its language means: also beneficial. In order to provide some kind of evidence for this beneficiality, Durkheim writes: 'According to Athenian law, Socrates was a criminal and his condemnation was entirely just. However, his crime – his independence of thought – was useful not only for humanity but for his country. It served to prepare a way for a new morality and a new faith, which the Athenians then needed because the traditions by which they had hitherto lived no longer corresponded to the conditions of their existence. Socrates's case is not an isolated one, for it recurs periodically in history.'[100]

The greatest crime of Socrates against Athenian society was a clear and unequivocal moral individuality. His activity could truly lead to the fall of Athenian society, in that the decline of hypocrisy is the decline of society. It is possible to say that no one has ever endangered the hypocrisy of society to the degree that personalities of the type like Socrates and Jesus Christ have. Let us not be misled by the fact that social moralities appeal to their names. If they did

100 Durkheim, *The Rules of the Sociological Method*, p. 102.

not do so, then they would not be moralities, they would not be good appearances. We have shown that a very high level of active selflessness is very welcome in society, and that, although moral virtue evinces such selflessness, it is nevertheless unacceptable for society on account of its individuality. Therefore, social moralities can make very good use of dead moral giants, but on the other hand *must* get rid of any living moral giants. How grotesquely tragic is the fate, for instance, of Christ! How it is tragic twice over, I want to say. I know of no more diabolical paradox, no more hopeless symbol than the crucifix on the table of the inquisitor and the judge.

Theory, no matter whether it proceeds from below (natural sciences) or from above (spiritual science, theology), reduces a human being to nothing. It transforms him into a rudiment with chemical, biological, psychological, sociological, and other elements. According to the classic account of Alfred Espinas,[101] on the one hand a human creature is 'in reality composed of millions of miniature beings', while on the other hand 'society is in reality a living being'. In this strange argument *per analogiam* a human being always draws the short straw: one time he is only a compound of millions of small beings, while another time he is merely one millionth of some kind of living being. He himself is never a living being.

Human being, you are nothing. But woe to you, if you fail! When they chop off your head, they will say: that was a close thing; he almost shifted the world out of its orbit. In theory you are less than nothing, you are a mere appearance, but in practice you are the pillar on which everything hangs.

I know the intention is a good one: to find a guarantor for a person, to construct scaffolding for human beings, and thus to relieve them of the load of responsibility and of providing a guarantee. What we see however is this: to relieve someone of providing a guarantee means to get rid of reality. Therefore, for you, human being,

---

101 French thinker (1844–1922).

there is no other way out: either you are a guarantor, or you are an apparition.

God was a support for a person's conscience in his dispute with the church, with the state, with society. Jesus, not Caesar! God was overthrown and Caesar has become caught up in God's legacy as well. If you cannot render unto God the things that are God's, because there is no longer any God, then Caesar will request the things that are God's. And today there is no one to whom you can appeal against Caesar; you remain alone. And this is fateful. To be alone against Caesar, this makes you into a 'pathological phenomenon', a 'social case', an abnormality, a monster, a scoundrel.

Bergson appeals to humankind and postulates a fundamental difference between humankind and a socially moral society, because he is well aware that we cannot achieve moral virtue by any kind of extending social morality. However, if he fails to attain a morally virtuous act in society, he achieves it all the less in 'humanity'. In reality, as Bergson says: 'The object is too vast, the effect too diffuse.'[102] The direction in which we must set off is precisely the opposite one: from the most diffuse toward the most concrete, toward the most elementary; toward a human being, toward an individual.

According to Durkheim, an individual cannot be the goal of moral virtue; neither oneself, nor other individuals, because, he argues, it is not possible to see why one individual should have precedence over another. But here this is not at all a case of giving precedence to one individual over another; the aim of moral virtue is primarily that precedence be given to an individual as such over mere 'parts of a whole', over a unit, an addend, an element of a map. A morally virtuous act can be performed only by a unique individual as a living creature, and not as a member of some society, a class, or a race; it makes itself manifest for a human being as a concrete person, not for some abstract 'species', class, society, humankind. A moral con-

---

102 Bergson, *The Two Sources of Morality and Religion*, p. 25.

science knows only an individual as a reality, but it knows nothing of society as a reality. It is precisely in this that the *all-encompassing humanity* of moral conscience lies: it contains not only everything human but everything living at all. Moral conscience says that the path to a living and real humanity leads to a concrete, unique, autonomous individual. *In this elaboration, a moral emotion makes itself apparent as an individual's defence against the levelling and uniformizing pressure of society.*

Here also the concept of freedom takes on a concrete meaning. What is natural, we have said, is of itself neither determined, nor undetermined. Naturalness does not arise either through coercion or through freedom. However, naturalness can be prevented in its manifestation. The concept of freedom and lack of freedom, therefore, only takes on concrete sense in the relationship of the internal world to the external world, or – if we have people in mind – in the relationship of a person to society. We have already earlier said that freedom is only another word for internal reality. So: the measure of freedom or lack of freedom are not chains, halters or bars in windows; it is not possible to talk about oppression where there is nothing to be oppressed. A flock of sheep, enclosed in a pen, can seem enslaved only to a person who notionally takes up the place of one of them in his imagination. However, there is evidently nothing in a sheep itself that feels enslaved by a pen. On the contrary, it is rather probable that it feels safer inside this pen, because when it is set free from the pen, it returns there again of its own accord. In short, a living creature cannot be oppressed from outside more than he is liberated inside, more than the amount for which he is a guarantor. If you set free a being that is internally unfree, if you open the gates for this being, then it will soon become helpless and will run back, urging you to run with it.

What, then, to do? Do not overlook that conscience intervenes for an individual – that is, conscience places responsibility on you for whom you set free; it obliges you to elevate him to yourself; to make him into a guarantor such as you yourself are. You will certainly realize that this is not an easy task; it is a superhuman task. Conscience does not know easier tasks. Conscience does not operate in an illusory world; you will not satisfy it by breaking the chains of the chained person; if conscience demands freedom for someone close to you, it asks you to make him *someone*, a guarantor, an individual. If you achieve this, then external freedom for him will be added to this.

A failure to clarify this has led to us welcoming science and technology as great liberators of humankind and to contend short-sightedly that a mere breaking of material shackles will make us free. However, science has not only failed to kindle and strengthen the guarantor in people, but on the contrary it has transferred the provision of guarantees to the imaginary world of natural laws, and by doing so it has deprived the human soul of all sense and purpose, or indeed of its very reality. And thus liberating us, it has taken as the price for this liberation our soul; it has liberated us at the cost of freedom. And so, thus liberated and unfree, we look once again for a way in which to bring our inner state back into accord with our external state, for a way in which we can quickly get rid of the freedom that demands a maximum of personal guarantees. And science and technology, which have so reliably been capable of breaking our shackles, are capable of fastening them once again just as reliably and willingly; even for those who have not only been liberated, but who are also free.

Science is a prospector of the 'given' and technology is a gold-digger who builds up ownership and material power, who owns this load-bearing pillar of the collective world of security. It is not important what name we give to this load-bearing pillar, whether matter, or spirit, or even God; what is decisive is that in all cases it is supposed to provide the same thing for us: security.

Before the birth of modern science human beings had always had their world of security in the church. The load-bearing pillar of the 'given' bore the name of God. A person amassed his capital with God, which was in practice in the hands of the church. Science deposed God and 'liberated' humans from the slavery of superstition and the church. However, a collective creature, thus deprived of its collective guarantees, required new guarantees. Science deposed God in the name of truth, and therefore it offered truth. However, what is an inhabitant of the world supposed to do with truth? God fell, because a human being apparently cannot live without truth. However, it has become apparent that a human without God can live quite well without truth, but that he cannot live without money, without property. Max Weber concludes that the spirit of modern capitalism is the spirit of Protestantism. But the Reformation was only the first step toward the dismissal of God from the mediaeval world. Protestantism played a part in the expansion of capitalistic society to the extent that it is an expression of the fact that God – as a material guarantee of a person's security – has fallen. Counting, measuring and weighing science liberated humankind in the name of truth. However, counting, measuring and weighing as a path to truth attracted all too few people; while as a path to profit, success and power it attracted practically everyone. Very few people care about whether science possesses the truth or not; it has become an instrument in the war of everyone against everyone else. For the same reason that a person in former times was afraid of falling into 'God's disfavour', today he is afraid of falling into poverty: a current-day Christian perhaps still acknowledges God, but he now rather relies on his property. Poverty and God's disfavour have merged into one for him.

The material pedestal of the world of security is today perfectly bare and exposed. The decline in hypocrisy destroys the old society. A person starts a new society, but the world in which he starts it is an old world: it is the world of scaffolding, the world of security and insecurity, borne by the given, the material. What is new about the person arriving on the scene is his greater sincerity – this is usually the case – but in all other respects he is the same as the old person. Therefore, his sincerity treats social morality in a strange way: it does not reprimand social morality for acting differently from what it preaches; it reprimands it for preaching something different from what it does. Up until now the hypocrisy of morality has made itself apparent to our conscience in that it preached a good thing, but performed a bad one. But this was conscience; this was the real world based on individuals. However, the new-yet-still-old pioneer of the world of scaffolding has discovered that his world is founded on material, and that he has reason and science to thank for this discovery, and not conscience. And this is why the hypocrisy of morality appears to him to lie in its acting correctly, but nevertheless preaching about an illusion. Therefore, whereas conscience demanded that people behave as social morality preached, and not as it acted, our pioneer requires us to act as social morality acts and not as it preaches. According to this, the greatest sin of the old society was that it did in a hidden, private and chaotic way what needs to be done publicly, systematically, scientifically, rationally, collectively and in an organized and planned way. Thus the prophets of the new society became economists, engineers, scientific specialists and technical utopians. If things are going wrong in a human society, then the cause must be sought in insufficient planning, rationalization, organization. All human problems – even moral, artistic, religious and similar ones – should be reduced to economic, professional and technical problems. This way of viewing the world is spread and propagated by those apostles of the new technology-driven society who do not have enough self-knowledge to be capable of differentiating between conscience and knowledge, and of rendering to the one and to the other what belongs to it. Such a utopian, being moral and intellectually astute, believes that he is moral because he is intellectually astute. What a surprise it is, then, that for such a person the renewal of mankind is a question of perfecter organization and improved technology. He also regards moral virtue as something that will naturally emerge of its own accord just as soon as the world has been technically mastered. Moral virtue, and all virtues in general, are characteristics of a perfect machine. Transform the world into a perfect machine, and you have made it perfectly moral. Moreover, in order to be able to transform it into a perfect machine, you must even rid it of any kind of virtuous notions whatsoever. In his book *The Mind in the Making*, James Harvey Robinson writes: 'In order that these scientific discoveries should be made and ingeniously applied to the conveniences of life, it was necessary to discard practically all the consecrated notions of the world and its workings which had been held by the best and wisest and purest of mankind. ... Intelligence ... must often break valiantly with the past in order to get ahead.'[103]

However, the following undoubtedly remains the truth: up until now, scientific discoveries have been used for good only in those cases when they have been in the hands of the best and purest of people. In the hands of the bad and impure, they have brought, and are bringing, the world only evil, disintegration, and destruction. Therefore, intelligence, if it is to 'get ahead', can possibly separate with the past, but it cannot separate with moral virtue and other 'consecrated notions' of humankind. There is no other option than to repeat over and over again: science and technology as saviours of mankind presume morally perfect people; they presume people who no longer have any need of salvation.

When we learn that Nazi researchers have carried out the most inhuman experiments on wretched political prisoners and then handed over the dead and beaten bodies to a technician for industrial utilization, then our conscience is shaken to its very bottom. Why? If we make science into our highest value, our highest criterion, then what can we base our protest on? In the name of what do

---

103 James Harvey Robinson, *The Mind in the Making* (London: Jonathan Cape, 1923), p. 39. www.fullbooks.com/The-Mind-in-the-Making1.html.

we condemn them, if they have maintained all the rules of scientific research and technological approach? What is there in science that we wish to appeal to on behalf of human beings? What does science have to do with human beings? Does not a scientist have the right in the name of science to protest: Who is this human being? I have never had anything to do with any such thing, so what then are you accusing me of? As a physicist and a chemist I was concerned only with a conglomerate of physical-chemical reactions, with a whirl of atoms and molecules; as a biologist, with a promenade of primordial juices; as a psychologist, with sense perceptions and similar elements; as a sociologist, with abstracts and products of society; but with a human being as an individual, with an actual person as a reality? I have never encountered any such thing!

As a guarantee of truth, we have demanded a science purified of any human element, and when a scientist presents us with it in this form, purified of anything human, then we are stricken with horror and disgust. When we read 'diagnoses of the spiritual illness of our era' which are written by men representing the conscience of today, we cannot escape the impression that we should search for the root of all moral poverty in the fact that life is so far not sufficiently scientific, in the fact that science has not been sufficient purified of the human. Ortega y Gasset connects the 'highest type of life' with a 'technical creature' and Johan Huizinga considers that 'the new will to exalt *being* and *living* over *understanding* and *valuing* appears, therefore, against a background of ethical disarray. This will, which scornfully rejects guidance by the intellect, can find no guidance in a type of ethics which knows itself to be founded in "knowledge".'[104] For Huizinga, 'The exaltation of being over knowing contains one other consequence worthy of attention. The repudiation of the primacy of the understanding means the repudiation of the norms of judgment as

104 Johan Huizinga, *In the Shadow of Tomorrow*, trans. by W. H. Huizinga, (New York: W. W. Norton, 1964 – orig. Dutch, 1935), p. 138.

well, and hence the abandonment of all ethical standards.'[105] – Is it really so difficult to see that moral cognition gives birth to moral virtue precisely as little as natural science engenders nature, or aesthetics generates art? If someone does not feel the obligation of norms of moral virtue, gained through I know not what research and cognition, then how do you intend to force him to accept this obligation? If you achieve this through promises or threats, then you give birth to social morality, good appearance, but never moral virtue. It is strange that even such clear-sighted men are not immune to the deceptive notion that their conscience issues from their knowledge.

Huizinga asks rhetorically: 'But what then remains to guide and direct this will if guidance is no longer sought in a metaphysical belief centred on a extra-mundane and incorporeal weal, nor in truth-seeking thought, nor in an all-embracing and generally recognized moral order containing such values as justice and charity?'[106] And he replies thus: 'Only life itself, blind and inscrutable life'[107] is left to serve as such a guide, to serve simultaneously both as a guide and as a subject. – But I ask: What is the guide of conscience – intellect or blind and inscrutable life? What is the guide of creation and beauty – intellect or blind and inscrutable life? The answer is unequivocal: Blind and inscrutable life! However, if the reply is such, why not invest the same trust in it as we did when we called this a just and invisible God? The entire value of God was comprised in the fact that human knowledge did not match that of God, that it was not sufficient to apprehend God. And I do not hesitate to contend that the entire value of life comprises in the fact that human knowledge is not sufficient to apprehend it.

A scientist speaks in such a way: 'Science discovered dynamite; but when a terrorist then makes use of this, what does this have to do with

105 Ibid., p. 126.
106 Ibid., pp. 138–139.
107 Ibid., p. 139.

science?' The failure of science in the fundamental questions of life gives us hope that life will never become a plaything in the hands of anyone; that the calculations, intentions, and caprices of technicians, economists, politicians, warmongers, parvenus, or the such are never going to decide on the reality and value of life; rather such decisions will be made only and exclusively by the 'internal equivalent', by the feeling of being and non-being, by an internal, vital, and individual process. Either reality and value reside in nature, or there is no saving us. Either conscience, goodness, and moral virtue constitute what we cannot control and dictate by our knowledge, but are rather something to which we 'submit', or we are given up to the mercy of even more obscure and inhuman forces than are 'blind and inscrutable life' or the 'mercy of God'.

I know what seduces and confuses us the most: when a human individual or a gang of humans murders and pillages, we view them as a jaguar or a pack of wolves, driven only by 'blind and inscrutable life', driven by their nature. But neither a jaguar nor a pack of wolves do anything morally worse than a housewife who cuts the throat of a chicken. After all, it is not even moral reasons, but rather economic considerations, that lead her to cut the throat of only one chicken rather than those of the entire coop all at once.

But so be it! The actions of an animal must be charged entirely to the account of 'blind and inscrutable life'. However, since reason has not intervened in the animal world, and has not therefore divided it into a dual conditionality, it is not possible to speak here either of morally virtuous behaviour or of socially moral behaviour, by which we are stating that all questions of the badness or goodness of nature must be limited to human nature. So, how will it be in the case of human nature? We already know that the intervention of reason divided it into a moral bipolarity – that is, into an egoistical side of human nature and a self-sacrificial one; and we know that the first egoistical side seeks through reason to assert itself as the whole of nature. Why through reason? Because the world of reason is a collective world – that is, a world of transferable, reduced guarantees. Quite simply, let us sum up: *What is morally negative in human nature - that is, what can hardly be acceptable to the conscience - appears as an inclination to take on a collective form, to strive for a minimum of individual guaranteeing.* What is despicable in humankind, this appears as an inclination to clothe oneself in moral obligation, in obedience to external authority and power. Conscience says clearly: in order for me to live can never be a reason for another person to die. However, conscience is silenced, and the existence of my own personage becomes a sufficient reason for slaughtering another, if I speak in this way: in order for *us* to survive is sufficient reason for the other person to have to die. And thus a person does not kill on account of himself, but rather because of his family, group, class, nation, or state, or even on behalf of humankind and humanity.

If a person acts according to the egoistical side of his nature – that is, against his conscience – he seeks to act as a socially moral creature, and not as an individual, as a personal guarantor of moral virtue. If we follow the court trials with the organized mass murderers of the last war, we will hear from the biggest to the littlest the same old story: I am innocent, because I was obeying higher orders – and he is sincerely surprised that he is supposed to bear personal responsibility. In contrast to the judges and many other people, I personally am more willing to believe that many of them are really sincere in this.

Our hitherto deliberations already outline a natural – that is, real – path to moral virtue. The only real soil of moral virtue is the human soul. This must be overturned, loosened, sewn, and seeded. And the only path to this is provided by the actions and living example of morally virtuous individuals, by their direct influence from one person to another.

Institutions, churches, the state, organizations give birth only to social morality; and if you change institutions and social forms, then you only change this outward morality; you do not touch moral virtue, you have not moved human conscience. A utopian society without classes, without a state, without police officers, is unthinkable other than as a society of individuals – that is, personalities, guarantors. An upbringing for citizenship of such a utopian world would be an upbringing for individuality. This can hardly ever be expected from societies and institutions; if only because some such thing is never going to be in the interest of their existence. In the best case, they provide their members with knowledge and education; more often, however, only with social morality, but never with moral virtue. The final argument by which they rule and aspire to rule is physical and material power, and they also implement this power in order to maintain their members in discipline and obedience – that is, in a state of readiness before the enemy. Precisely because the existence of these societies and institutions is grounded on the egoistical side of human nature, they are forced to arrange their social structure hierarchically and, in accord with every higher level of disciplinary powers and responsibility, also to increase proportionately personal privileges, external distinctions, and material advantages. It is evident that in this function a person can never be a morally virtuous agent, but rather always an agent of social morality. If we think that to create moral virtue means nothing less than to create personalities, we can easily concede that the praxis pursued as a condition of their existence by all societies that have ever been, and evidently also by all those that ever will be, is something entirely different than moral virtue. If the moral example of an individual and direct influence from one person to another is not sufficient, then there is no longer any other path to shaking and arousing the human soul than the path of tragedy, catastrophes, and apocalyptic frenzy.

It would seem that the sincerity of the new-yet-still-old person, who discovered a material basis for his collective existence, will found a new society without social morality, without good appearance. What is there to pretend, when we have sincerely and openly revealed that we have pretended and what we have pretended? However, the snag is in the fact we have not revealed everything. We have admitted sincerely and openly to the material conditionality of our existence, and to the egoistical side of human nature, but in spite of this our conscience is not abated. However, we do not admit to this unabated conscience. Why do we not admit to this? In order to prevent it becoming apparent that the material pillar on which our collective world is based would not be sufficient to bear the weight of this world, unless it was itself supported on the shoulders of someone, on the shoulders of a participant, an unconditional guarantor, whose intercessor is precisely conscience. This intercessor never ceases to remind us that the sin of the old morality was not in what it preached, but in what it did, and that therefore the sincerity that divorces us from moral virtue, love, compassion, and other 'sacred notions about human beings' hardly serves life better than a social morality that acknowledged these things only in word. This intercessor says that real evil cannot be narrowed down and reduced to ownership relationships. It tells us that not only can the problem of moral virtue not be resolved on a material basis, but that a thorough resolution of this problem would sweep away this material pillar itself. However, conscience is precisely such a thorough resolution and it inexorably designates the 'given' as misappropriated.

So, if we want to maintain the material pillar of the collective world, it is still essential to barricade this conscience with a collective morality. From where can we take this collective morality, when we have previously exposed the old, religious, and bourgeois morality and revealed it to be mere good appearance? Where can we find a new good appearance? Where can we seek a new social morality, if this can no longer be the one that pretended moral virtue, love, and compassion? Well, why not in the thing that helped us get rid of the old morality: in science? Theory is amoral; it is outside of emotions like love and compassion. Why, then, can its theoretical 'given' – that is, an amoral one – not shield us from the practical 'given' – that is, an immoral one? An amoral theory supplies us with a social morality, and thus conceals immoral praxis.

And, lo and behold, a new collective morality is born; its name is science. Clothed in its uniform you will never steal and misappropriate, but only find the 'given'. You will behave just as egoistically as before, but you will no longer guide your behaviour by moral reasons but rather by scientific ones. If you achieve power and material success, or at least you are aiming for this, you will no longer appeal to your virtues, noble feelings, and moral will, and you will no longer even have to appeal to the favour of fortune or Providence, but rather exclusively to the scientific nature of your thinking. You can continue to cheat your fellow human beings as you have done before, but rather than appealing to moral teaching and the bible as a justification for your actions, you will appeal to scientific textbooks. And any daring escapades – such as, for instance, chopping up your fellow human beings and then cooking up their fat to make soap – which previously you would have had to have justified by admitting a temporary loss of your senses, now on the contrary you can justify by claiming that you have concentrated and sharpened your thinking into a state absolutely free of any human element, into a state of absolute scientific character.

Today, science and technology are taking over those functions in society which during the period of the church's hegemony were represented by dogma and sacrament. This is the reason why today any person who expresses doubts about the redemptive power of science and technology is proclaimed as a heretic just as before any person who pronounced doubts about God and the sacrament was proclaimed to be one. A religious heretic was 'possessed by the devil', while a scientific heretic is a 'pathological phenomenon'. Not to believe in God is today a private matter; to be sceptical toward theories, ideologies, programmes, and technologies makes you 'antisocial', an enemy of the people, a saboteur and traitor of a group, a class, a state.

In this way, science and technology, the amoral preaching and the immoral praxis of the new-yet-still-old person, is sufficient for everything. But never before has the need for individual moral virtue been so urgent and intense as precisely today. Modern-day moralists formulate the biggest problem of modern scientific and technologized life as the question of how to lead a person to moral virtue without supernatural hopes and fears. Concealed within this question is the conviction that supernatural hopes and fears led to moral virtue, and that in general hopes and fears undoubtedly play a fundamental role in moral virtue. This is the source of the notion that, if a person is to be brought to moral virtue by a 'natural' path – that is, one without religion – then it cannot promise him, or indeed threaten him, less than religion promised and threatened him. What promise is at stake here? In Driesch's book *Man and the Universe* we can read this: 'If dying means ceasing to exist, then life in its deepest essence is actually indifferent. I will make of my life whatever makes it the least unpleasant for me. To the devil with this illusion of moral virtue. ... I dare to contend that moral conscience will only truly be a pressing matter for someone who accepts the notion of immortality, in whatever form – in the case of a philosopher this will not of course be any childish kind of form. Not that this person will think about a reward. This thought would spoil his own moral virtue. But he may think about *justice*.'[108] Science has become the inheritor of religion. Driesch, therefore, says about science: 'If knowledge is to make moral virtue into a pressing matter, then it must aim literally in the direction of immortality.'

We know already that for someone for whom 'moral conscience is truly a pressing matter', it is pressing because it is pressing, and not because it promises something, or threatens him with something, or simply that it knows something. We have tried to clarify what nature consists in, and why moral virtue, just like creativity, is therefore natural. We thus came to the conclusion that *a person is either morally virtuous, or he can be held to a social morality; a person is either creative, or he can be held to work.* Moral virtue and creativity

[108] Hans Driesch, *Man and the Universe* (London: G. Allen & Unwin, 1929).

are natural, 'instinctive'; social morality and work have to be justified and imposed on human beings. If religion failed to lead a person to moral virtue, but rather merely provided a justification for imposing a social morality on him, then neither can we expect any more than this from science. A socially moral being – we have seen – did not exchange a religious morality for science, but rather only for a new morality, for a scientific morality. As we have shown, the ultimate argument of every social morality is physical and material coercion. However, before a moral collective turns to this ultimate argument, it attempts less drastic means. It offers advantages and punishes with disadvantages; it promises and threatens. The promise of immortality is one of these means.

Death is a member of the spectator's world. For the spectator, the real world is transformed into a world of mere phenomena under which, behind which, or above which the lost reality is located as an essence, an ultimate reality. A 'phenomenon' is fleeting, but 'ultimate reality' is 'always' and 'everywhere'. It is eternal. As mere fleeting appearances, living creatures do not have any reality for a spectator; by an analogical understanding of himself as a mere appearance, the spectator arrives at a notion of his own fleeting nature. He arrives at a knowledge of his own death. Death is a shadow thrown by a soul blinded by reason. Death is the destiny of someone who wants to find as given something that he should guarantee. Nature punishes a desertion from participating to observing by driving a person out of the real world into a world of danger and death. A spectator expelled from the real world, expelled from the present, can never reach his goal, and death eventually appears to him as the conclusion of everything. Death becomes the spectre of his existence, and all his actions are aimed at getting rid of this phantom. He does not know why to live, and therefore he wants to live securely, comfortably, and for as long as possible; he does not know what to die for, and therefore death has the last word in the question of his existence; his life has lost meaning, and therefore it becomes for him his dearest possession; his egoistical effort at self-preservation reaches its culmination because he has nothing to preserve. The world of reality, the world of the present, does not know this death; a participant is always at his goal; his life is fulfilled at every moment, and therefore death has no access to him. We can be sure that 'nature' knows nothing of death. An animal does not defend itself against death, but always only against manifest violence.

A person is inclined to a belief in immortality to the extent that he succumbs to a notion of death. And he succumbs to this notion all the more, the less he is a participant and a guarantor – that is, a creative and morally virtuous individual; or to put it another way: the more he is an inhabitant of the collective world, the external world. Because this belief in immortality has a tendency to be expressed collectively, it provides society with an ideal means of discipline, a method of social morality. The most effective form of this is offered by religion, which in the form of an all-powerful technician guarantees to human beings that transubstantiation 'from a mere phenomenon into an ultimate reality' which is absolutely essential for immortality. God as a person, as a heavenly ruler, is much more advantageous compared to all other substances, because he gives a person the greatest assurance that he will not lose his I, his personal identity, in the process of transubstantiation. In contrast to this, a promise of human immortality from the mouth of science seems absolutely trivial, when we bear in mind that science has not only denied the existence of a heavenly prime mover, but of any prime mover at all, and that it only acknowledges material as a substance. This is why we demand from science – rather than immortality after life – 'pre-death' immortality, immortality without death.

We should note how, from a *hope* of immortality, a *claim* to immortality arises, and this even in the name of justice. A person living under the threat of death, but not however otherwise subject to external pressure and not coerced to certain actions and behaviour, would never proceed from a mere desire for immortality to a claim to it. Face to face with himself, he could not deny that he wants to take without giving. It is known that people who are terminally ill, threatened by an imminent death, feeling freed from social chains and left to their own selves, make all kinds of promises to God, to those close to them, or at least to themselves. They often promise no small sacrifices and renunciations in the future, 'if they get better'. In this way they attempt to negotiate a claim to live from their desire to live. Well, a claim to immortality is acquired in a similar way, but by an approach that is in some way opposite. A person, not threatened by immediate death, but aware of this threat, manifests a willingness to bear an immediate sacrifice, to commit some harm to his life, if by this he in some way ensures a future life. It is evident that he will welcome it if some institution can be found that is powerful and trustworthy enough to be capable of taking on the entire transaction as its own, and that can measure and also enforce the payment of 'instalments' for the future good of a living client. In fact, it is only this pressure from outside, which allots self-sacrifice and renunciation to a person without regard for his natural inclinations, that first founds a person's 'natural' claim to a future life. The most favourable soil for the establishment of a personal claim to a future life is a society with a strict discipline and a stern morality that imposes an excessive load and sacrifice; this claim to a life tomorrow displays an inclination to extend itself into a claim to immortality, and therefore it takes on a religious character. In support of this claim, a person is even willing to acknowledge the supremacy of 'natural' law – that is, God's law – over himself.

A hope for immortality is not yet a belief in immortality; it is only the claim for this immortality that first strengthens this hope into a belief.

The claim to immortality also has a paradoxical reverse side; a *duty* of immortality, a duty of further existence. However, this immortality is nothing other than an intensification of the state of death and non-being. In order that the loss of, and harm to, this life be alleviated, and the after-death reward multiplied, the punishment of death is intensified for those who make no sacrifices, suffer no losses, in this life by consigning them to hell after death. This moral calculation is further complicated by the teaching about original sin, which is supposed to reconcile a person to those sacrifices and losses which he does not wish for and which he does not store up as a claim for a future life, and which therefore he would feel as iniquity and injustice, which injustice he could try to redress wilfully through revolt, robbery, and violence. Buddhism, which has identified life with suffering, seeks to justify them in its teaching about karma as some kind of duty to expiate the evil committed in previous lives.

If a person raises a claim for gaining life tomorrow in return for today renouncing an act designated as bad and immoral, this means that his actions today do not bring him any feeling of vital living gain, but rather a feeling of loss in life; he gives up being today in favour of being tomorrow. Such an act can never be a morally virtuous act. A virtuous act does not bear within itself any expectation of some future being, because for it there is neither tomorrow nor yesterday. For a feeling of satisfaction, it is quite enough that this act actualizes itself, that it makes itself into a real fact. It derives from the feeling of being and non-being, and therefore through such a virtuous act life is made real, fulfils itself, and therefore it has no reason to make any claim to some future actualization and fulfilment. This is popularly captured in the words that a good deed is its own reward. By this of course is stated that a good deed cannot be felt as a sacrifice, as a loss, and stored as a future claim. A good deed is a gain of living reality and its countervalue is the same as the countervalue of any reality: a psychological equivalent, which in a vital living process gives rise to reality.

An understanding of moral virtue as a loan granted for repayment in a future life corresponds to a tendency on the part of reason to interpret the world as 'given', and not as created. If life is given, then of course we have it free of charge, and therefore we cannot understand any eventual harm or injury suffered as an item paid to current, 'given' life. Moreover, we will understand all productive activity whatsoever as some kind of constant acquisition, accumulation, and storing up, as a constantly growing something in addition to the given – that is, as a constant ascent to something. However, what is the point of this accumulation and storing, and what is the point of this ascent, when at the end of everything, death and extinction are grinning at us? This is why John Fiske,[109] for instance, asks: 'Are Man's highest spiritual qualities, into the production of which all this creative energy has gone, to disappear with the rest? Has all this work been done for nothing?'[110] If he had asked who will pay us for our current being today, then this question – 'Has all this work been done for nothing?' – could not possibly have occurred to him.

If life is given, then of course whatever we renounce in life – whether voluntarily or by coercion – cannot be lost: it is stored up on our behalf and credited to the benefit of a future life. We have said that the 'given' as a moral concept expresses an ownership claim; it is an expression of the egoistical aspect of human nature. To renounce life means then to suppress and restrict the egoistical side of human nature, and this is regarded as the source of a just claim to future being. It is clear that the renunciation of life here today and the demanding nature of an immortal life offer society an ideal means of discipline, and thereby also of power. The church, which seized this means of discipline, grew into the most powerful and long-lasting organization in the whole of human history. We should note that it has succeeded in something that all kinds of secular societies have tried to achieve in vain; it has forced an egoist to behave in a way that is intrinsic only to moral virtue, without having in the least to accept what is unacceptable to it in this moral virtue: individuality.

---

109 American philosopher (1842–1901).
110 John Fiske, *The Destiny of Man, Viewed in the Light of his Origin* (Boston, New York: Houghton, Mifflin, 1884), p. 144.

It has succeeded in achieving a simple transposition of the egoistical instinct into a life after death, into a fictive world. The fact that it was not concerned with real moral virtue, but rather – like every society – with blind obedience and social morality, has been shown to us more than sufficiently by its history. What other use would it have had, for instance, for its hierarchical organization, its ceremonial and ritual acts, its material and political power, its dogmas and beliefs such as a 'shroud with an image *in bianco* (white)', and so on? 'The standing of a Christian in the church can only be a standing of systematic immaturity,' says Auguste Sabatier.

Religion arose from the need of a socially moral being, not from the need of a morally virtuous individual. Moral virtue and immaturity exclude each other. For moral virtue a guarantor is required, and not a child who constantly requests forgiveness and reckons with this forgiveness. '[My] curse shall be Forgiveness,' says Byron in the words of one of his characters.[111] Similarly, F. X. Šalda writes: 'Forgetting is the only forgiveness of the proud and the strong; the only sincere forgiveness.' Let us not repeat these strong words about the proud and the strong, but rather say simply: of the mature and the responsible. Religion arose for the benefit of the collective world of scaffolding, the world of security and insecurity, the world of egoism and death, and with respect to this world the Roman Catholic Church represents the most successful religion that so far there has ever been. However, religion does not have anything to do with moral virtue. There is self-sacrifice in it, but this is a sacrifice to a God-Moloch. Can you describe as moral virtue the determination of a saint to go and live among pagans *in order to* find a martyr's death there? Can you designate as moral virtue the exultation of Japanese young men who hurl themselves into a waterfall to thereby merge with God in death? Or the acts of a fanatical creature who sacrifices himself for his leader? Such a sacrifice of life is the act of the mem-

---

111 Lord Byron, *Childe Harold's Pilgrimage, Canto IV,* stanza 135.

ber of a cult, not a morally virtuous act. Moral virtue is not sacrifice, and therefore it does not even seek death. It can be said: the act of a cult member is performed with a discarding of conscience. The God-Moloch, the leader, or the mass group nature of the act (it does not matter whether this mass nature is actual or merely imagined) absolves a person of giving an individual guarantee and supplants his conscience. This is precisely the difference between individual participation and the mass group nature of fanaticism: the most awakened conscience as against the most dimmed conscience. Auguste Sabatier writes the following about the difference between religion and moral virtue: 'The religious is so different from the moral sense that, at the outset, it exists by itself, and expresses itself in the most selfish and ferocious manner.[112] A religious society, no differently from any other society, provides a place for what is negative in human nature – that is, behaviour which does not stand up to the examination of conscience and which therefore has an inclination to take on a collective form. History provides more than enough lessons showing that the name of God does not have influence on the moral quality of collective actions.

Even today – and perhaps precisely today – current-day thinkers and moralists have no other answer to the burning question of how to bring a person to moral virtue than: religion. For instance, in his book *The Current State of Ethics* Jan Blahoslav Kozák surveys modern ethical theories and teachings and in the end says that he has 'looked for an ethics that would explain an appeal to personal decision and absolute responsibility without religion', but that he has 'sought in vain'.[113]

If I say: I am morally virtuous because there is a God, then so be it! Religion is then an explanation of moral virtue, just as natural

---

112 Auguste Louis Sabatier, *Outlines of a Philosophy of Religion Based on Psychology and History*, trans. by Rev. T. A. Seed (London: Hodder and Stoughton, 1902), p. 111.
113 Jan Blahoslav Kozák, *Přítomný stav ethiky* [The Current State of Ethics] (Praha: Dědictví Komenského, 1930).

science is an explanation of nature, or aesthetics is an explanation of art. This is the way in which Kant proceeded from conscience to the postulates of God, freedom, and immortality. This is 'cognition' of moral virtue. If I stay at this point, then very well! However, if I want to proceed from cognition to action, and if I then say: there is a God, and therefore I am morally virtuous and therefore also you, who are not morally virtuous as I am, must be morally virtuous – here we have parted company with moral virtue and found ourselves in the world of social morality, of technology. Through cognition, conscience loses its reality: that is, it ceases to be an imperative 'here' and 'now' and becomes a doctrine for 'always' and 'everywhere'. If we move from 'cognition' to practice, we request from this doctrine a pure impossibility: for it to become a conscience 'here' and 'now'. In order for us to force a person to the required action, we must use pressure which gives this doctrine the obligatory character which it lacks compared to conscience. However, here this is a case of external obligation, of a socially moral obligation, imposed from outside and enforced either by a threat or by a promise, and whose ultimate argument is physical violence.

Social morality, like every technical means, presumes rational instructions, teachings, rules, and norms. However, if we overlook the fact that the teachings established by natural science do not govern nature, but rather technology, then in all probability we will also confuse moral virtue with social morality, and we will consider as binding for individual conscience those norms that are binding only for the external behaviour of a collective body. We started out from 'cognition of oneself', we rationalized our consciences, we objectivized the 'moral law in us', we transformed the conscience of 'here' and 'now' into knowledge 'always' and 'everywhere'; the 'inscribed tablet of objective moral norms' is written. If we want this to become obligatory for human conscience, what exactly do we want? Nothing less than that what we feel as obligatory for ourselves to become obligatory for everyone. We, who have deduced a scale of moral norms from our own most personal and individual inclinations, now declare it to be not dependent on any personal inclinations, and we see in this non-dependence its true moral value. It does not bother us at all that it is precisely on account of this postulate of non-dependence on personal inclinations that we cannot give our scale of moral norms validity other than with the help of coercion and violence. But this is just the start of several paradoxes. Let us have a look at some others!

The obligation of moral virtue, the reality of conscience, lies in the vital process by which it is actualized, made real. But imagine that you understand moral virtue in a technical way – that is, that you make its actualization dependent on cognition. As soon as you change the task of a participant for the task of an onlooker, moral reality is deflated into a mere 'moral phenomenon' behind which or above which you seek for the true reality. Consider: instead of moral virtue as actualization 'here' and 'now', you seek for moral virtue as *given* 'always' and 'everywhere'. That which should be actualized, made real, all of a sudden becomes something that has already been actualized since the very start of time and for ever.

What should conscience do with such givenness? What work is left here for conscience? Should it make real something that has already been made real, or actually transform this reality into mere appearance? Should it guarantee something that has already been guaranteed for ever? Should it fight and die for something that has long ago been won? What is the point of maximum risk, when there is nothing to risk for? Whatever conscience is, it is certainly not Platonic. J. B. Kozák writes: 'To believe, *justifiably* believe, that we are not aiming towards a fiction, but rather towards final, even if unknown, goals, for whose victory our assistance is also necessary, but which will nevertheless one day be victorious even without us, or even in spite of us.' What does your conscience say in response to this? It says: If the triumph of good is given in advance, then why do you discredit and devalue it by fighting in its name, even by using violence and increasing the amount of evil? And why do you also devalue yourself by putting yourself at risk for something that is won? Do you not yourself place the seal of dubious character on the foreheads of those who join with a victor in order to help him finish off the defeated party and then take a reward from him for this assistance? If God is from the start the absolute victor, then an appeal to our conscience to help him and sacrifice on his behalf borders on immorality and cynicism. It is an appeal to join a cult, not an appeal to moral virtue. Here it will be moral conscience itself that leads me to Satanists, to the decadent, to Titans.

If God is all-powerful, then is not every 'good deed' for his benefit merely an insane provocation? Is it not, then, 'more natural' to give oneself up to his will and wait for his mercy? After all, as such, he best fulfils the role for which he was created by mankind, and which was then taken over from him by science and technology: to bring humankind to eternal doing nothing.

J. B. Kozák wants to have someone guarantee that his tomorrow is not a fiction. I think that the fictiveness of tomorrow merely reflects the fictiveness of today and that all our powers – that is, including those that we expend for tomorrow's being – are therefore hardly sufficient to guarantee us today's being.

If a person consents to act in accordance with the prescribed moral norms and does so with a feeling of renunciation, of sacrifice, of harm and loss to his life, then – as we have said – his desire for immortality is transformed in him into a claim to immortality. Moral cognition, or the science of morality, supports this claim theoretically by positing moral virtue as *something given* – that is, as an unchanging, absolute substance of moral virtue, underpinned by a succession of variable and momentary moral phenomena. This something given, if it is to remain something given, must be moral virtue 'always' and 'everywhere'; if, however, it is maintain its moral character, then it must be an individual, analogical to a person. The only thing that is capable of fulfilling this dual condition is religion, which in God has a being who is a morally perfect, and at the same time ever-present. It is in this given moral virtue 'always' and 'everywhere', in the realm of an eternal and perfect God, that a person localizes his immortal being. And so, in contrast with the earthly world, the realm of God emerges as a place in which all sacrifices and renunciation, all wickedness and bad deeds, all iniquities and injustices receive a just recompense. This just recompense consists in all this renunciation undergone and harm suffered in this life being compensated in the form of life after death. If you renounce this life, then you are ensuring a claim to the next life. And since that world, the after-life, because it is for ever given, is the real and actual world, and this world accordingly merely a momentary fleeting appearance, then to renounce it is simply to recognize its illusory nature, and therefore to deny its reality. And since here in this context renunciation must be understood as the suppression of the egoistical side of human nature, a human being as an egoistical being is a member of this world, the world of appearances and mere phenomena, and he is therefore himself only an appearance, an ostensible phenomenon. To act in a morally virtuous way, then, means renouncing oneself as an earthly and momentary being for the sake of oneself as an eternal being. In this way we arrive at the strangest paradox of all moral teaching: the concept of a morally virtuous act as a denial of the will to live, as self-denial, as a denial of all earthly being. Paul Deussen – who in his *General History of Philosophy With Particular Reference to Religion* traces this idea from Indian thought, through antiquity and Christianity up to Kant and Schopenhauer – concludes: 'If it is thus shown that, as a consequence of the spatial detachment of individuals, egoism is the only possible motivation of empirical action, two important conclusions can be drawn from this sentence: *firstly*, that all actions whose motivation is not egoism cannot be understood from the natural order, and that another principle is necessary for their explanation, and *secondly*, that the suppression of egoism is only possible through the suppression of all empirical being. ... All morality in its varied forms (such as disinterested justice, self-sacrificial love to those closest to you, renunciation, and selfless engagement for some great task in life) consists in self-denial, as Jesus says, in the denial of the will to live, as Schopenhauer says in different words. ... What the bible calls sin lies not in individual acts, which necessarily proceed from egoism, but in this egoism itself as our innate empirical character, and all deep religions require the suppression of this egoism as the highest task and actual purpose of earthly being.'[114]

According to this, a morally virtuous person does not act for the good of this life, but rather for the good of some kind of next life. However, this means that the measure of good and evil is not in this world, but rather in the other life, in what 'no eye has seen, nor ear heard, nor the heart of man imagined'. (1 Corinthians 2:9) How, then, can a person recognize that he is acting in accordance with this? Either the moral law of God is given by our conscience, in which case it serves this life, or God's measure is different from ours, and then we can discharge God from our thoughts entirely, because when we do good we do not know whether God receives this as good, or when we do evil we do not know whether God receives this as evil, and on the contrary when we experience evil we do not know whether God is punishing us, or rewarding us, and similarly we do not know this when we experience good.

Apart from that, if moral virtue lies in the suppression of egoism, in a denial of the will to live, in a rejection of this world, how then can we concede to God a moral character, when he is quite free of any egoistical conditionality, and therefore does not have anything to suppress? If moral virtue is induced by a feeling of harm to one's life, and this feeling of harm thereby founds a claim to a future life, what harm could God experience in his being, and what claim

---

114 Paul Deussen, *Allgemeine Geschichte der Philosophie unter besonderer Berücksichtigung der Religionen* [General History of Philosophy With Particular Reference to Religion] (Leipzig: F.A. Brockhaus, 1915).

would arise for him by this? If we understand moral virtue in this way, it is evident that we are initiating some kind of chain of loans and claims reaching *ad infinitum*. In order to relieve God of this embarrassing role, we would have to attribute to him a morally indifferent character and view him as a mere impartial accountant of human moral claims. However, how could he perform this impartial accounting, when – not being a moral being – he would have no scales for measuring moral and immoral, and therefore would not know which of a person's actions to assign on the 'Gave' side of this person's account and which ones to assign on the 'Should Give' side? As soon as we tie moral virtue with the idea of justice, we will never extricate ourselves from such accounting difficulties.

If moral virtue lies in rejecting this life, then why should we find moral virtue in 'engagement for some great task in life'? Why should we find moral virtue in the act of a person putting his own life at stake to save the life of a person close to him? I preach that moral virtue lies in a rejection of life, and I see its greatest expression in an act of saving life. Why should I act morally 'in order to live for a long time and in order for me to get along well on this Earth'? Why should I not rather see immorality in behaviour that renounces some desires today in exchange for the prospect of being satisfied many times over later? Deussen argues against this objection with the well-known evasion: in his opinion, it is something entirely different if a heavenly reward is a *reason* for moral action, or merely a *consequence* of it. I think that with respect to moral virtue this is a matter of absolutely no significance. If I know, for instance, that a jump from a high place will have as a consequence the breaking of limbs, then this consequence is a reason for me not to jump from a height. What is decisive for moral virtue is either knowledge, in which case the consequence of a moral act is its reason, or knowledge is not decisive here, in which case a moral act lies neither in consequences, nor in its reasons, but rather it is simply a unique living reality, a vital event of 'here' and 'now'. However, if it has to be linked to a consequence – that is, inserted in a causal chain – then this is doubtlessly because it is not a reality, and that therefore it is necessary to explicate it by something else, to transform it into something else, in this given case into 'the next world', into 'life after death'. It is evident that 'the next world' is simply an expression of a loss of the real world, an expression of the fact that certain behaviour, apparently morally virtuous, is not felt as a living reality, as a gain in life, but rather as a loss and injury in life, by which a claim arises for recompense in the form of a future life. Moral virtue is not a case of merit. It is social morality that interprets moral virtue as meritorious – that is, as worthy of reward.

God was a transposition of the egoistical side of human nature into the 'next world' under the veil of moral virtue. Science swept away 'the next world' and thus brought the egoistical principle back down to Earth again. This principle – we have said – has a tendency to take on a collective form, which conceals it under its social morality. Religious morality was swept away along with 'the next world'. The authority of the new morality will no longer be God, but rather God's vanquisher: science. A society of the new morality will no longer cite God and his will as a justification for its standing as a chosen nation, race, or class, for its moral, spiritual, or some other form of superiority over others, and for its 'natural' right for rule over the world. Rather it will cite science and its laws to justify this. However, the truth of science has not made even the slightest impact on the souls of immature beings, and science as such is not doing any better in this respect than God once did. We can judge this from the fact that, just as a human being once signed a blank cheque without even blushing as far as the content of faith was concerned, now he is willing to sign a blank cheque as far as the content of science is concerned. However, never in the world of religious morality was there such a pressing need for real moral virtue as there is in the world of the new social morality. Why? Because there is no longer any transposition of the egoistical principle into 'the next world' and only this world remains to digest this egoism in its entirety. It is true that there is no lack of visions of utopian future realms and worlds, but these realms and worlds do not even guarantee personal immortality, and neither are they so close and sure as to give hope of a reward still in this life. Quite simply, there are no inhibitions in the form of the notion of a higher justice, God's justice, that would prevent an egoistical creature – under the protection of the collective – from taking his reward at any moment that it is offered to him at the expense of any other person whosoever. Neither is it possible to overlook that the old social morality covered a moral authority which prescribed moral behaviour both for the purpose of good appearance, but also for a personal claim to immortality. In contrast to this, the new social morality is backed by the authority of science and it conditions entry into utopia on a theoretical justification and technical performance. If it concedes any role at all here to moral virtue, then only as an accompanying phenomenon of perfect organization, engineering, and economy. The consequence of this is that the ideal figures of the old social morality – the ascetic, the saint, and the missionary – have been replaced in the new social morality by the ideal figures of the sportsman, the chauffeur, and the engineer. The loss of the assurance of the afterlife as a result of an insufficient internal certainty leads to the paradoxical phenomenon: to increased external dynamism, to dynamism in the world of the spectator, in the world of scaffolding, which was initiated as a means of escape for the spectator from internal dynamism, from the dynamism of the real world, the participant's world. This external dynamism, the measure of which is tempo, record performance, task-directed performance, quite simply the achievement of above-average quantities and numbers, has no other purpose than to deafen the deathly silence and the deadly immobility within through the din of machines and the attainment of bigger quantities. The consciousness of security increases with bigger amounts, increasing numbers, greater quantities. But the pressing need for a real individual moral virtue reaches an intensity never before felt.

And today's moralist has no other method to save him than the old moralist did: if science is to bind a person morally, then it must aim toward immortality. How can we understand this? We have lost faith in an immortality that begins with death; we have lost faith in a heavenly garden which is entered by a fall headlong into a bottomless black hole. The modern technological soul does not fall for such nonsense. It knows that technically this is nonsense, and what is nonsense technically is nonsense full stop. Therefore: either the heavenly garden without a black hole as an entrance gate, or immortality without death, or – there is no point in continuing. If a technician cannot succeed in achieving this, then no one can. Immortality without death: such must be the ideal of natural science. What are the prospects for this?

Natural science is actually working with the assumption of immortality. Its 'ultimate reality' is precisely this eternal and immortal, all the things that being stores and guarantees. Today, for instance, this prerogative of immortality is assigned to electrons, protons, photons, and suchlike. Viewed in this way, a science that was supposed to endow a human being with immortality would have to make him the ultimate reality or essence; however, as such, a human being would then become the essence of everything, and would change everything, except himself, into a mere phenomenon, a mere appearance, and a false problem. However, if the ultimate reality is already *given* in electrons, it would be a crazy idea to want to transform it into something else. Therefore, for a person to achieve immortal being, nothing more is necessary for this than for him to die. However, a human being is not interested in such an immortality. He was interested in immortality in religion, where through death he was transposed into the substance of God; but who would be interested in immortality in the form of electrons and ether waves?

Science cannot, therefore, offer a human being the kind of immortality that religion offers him: it cannot turn him as a mere appearance into the opposite of this – the reality of himself. For science, a human being is nothing more than a sum of physical-chemical and other conditions, and only this sum of conditions can have any kind of hope of becoming eternal. An immortal human being, therefore, is only conceivable as an immortal phenomenon, a semblance, a false problem. This is a somewhat embarrassing notion, but if it does not bother the majority of us now, then I think that it will bother us all the less later.

The path to immortality as an eternal immutability of conditions has been indicated in a practical way so far only by Carrel's experiments with living tissues. However, even if there were not other difficulties here that seem thus far insuperable, one difficulty seems to be insuperable for ever: an eternal immutability of conditions is dependent on a mortal human being. The task, therefore, is this: a mortal human being is supposed to introduce and eternally maintain conditions which would make him immortal. Or, in other words: a human being should create eternity in advance, so that this eternity can then make him eternal. Religious human beings created this eternity in the image of God, and from him they promised eternity for themselves, However, natural science thus far does not know any other eternity than that which is represented by elementary particles and the immutable laws of their movement.

Practical attempts at immortality have had at least this indubitable result: that they have forced us to part with the notion of eternal life as an eternal doing nothing. There is nothing and no one who would provide us with such eternal hospitality. Living reality is something which must be purchased and paid for in hard cash, 'here' and 'now'. Those people who request immortality for what they are doing now, for how they are behaving now, admit on the one hand that they must pay for their being, but strangely, on the other hand, only for some kind of future being, while for their current being ... Who do they think will pay for this? In his book *The Universe Around Us*, James Jeans predicts that in the 'far distant future [when] disease, and perhaps death, will have been conquered, and life will doubtless be safer and incomparably better-ordered than now, it will seem incredible that a time could have existed when men risked, and lost, their lives. ... Life will be more of a routine and less of an adventure than now.'[115] – I would say that, if the time ever comes when life is 'more of a routine and less of an adventure', then this will more probably mean the end of the human race than its culmination. I consider that the old debate about the price of civilization and culture should be concluded thus: civilization and culture are an ascent for those who create them, but a decline for those who merely make use of them. The pioneers of civilization have rarely lived or live in a civilized way; and in the eyes of the common consumer of culture the real creator of culture rarely lives in a cultured way.

Life does not become a habit until the moment when the all-powerful Gods or all-powerful laws relieve us of the burden of providing a guarantee. The great campaigns of theology and science, which were supposed to seek out a guarantor, have ended in the conclusion that there is no such guarantor, other than in theology or in the researcher himself. As a researcher you are guided by reason; as a person you are guided by conscience. By critical reason you want to ascertain a truth that would bind your conscience; but conscience dictates to your reason what to find truth in, and what not to find it in. Reason searches for a law as a guarantor of truth – a guarantor that is external to human beings; however, conscience demands you as a guarantor of law and truth. You attempt to demonstrate that the world is based on an objective law; however, your conscience leaves you in no doubt that the world is based on you. For the salvation of a human being, you say that God is required, or nature is required, in order for them to prove their worth – the first in one way, and the second in a different way; however, in truth this salvation requires a human being to prove his worth. However, the same burning questions remain: How can we measure whether

---

115 James Jeans, *The Universe Around Us* (Cambridge: Cambridge University Press, 1929), p. 364.

he has proven his worth, or not? How do we recognize this? Where is this scale of absolute values, and how can we escape from this disintegrative phantom which is concealed in the word 'subjective'? Well, there is no other answer than this: this scale is in me, in my conscience, and nowhere else. The problem of absolute values is not a problem of cognition; it is a personal task to make binding for others what I feel as binding for myself – that is, to make them into guarantors, such as I am. However, what do you make them into, if you entrust this task to cognition and arrive at some objective or absolute inscribed tablet of values? This inscribed tablet does not have any more internal moral reality – that is, moral obligation – than a pronouncement on the town-hall noticeboard. If you want to impart any obligatory nature to this, then you must post a police officer next to it. You have not, therefore, brought people to moral virtue, but you have given them social morality under a power that will enforce this morality. You were supposed to make them into a guarantor, but you have entrusted them to someone who needs to keep them inherently immature.

On your inscribed tablet of absolute norms you long to construct some kind of absolute conscience, according to which people would set their own consciences, just as they set their watches according to the official town clock. However, the obligation that forces me to adjust my watch in accordance with a central clock as 'correct' is not imposed on me because this official clock runs more objectively or absolutely then my own watch. If the main official clocks show solar or stellar time, this does not mean anything, because it is not possible either objectively or absolutely to decide which is running correctly: whether the sun, or my watch. This question does not even make sense, because the notion 'more correctly' does not contain anything objective. The question of what is running correctly – whether the sun or my watch – is a matter of agreement, of convention. If I were to claim that my watch is running more correctly than the sun, no one could prove that I was lying or indulging in deception. However,

I could quite rightly be accused of intolerance, of revolting for the mere sake of revolting, of pointless resistance, of playing the fool and making a cheap attempt at being original, of being crazy, and so on. However, it is quite another matter, if in a given case my conscience commands me to behave otherwise than as commanded or forbidden by the inscribed tablet of moral norms. Neither here is there any objective or absolute measure that could prove me guilty of a lie or a deception. But nevertheless I cannot be accused of any of those vices of which I was accused in the case of my watch. Why this difference? Because my watch does not have anything to do with my internal being or non-being, with what I am or am not. But my conscience does. Watches are interchangeable, they can be exchanged between people, while conscience cannot. Watches in their function constitute knowledge 'always' and 'everywhere', while conscience is 'here' and 'now'. Watches are knowledge of the collective world of scaffolding; conscience is the reality of an individual's world. In a process of synchronization with central clocks, watches remain the same thing that they were before, or we can even say that it is only through this process of synchronization that they first become watches in the true sense of the word: that is, that they fulfil the function of watches. However, through synchronization with an objective inscribed tablet of moral norms, conscience loses its reality: it ceases to be a conscience of moral virtue and becomes socially moral knowledge. It loses its natural function, and in doing so it also loses its internally binding nature. Socially moral knowledge, if it is to be binding for a human being, must be presented to him as binding from outside. A grotesque case occurs when two or more 'central clocks' – social moralities – stake a claim to the synchronization of your conscience. In order for one to paralyse the influence of the other, it must appeal to your conscience; however, in order to then submit your conscience to its own social morality, then it must deny your conscience. This is the sense of the theologian's statement: 'Conscience is not the final lawgiver; it was created, and therefore it is not a moral sovereign.'

With respect to one social morality, for instance a secular one, your conscience is a lawgiver; however, with respect to another social morality, for instance that of the church, it is not the final lawgiver.

The spectre of subjectivity drove G. B. Shaw to the statement: 'If conscience allows someone to steal watches, then I am not much in favour of conscience.' A lack of conscience is not conscience. However, of course: if there are no objective norms, then where is the measure for what is conscience, and what is not? Meanwhile, we need not be totally at a loss here. If you are in doubt about someone, try to bribe him, to buy his soul. Let him go through temptations, just as Christ was ordained to go through them. And in this way you will recognize what is more important for him: whether to take or to give. Someone for whom to take is more than to give – that is, he who feels himself poor – is not capable of approaching another person with pure intentions. Neither love nor friendship buds from poverty. The poverty of current-day Christianity is that it is a religion of those who consider themselves to be piteous wretched fellows. But Christianity is not for wretched fellows; it is for those for whom to give is more than to take. This means to give, and not to lend at fat interest rates.

In fact you do not even need to subject those persons close to you to such tests, because life itself already does this and it does so with all of us. After all, the fact that we can say about conscience that everyone knows what it is, we owe to the fact that life itself ceaselessly leads us into such temptation, bribes us, and entices us to betrayal, to betrayal of ourselves. And so life itself chooses for us those whose voice is worthy of being heard. And if these chosen ones preach to us about objective norms and truths, then we feel behind these norms and truths primarily strong and uncompromising guarantors. What would their objective values be without these guarantors? In truth, these chosen ones are the only ones amongst us who unflinchingly follow their consciences and their own 'subjective' truth. So, everyone should really follow their own subjective truth, and not some good appearance. So, everyone should openly follow their own subjective truth and undergo with this truth the test of life. You can be sure that life and the world will harvest only good from this, as always until now.

A strange thing: as I feel something that – as it seems to me – other people do not feel, then I request for my feeling an objective validity. If the feelings of all of us were the same – that is, if they were to have objective validity – then such a request would not even occur to me. However, if anything at all were to be objective – that is, given entirely outside of me – then why should this be binding for me? If my guarantees are not necessary for this, if this is valid even without me, then why should this be binding for me? If the world was given, then why should I have any feeling of obligation at all, why should I be at all? I cannot resolve this in any other way than by accepting that the more pressing the feeling of obligation is, the greater the dependence on an individual guarantee doubtlessly is. If your reality was 'the same' as my reality, why should we have two? Why not just one? If your truth was the same as my truth, why should you be someone, and why should I be someone? Would not such a 'truth of all' be most successful where everyone is no one, where everyone is one, a uniform?

If the word 'subjective' frightens us so much, let us use a more appropriate word. Indeed, if objective truth exists, a truth 'for no one', if the thing in itself exists, a thing 'for no one', then the 'subjective' is an assemblage of all vices and errors. In that case, it is quite appropriate to blame it for everything accidental, arbitrary, wilful, recalcitrant, self-deceptive. However, if the thing in itself and truth of itself do not exist other than in a concept, in a thought, then the 'subjective' cannot be found guilty of 'objective' untruth and deception. Then, on the contrary, what is not subjective is not guaranteed, and therefore is not real. Of course I can declare whatever I like as reality and unreality, but that is drivel, and not subjectivity. The only thing that is really subjective is what is absolute, what internally binds me absolutely. No one has ever propagated and fought with all his personality, and with ultimate risk, for values that he has not felt as absolute. Whatever is derived from individual guarantees, this bears within itself absolute obligation. A value for which no one provides a guarantee is not a value. An absolute value is an immanent value; if I collectivize it, then natural obligation degenerates into forced obligation, obligation demanded by social morality. Nature has created absolute obligation for an individual, not for a collective; indeed, it does not even recognize such a collective. Human reason perceives this obligation without its reality – that is, without its obligatory nature – as a 'phenomenon', and searches for this reality, for this obligation, in some essence, in a law, in God. However, so long as the absolute remains an internal reality, this essence means less than last year's snow. 'So long as men can use their God, they care very little who he is, or even whether he is at all.'[116] However, such a subjective God is not what social morality requires. Nevertheless, since God cannot be simply argued away, social morality does not see any other way out than to declare him as a being that is simultaneously both transcendental and immanent. If a person is punished or rewarded by God, then this cannot be understood in any other way than that God in his transcendental function is punishing or rewarding a person for his, God's, own negligence, or respectively vigilance, as tested in his immanent function. And how about when the church authorities punish or reward a person for this negligence or vigilance on the part of God!

If yesterday's heretic today becomes pope and has today's heretics burned at the stake, then this is merely an expression of the desertion and betrayal that a human being commits on nature by collectivizing personal obligation, by violently imposing on others the obligation that was imposed on him himself. Nature obliges a heretic primarily never to become himself a pope. It commits him to make other people the same guarantors, internally free beings, as he

---

116 Professor James H. Leuba as paraphrased by William James in *The Varieties of Religious Experience* (New York: Longmans, Green and Co., 1902), p. 498.

himself is. His duty is to actualize the world of individuals, the real world, a community without classes, without authorities, without organizations, without social moralities, without violence: a society of mature beings, a society of guarantors. However, if he entrusts his task to sword and fire, then he betrays this world for the world of social morality and material power. He entrusts his task to predators, and by doing so he loses. As long as human beings call God that absolute obligation by which they themselves feel bound, then God is a blessing for the Earth; however, insofar as they give the name God to that obligation which they impose on others as absolute, then God is an affliction and a curse for the Earth.

It is evident that, if the absolute is identical with the subjective, then the objective is not any kind of middle point between them. The objective is the mapped – that is, reality and obligation divested of the subjective, or respectively of the absolute. The relativity of values is connected to their subjectivity. In the real world, there is no relativity. We speak about the relativity of values, if we compare them on a map. It is the same case with the absoluteness and relativity of values as it is with the absoluteness and relativity of movement. If I observe myself and compare myself with those around me, I can deliberate about whether I am moving only apparently, or relatively, or in some other way. However, in the fact whether I am walking or lying down, the difference is not apparent and the relationship is not relative. *My* lying down or *my* movement is not a relative thing, and it is also not a mere appearance or semblance.

The loss of subjective obligation has turned values into mere precepts or propositions. The proposition two and two are four represents 'absolute knowledge', but precisely because of this no individual obligation. It is ideally communicable, perfectly interchangeable between consciousnesses; it is simply 'self-evident' to everyone. Why, then, should it impose on an individual any kind of obligation, even perhaps an absolute obligation? Why should anyone confirm it by losing even a single hair from his head, let alone his life? Such is the aim of the spectator and such is the aim of science: to replace absolute obligation with absolute knowledge. In this way, science has proceeded from 'subjectivism' to universalism, but at what price? At the price of almost absolute separation from humanity, an absolute dehumanization. If knowledge is sufficient, then obligation is not necessary, and so what is the use of a living individual and his subjective guarantees?

Nietzsche objects: 'It is so little true that martyrs offer any support to the truth of a cause that I am inclined to deny that any martyr has ever had anything to do with the truth at all. ... The martyrs have damaged the truth. ... Is the worth of a cause altered by the fact that someone had laid down his life for it?'[117] If someone lays down his life for something, certainly this need not change anything about the worth of the thing *for me*. The wisdom of such statements becomes considerably hollow, if we reverse them into the question of whether it changes anything about the value of our truth if Mr. X. Y. does not show any willingness to lay down his life for it. A truth for which we would all be willing to lay down our lives, would not actually compel even one of us to lay down his life for it.

What is truth? The more books you read, the more debates you take part in, the more universities you attend, the more clearly you see that there are no reasons that are sufficient to endow truth with a certainty that could not be shaken by other reasons. And eventually you see that the only thing that cannot be shaken is not reasons, but rather a personal guarantee, the confirmation of truth by life and death. The arguments of Socrates, Christ, Giordano Bruno, Jan Hus, and others are or may be disputable, but their example and their sacrifice of their lives, this seal of certitude imprinted on their truth, is beyond any dispute. And even if you search around for an eternal truth, then this example and sacrifice is the only thing that

117 Friedrich Nietzsche, *The Antichrist*, trans. by H. L. Mencken (New York: Alfred A. Knopf, 1923), section 53, p. 150.

truth has that is certain and forever irrefutable. This is the final and unshakeable pillar of truth. If, then, you ask what is truth, take a reply here: How are you capable of providing a guarantee for everything that you have and that you are? Do not ask, therefore, what is truth, but rather ask: What am I capable of guaranteeing? Well, actually: What am I guaranteeing?

By saying that we cannot live without truth we are saying that the world cannot get by without our providing guarantees. We do not arrive at non-personal truth so long as the world needs our guarantees for its being. We do not arrive at eternal truth until some all-powerful God or immortal electron takes the directing of the world into its hands. However, when that happens, we will already be superfluous in the world and truth will not be needed.

For Nietzsche, the mark of truth is the will to power. Truth is an opinion which proves its worth 'biologically', even if theoretically it is quite false. For Socrates, Christ, Bruno, and others, their truth did not prove its worth biologically, because they were executed. By whom? By nature? No, on the contrary, by society, by social morality. If, therefore, these men have failed to prove themselves in some way, then they have failed to do so socially, in terms of social morally, but 'biologically' they did indeed prove their worth – if by this 'biologically' we mean 'biological' nature. In terms of social morality, they were not successful because they were strong individuals, maximal guarantors. Nature does not demand anything more from a person; naturally, 'biologically', their truths have proved their worth perfectly. Precisely because of this they had no need of the will to power – that is, the will to a diktat to impose their truths on others, which diktat is the characteristic of social moralities. For Socrates and the others, truth was not a coat, a good appearance; it was a living reality, it was the will to make this world real, and therefore it was not necessary for them to subjugate the world to their will.

If moral virtue does not have martyrs, it must be said that truth on the other hand does have martyrs. If a human being were only a spectator, or only a participant, it would be easy. A spectator, who by death sacrifices everything, would simply not make this sacrifice; and if he did make it, then only with the assurance that death is not death, and that a sacrifice is not therefore a sacrifice, but rather only a loan: such perhaps is the case of religious morality. A participant, who does not know the spectator's notion of death, would submit to it without sacrificing anything; this is perhaps the case of moral virtue. However, a human being, as a spectator and also a participant, is not faced with a simple choice between life and death; a human being oscillates between preserving its existence at the cost of its being, and preserving its being at the cost of its existence. A human being is a duo, but it has a need to be a unity. It attains this unity in truth. Truth assumes that a spectator renounces cognition on his own account; that he entrusts the question 'What is this thing?' to the participant and does not search for a guarantor of things at the notional end of a causal chain. In truth, words cease to be *concepts* (that is, logical constructs) and become what they originally were (that is, *statements, expressions*): an explanation is an 'external' construct; it is articulated 'linearly'; each member of the construct refers to its neighbouring members as to those that explain it (that is, to a connection) and therefore the reading of this construct is also 'horizontal'. Truth, in contrast, is an internal *expression*; it has no horizontal connection, but rather each member is reinforced separately, 'vertically', supported by the bottom, the inner soul. If we were to envisage an explanation as an interconnected floral decoration woven into the pattern of a carpet, then we would have to envisage truth as a flowering meadow, in which every flower has its own roots in the earth. Because truth does not have a horizontal connection, it is not possible to 'read' it; it can be neither accepted nor rejected. If we nevertheless attempt to read it, then we are conceiving it as an explanation – full of contradictions certainly – which it simply is not. All the one-sidedness and coerciveness of theories derive from an attempt to make do with horizontal reading. Theory is depersonalized, while truth is the expression of an individual. In the case of theory, the personality and the life of the explicator are minor incidental matters, while in the case of truth they themselves are what constitutes its very reality. Scientists, for instance, usually remain in the background behind their science, while apostles of truth – so to speak – go ahead of their truth.

We have said that truth, in contrast to moral virtue, has its martyrs. How can we explain this? If we were to describe moral virtue as something that *I may*, *should*, *must* defend and enforce, this could lead to a misunderstanding. It could lead to the contention that I am setting some aim for myself; that I am convincing myself about something; that I am committing myself to providing a guarantee and to sacrifice; that I am simply appearing in the role of a moralist towards myself. However, as we know, this is not the case. If I act in a morally virtuous way, I do not do this because I may, should or must act in such a way; I act in this way simply because I act in this way. Moral virtue is natural, and that is why it manifests itself, makes itself real, and by this everything essential has been said about it. If egoism, as one side of human nature, were not compensated by the positive side of human nature, if it should be curbed by theory, by reasons, by promises, or by threats and punishments, then there would be nothing else left for us than to give up all hope about human destiny. However, the fact that moral virtue is natural, that it simply makes itself real, materializes itself, means that is also bears its reward within itself – that is, it is not any merit, and therefore it raises no claims, and precisely in this it constitutes moral virtue. If we commit the error of connecting moral virtue with *I may*, *I should*, and *I must*, then we arrive at a false notion of moral virtue as a duty, of moral virtue as a something 'that is independent of my inclinations'.

The case of truth is slightly different from the case of moral virtue. Truth is not in opposition to reason, as moral virtue is; truth is a unity of reason and heart. In the case of truth a spectator renounces external guarantors and becomes attached to an internal guarantor. He abandons the collective world of scaffolding, the world of the given and of technology, and submits himself to the individual world of creation. It would be a surprise if something of the spectator's character did not become attached to truth. We can perhaps best capture its share if we say that it imparts to *pure participation* the character of *conviction*. Conviction is participation accompanied by an *idea*. This idea does not have anything in common with what a technician calls an idea. A technician's idea is a mere proposal which requires that it be implemented in a rational way – that is, constructed, assembled, incorporated in a mechanism or a material construction, or established in an organization, an institution or something similar. In contrast to this, the whole actualization of truth lies in it *being expressed*. The idea of a technician is a programme for the construction of a collective world of scaffolding; truth, however, is wholly actualized, made real, by being expressed in the world of individuals. A theory proves or demonstrates. Truth does not demonstrate anything; truth reshapes itself, transforms itself internally. It opens the empty and barren abode of the soul to something newly arriving.

Even if a person does not receive an idea as imposed from outside, the mere presence of an idea is sufficient for it to seem to him as though it is at least imposed by himself, by his conscience, by which it really becomes something that 'I may', 'I should' or 'I must'. In this way a human being feels himself to be a servant of his ideas – he speaks directly of truth instead of speaking only about an idea. He moralizes himself. However, this individual morality, this internal discipline, does not have anything in common with a collective morality – that is, with coercion from outside. The feeling of service, of sacrifice, which a person brings to his idea, to his truth, is balanced by its realization – that is, its expression, and thus in spite of its particular character it can be said that truth also bears its reward within itself. The essential characteristic of truth is that it does not remain silent. If it were to remain silent – that is, if it were to renounce its own actualization – only then would it be an actual living harm suffered, an actual sacrifice in the moral sense of the world. It would, however, be a harm of an opposite character than an egoistical one; in this case, it would be a harm suffered by the conscience. If we were to interpret this harm, according to Freud, as a 'suppression', then we would have to think up some kind of 'angelic' complex for this, because the usual 'diabolical' complex would falsify the entire case and turn it one its head. Despite all its anti-moralistic tendency, Freudian ethics still demonstrates the same moral ignorance as sociological ethics.

Since the expression of truth is actualized truth, no feeling of merit arises from a feeling of service to truth, and thereby neither does any claim to some kind of future being arise from it. And if a person submits to death for his truth, he submits to this with a consciousness of making a sacrifice for truth, but without a feeling of merit or claim. After all, by this death a person makes the ultimate expression of his truth; he actualizes this truth in the ultimate way. Therefore, while it is true that there is something cult-like in the sacrifice of life for truth, this is nevertheless entirely a person's internal matter, which does not have anything in common with collective morality, with a morality that justly weighs merits and claims. It is true that in concrete cases of acts of martyrdom it is very rarely possible to distinguish between what belongs to truth, and what belongs to collective and religious morality – that is, to distinguish martyrdom not involving merit and claims from martyrdom that is meritorious and makes a claim to something.

Even though in terms of its ideological aspect, truth is not a part of moral reality, it nevertheless has the significance and import of a moral action in that it is a manifestation of a person's living soul against uniformity, official speech, and sterile phrases, against the duplicitous and hypocritical misuse of words as human expression, against a person's servitude to social morality and good appearance; in short, against the mechanizing, anaesthetizing equalization of the living human soul. The recognition of the moral magnitude of a martyr of truth is not connected to the acceptance of his truth. It is not necessary, and as a rule it is not even possible, for me to accept as my own the idea for which a martyr of truth laid down his life; it is enough for me to know that he died for *his* truth. In fact, every such martyr challenges us: follow me! But a social morality that appropriates a martyr misuses this to make a socially moral appeal: follow *my* truth, *my* idea! However, the entire real moral appeal of a person's martyrdom is comprised in the challenge: follow me – that is, be a guarantor, such as I am, and therefore follow *your own* truth! The *real moral value* of his truth and his death is contained in this and this alone.

Churches, either religious ones or secular ones, cannot save a person who can be saved only by truth and moral virtue. This or that dogma – this is always a teaching that salvation comes through obedience, and not through truth. Churches can save only the immature, minors, not guarantors. 'This abandonment of self-responsibility,' says William James, 'seems to be the fundamental act in specifically religious, as distinguished from moral practice.'[118] This is true not only for specifically religious actions, but for absolutely all mass collective actions. The existence of churches of all kinds stands and falls with those who do not refuse to sign a confession of faith as a 'blank cheque'. Where truth has no more value than a poor recruit's blanket, there truth becomes so sovereign, perfect and eternal that it no longer permits any other truth alongside itself.

An amazing thought is concealed in Christ's legacy: the idea of God as an Almighty being, a being that is Almighty because it loves without limit. This implies the following for human beings: whatever you achieve only by a path of violence and physical power, you have no reason to be proud of; you attain this only through the extent of your imperfection, small-mindedness, helplessness. The expenditure

---

118 James, *The Varieties of Religious Experience*, p. 289.

of human life in the name of anything whatsoever will never be a morally virtuous act. You can call it a 'necessary evil' if you like; in any case it is something that should shake your soul, and not comfort it. The really diabolical thing about evil is: that it forces upon us its weapons, its methods and means; that it forces us to perform its will of our own accord, and moreover 'in the name of good'. The diabolical thing about evil: it makes good into a 'necessary evil'. In this way it overcomes us; in this way it is victorious over us.

Both religious and scientific explanations of the world are rational, technical. However, because religion makes use only of a prime mover, without laws and material, it cannot rationally interpret this explanation other than as a miracle. If life and the world are to be explained technically, but without material and laws, this cannot be done other than by the prime mover himself in some way deputizing, intervening – that is, by changing into a supernatural being, into God. It must be emphasized that God and his supernatural characteristics are a postulate of reason – that is, a *rational* explanation of the world and of life, and that they do not constitute an *irrational* explanation, as many believe. An '*irrational explanation*' is in any case a contradiction in terms as such. To say that a natural event is irrational in its reality is to say that it is participation – that is, that it is neither cognizable, nor non-cognizable, because there is nothing to cognize, and therefore neither is there anything not to cognize; it is only possible to participate. God, whether knowable or unknowable, remains a rational explanation.

What is knowable but not yet known, and also what is unknowable – all this is a 'mystery'. Mystery is a requisite of a rational understanding of events. Mystery is either what our reason has not yet gained knowledge of, cognized, or what it will never know, cognize – either on account of technical obstacles or because of reason's limitations – but which could be known by a 'more developed' or 'higher' reason than ours and which is certainly cognized, or respectively known, by God's reason. God's *all-knowingness* – this, just like 'natural laws' of natural science, constitutes the rational principle of a natural event. Miracles and supernaturalness, therefore, do not point to the irrational, but rather on the contrary to a more perfect rationality. In this conception, God is a technician. If a person is not capable of discovering God's technical means and acquiring these means, then this is because his human reason is not on the same level as God's reason. Mystery is here a mystery for human reason, not for God's reason. Mystery is a veiled rationality, hidden from and inaccessible to human reason, human 'cognition'. This is the source of the state of immaturity and the source of humankind's relationship to God as that of a child to the father. However, this comparison is not entirely precise in that God does not rear a person to maturity, into a maximal guarantor, into a father, but rather keeps him in chronic immaturity. 'Mystery' is not revealed to a human being – at least not so long as he is alive. The mystery remains for ever something obscure, which the church, the representative of God on Earth, thunders over the eternal minor and thus maintains him in awe and obedience. If a scientist uses the term 'mystery', then by this he is saying: I know nothing, you know nothing, and therefore we are equal. If a priest uses the term 'mystery', then by this he is saying: I know nothing, you know nothing, and therefore you must obey me. And if a priest has more success in this than a scientist, then this is because for a person who is left at the mercy of mystery a diktat is more welcome than responsibility.

Scientific technique derives from a knowledge of laws and 'given' material. Religious technique is determined by mystery; it is evident that it cannot be anything other than a cult, a sacred ceremony, a set of norms for human behaviour. However, mystery as a teacher's ignorance is after all a risky means of upbringing and discipline. This is why the church has always attempted to embody this mystery in cognition, knowledge. The result of this effort is dogma. Dogma – this is a mystery that is not ignorance, but rather knowledge. By relying on dogma, the church can speak about mystery not in the sense: I know nothing, you know nothing, but rather in the sense: I know, while you do not know. A quite logical and necessary culmination of the dogmatic line is the dogma of infallibility. It is only through this dogma of infallibility that the other dogmas acquire appropriate theoretical sanctions. By relying on this dogma, the church can communicate new religious *pieces of knowledge* to believers, without having to consider the conditions that are connected to every piece of knowledge: the condition of comprehensibility and the condition of verifiability. This dogma was not essential, all the while that modern science did not exist; however, today, when religious morality is losing ground to scientific morality, the dogma of infallibility is a necessary act of self-preservation – not merely on the part of the Roman Catholic Church, but also on the part of religion as such. In opposition to a science that preaches: whatever you do not understand, you *must not* believe – religion cannot do other than to seek for protection in an authority that allows it to preach: whatever you do not understand, you *must* believe. In contrast to Sabatier, who considers that the infallibility of the church comes from its power, I would rather say that it actually comes from its powerlessness. It really seems that, of all the Christian churches, it is only the Roman Catholic Church that is fully aware of the danger facing religion today. I think that it is the only church to which it is evident – even though it does not say this openly – that the current-day crisis of religion does not concern either truth, or moral virtue, but rather exclusively social morality. People are not turning away from religion on account of moral motives, or out of a desire for truth, but rather primarily because they have become enchanted with a new technique, primarily by a technique based on the natural sciences. This has given rise not to a new truth or moral virtue, but rather to a new social morality, a 'scientific' morality, and it is only because of this – and nothing else – that science has become a mortal danger for the church and religion. Against this scientific morality, religion has no other defence than to insist tenaciously on its *'credo, quia absurdum est'*, and bide its time. If it falls nevertheless, then there were simply no paths for it to avoid this fall.

However, there is no more dubious path for religion than making a pact with the new morality, or – as the saying goes – seeking a reconciliation with science, providing scientific justifications for elements of religious faith; in short, verifying religion by science. This means sticking one's head into the lion's paws. If religion makes even the slightest concession to science, this signals the beginning of a process of making concessions to which there is no end, or only with the end of religion. As far as Christianity is concerned, the majority of its so-called reformed churches have stepped out on a slippery slope that has only one direction of movement: downwards. During the hegemony of the church the dispute between religion and science turned out to the disadvantage of science; if science wanted to advance, it had to hide behind a dual measure of truth. Today the situation has completely turned around: 'An agreement of religious faith with scientific knowledge is a strengthening of this faith, while an evident discrepancy is a weakening of it.'[119] (František Linhart)[120] – This is what is called capitulation. We should notice how this turns out for God: 'Not even for God is everything unconditionally possible. God cannot perform something that is contradictory in and of itself; he cannot do something that has already been done; he cannot make what is true untrue; he cannot make a part equal to a whole; he cannot create a square circle. God cannot act in contradiction with his own nature.' With what nature? This entire passage seems to me to state only that God cannot act in contradiction with human reason, with science, or with scientific technology. So, what use then is God? From here it is only a small step to throwing God,

---

119 František Linhart, *Úvod do filosofie náboženství* [Philosophy of Religion] (Praha: Sfinx, 1930).
120 Czech theologian and philosopher (1882–1959).

along with religion, over the wall, and science with its techniques will then rule the entire field for good. Such are the prospects for a reform that views the crisis of religion as a crisis of moral virtue and truth, and which seeks a way out in a greater rationalization of religion. It looks at religion as at a predecessor of science, and this usually means a view looking backwards. However, would we not catch religion in the same role even if we were to look forwards? In this case also in a role of orthodoxy, dogmatism and intransigence. – Elie Faure says about Michelangelo that he laid 'on the threshold of the modern world, which dates from himself, the fundamental tragedy of the spirit, which is to destroy mysticism through knowledge and then, having reached the limits of knowledge, to have no choice save between mysticism and death?'[121] – If the world consists in creation and participation, and not in what is given, then a systematic and thorough search for the given must end up at nothing.

Indian spiritualism is marked by a favouring of the rational side of a human being: 'Salvation lies in *cognition*!' Meanwhile, a seeming paradox here is the rampant growth of ceremonial and ritual activities, of mystical and magical tasks. I say seemingly paradoxical: India can teach us about the aims and the ends of cognition. The Indians have ended their cognitive activity in mysticism. There is absolutely nothing forced about this; there is no sudden turnaround. It is also possible to understand Christianity as the mystical end of Greek rationalism. Each attempt to acquire knowledge of the 'essence of life and the world', when vain searching has exhausted itself, ends up in recognizing as a fact what hitherto had been grappled with as a problem. An enigma which was hitherto a problem, finds its resolution in mystery. Mystery becomes itself reality. The entire behaviour of humankind shows this: whatever

---

121 Elie Faure, *History of Art: The Spirit of the Forms,* trans. by Walter Pach (New York and London: Harper, 1930), p. 454.

was previously investigated as an enigma, is now worshipped as a mystery. Cognition and science are replaced by cult, ceremony, ritual, piousness.

The mysterious emerges as a supplementary component where nature has been exhausted by knowledge, where nature is viewed as a technical process. But nature is a vital process. It wants neither to be investigated, nor venerated; it wants to be lived. However, if we refuse to live it and want only to measure and calculate it, then it forces us to venerate it. If we only want to venerate it, then it forces us also to investigate it.

Science, therefore, evidently has a choice between extinction and mystery. This mystery will no longer be a question, it will be an answer; it will no longer be a problem, it will be a solution; it will no longer be a motivation for research, it will be a motivation for a cult; it will no longer be scepticism, it will be dogma. Well, if this is how things seem to us, then we must wonder at a church, which at the moment of the triumphant onset of science and scientific morality, announces a dogma about infallibility, and thus puts a seal on its efforts at a transformation of mystery as not-knowing into mystery as knowing; a transformation of mystery as a question into mystery as a reply and a solution.

Lo and behold, a religion that is doing everything for the fruits of science to fall into its lap.

The perspective adopted by Elie Faure, which outlines the end of cognition as an alternative between mysticism and death, does not seem to me so simple. After all we can leave death out of consideration; if death is not conceived and foreseen as the mutual mass murder of people by some marvellous technical means, then it is mentioned here only for stylistic effect, in order to underline the fact that the only thing that is left will be mysticism. Why death, when there is still another way out? The world of cognition is inhabited by a handful of researchers, but it is overflowing with technicians and people representing all types of social moralities. Are we supposed to think that all these people will become mystics? The inclination to mysticism, or at least to metaphysical idealism and spiritualism, is becoming characteristic for those current-day researchers who demand more from their science than mere findings, mere precepts. The existence of these researchers therefore confirms Faure's perspective. But the number of these truth seekers is negligible. An overwhelming majority of the members of our scientific age do not search for truth in science; they have science only as a social morality, as a technique, as a profession. This majority do not, therefore, exchange science for mysticism, but rather the current social morality for another social morality; nothing in their souls is shaken, nothing dies, nothing is reborn; they take off the old uniform and put on a new one.

It is precisely this moment that religion is waiting for: it knows that the crises of society and of collectives are not crises of internal moral values and truth, but rather crises of social morality and technique. Whether it will actually ever experience this moment is, however, a different matter. We are witnesses of how modern material and machine technology intensify a crisis, once one has occurred. While technology was born in order to provide humankind with a shield against the phantom of death, today this technology itself is becoming the most terrifying memento of death.

If a researcher wants to evade mysticism, or at least metaphysics, then – as we have seen – he has no other possibility than to deny his science cognitive value, its capability to produce truth. However, this escape is merely apparent. If he transforms science into a mere producer of precepts and practical findings, then the only consequence of this will be that he will go and search elsewhere for what he expected and sought for in science. Science will no longer be the focal point of his life; he has made the first step toward replacing it with something else. It he holds on to it, then only as a profession, a social morality, a conventional and ready-made attire prescribed by society.

Mysticism is the conclusion of cognition; even for a mystic. The mystic's aim is cognition of God, the absolute, the eternal; in short, 'ultimate reality', the essence. The beginning of this mystic process is explicitly rational; it begins with deliberate preparation, with an effort at turning attention away from the self and at concentration. Oriental mysticism in particular is known for constructing whole systems of practices and techniques for this purpose. What is the aim of these practices? They are aimed at cutting off all connections with the external world, at subduing the senses, reason and desire. What does this lead to in an extreme case? To a spiritual state that mystics describe in words like boundless love, an ocean of joy, a oneness with God; Jakob Böhme even uses the word 'nothing'. My own self, the I, vanishes into everything, into the divine, into an immanent essence. If we attempt to characterize this in our terminology, then we can say that *mysticism is a path from a spectator to a participant*. This I, this self, that the mystic loses is the spectator; the immanent 'essence' which he attains is bare, pure participation. The process of cognition culminates in the spectator leaving the field entirely to the participant. What makes this phenomenon exceptional – that is, ecstasy – can evidently be attributed to the intensity, dynamism, and speed of this process of replacement, which takes place in a short time from one extreme to another. This is also possibly why it passes away so quickly. From the extreme point of the spectator's world, the mystic falls, so to speak, at one stroke to the very bottom of the participant's world.

A mystic cannot be understood as a mere participant; he is a person of unusual sensitivity, who feels himself to be a constant prisoner of the collective world of scaffolding, a world of concepts, notions, and phenomena, the world of *maya*[122] (illusion). Gener-

122 In Indian Vedantic philosophies the external world is regarded as the world of *maya* (illusion). See Paul Deussen, *The Elements of Metaphysics*, trans. by C. M. Duff (London: MacMillan: 1894), pp. 332–333.

ally he consumes most of his effort in escaping from this prison for a short time and gaining a moment, the living intensity of which increases in proportion to the shortness of its duration. However, this 'singularity', which the mystic is aiming to achieve in this way, is not a compound of the cosmos, it is he himself: an individual who has escaped the collective world and identified with himself. The short duration of the moment and the fever of ecstasy do not allow him to open his eyes enough to see that the thing that he calls God, the ocean, the cosmos, is nothing more than the people close to him, his friends, transformed in the same way as he himself is. Only in this way would he first understand the full and concrete meaning of the love which floods over him, and he would not compare it to breaking waves that, not finding a shore that would embrace them, consume themselves. If you want to call this religion, then so be it! Then, religion – in addition to its collective morality, and in opposition to this morality – also has its own reality.

We should notice that scientific cognition starts with focusing attention on the external world, but in the course of time this process of concentration has cut itself of from emotions and demands, and reduced the significance of the senses, and even of reason itself, so much that the external world has actually disappeared and all that has remained is mathematical speculation. It would be possible to compare science to mystic thinking, but with the difference that science undergoes very slowly – that is, soberly, coldly and cautiously – the path that a mystic soars through all at once, in a state of passion and ecstasy. However, science is only granted to go halfway along this path; it loses its name at the moment when it touches the extreme point of the spectator's world, the world of the collective, the world of appearances – that it, at the moment when it finishes up at nothing. Up until that point it would be possible to call science some kind of a protracted, chronic form of 'acute' mysticism. Beyond that, it does not have any further access to the world of participation.

Such, then, is the retrospective and the perspective: science starts out as a liquidator of the world of the participant and a constructor of the world of the spectator; it ends up by liquidating the spectator's world and clearing space for the participant. What an idea on the part of religion: to part company with mysticism and get into a raft on which science is floating!

7
THE TIGHTROPE WALKER DANCES

WELL, since each of us – of the people in Robert's milieu – has accepted his share from the hands of the man on the tightrope, let us also let Robert himself accept his share.

The aim of religion is where life is at an end, where there is no longer life; the aim of science is where life is at a starting point, where there is not yet any life; the aim of art is where life culminates, where life is fulfilment. The analyst and the visionary, left to themselves, repel each other mutually in opposite directions: the first rushes off into the mist of the past; the second into the mist of the future. The artist anchors himself in the present, in what is past reality and also future reality. Past and also future – this is a pole created and used by the man on the tightrope for walking more surely, for achieving greater stability and a greater variety and area of movement. Only art knows that the pole was made for walking, and not walking for the pole. Art alone rotates the pole to the rhythm of its step, which then changes into a dance at the point when the others, paralysed with vertigo and fear, clench their pole in the belief that the railings which are guiding them – a cord held tight by the hands of all-powerful Gods and laws, anchored in eternity backwards and in eternity forwards – are given and unchangeable for ever. No surprise that in the eyes of these serious and apprehensive people, art is a frivolous game and a carefree activity. However, all the equilibristics of the tightrope walker, all the hazardousness of his movements, this entire dancing and light-legged walk – all this has no other aim than the most necessary one: to maintain the man above the void. Only art is not mistaken about the nature of means and ends, of tasks and aims: it knows that the real aim of aims and task of tasks is in the present, in the necessity of preserving life today, of maintaining it above the void now. Art knows that it is not a mere diversion, a parade, a game somewhere beyond the knowledge and supervision of illusory Gods and rules; it knows that it is fighting for life and that it is guaranteeing for life; it knows that the reason why it came into the world is that there are no all-powerful guarantors and lawgivers.

The thing that shocks and provokes us the most about art is that it refuses to cling on to the safety-ropes and allow itself to be led along them. In comparison with art, science demonstrates exemplary behaviour. 'In science the spirit, in unconditional obedience and submission to the dictates of the perceptive and critical faculties of the intellect, and under the requirement of utmost exactness, is carried along to heights and depths from which it cannot return. It must needs go ever further. Its path is clearly marked. To follow this path is a voluntarily accepted service to a master called Truth. In art there is no such external compulsion. There is no duty of exactness. Art (or rather many of its servants) has come to the complete abandonment of the principles of observation and thought by its own volition. ... For art there is no absolute imperative. Art is not restrained by a discipline of the mind. Its creative impulse is centred in the will. And here the important fact reveals itself that art stands much closer than science to the modern life-philosophy which sacrifices understanding to life.'[123] – Let us not beat around the bush: modern art and the 'myth of the twentieth century' grow apparently from the same ground. They are expressions of a spiritual crisis whose explanation we should seek in the move away from the rational to the irrational.

Well then, the myth of the twentieth century, or Aryan racism, owes its origin to modern-era collective morality, 'scientific' morality, just as, for instance, Israeli racism or later Christian racism were a result of the morality of that time, a religious morality. The aim of this morality was to cement together a certain collective into a state of readiness against the 'enemy'. We should note that today it is regarded as necessary to refute racism in the same way that attempts are made to prove it – that is 'scientifically', even though it is evident that racism is more opposed to moral feeling than to science. The new morality has already taken such a hold that the voice of conscience –

123 Huizinga, *In the Shadow of Tomorrow*, pp. 196–197.

that is, precisely the irrational – is not regarded by any of us as a sufficient argument against racism. Racism is moralized science: biology, anthropology, psychology, sociology, and so on. It is a hypothesis and a precept that pretends truth. It is scientific kitsch.

To present racism as irrational, and at the same time refute it scientifically, is at the least a misunderstanding. The fact is that a scientist as a scientist never encounters the irrational and that for him there is no irrational at all. He uses the term irrational for the circumstance that certain rational processes that enable the investigation of a human being do not go through the consciousness of the person examined but rather only through the consciousness of the scientist himself. According to this notion, a person who acts under the influence of the 'irrational' actually acts under the influence of the rational, only that he himself is not aware of this influence. If he were aware of this – that is, if he would allow himself to be informed by science – then he would act differently, more reasonably. Why? If his action is a result of rational processes outside of his consciousness, then what does this action gain in rationality if these processes become conscious ones? What does it matter if he is conscious of them or not?

The indiscipline with which we reproach art is the same indiscipline with which we reproach 'blind and inscrutable life', nature. Nature is undisciplined because when, for instance, it arrived at a salamander, it did not arrange for all time a planned and serial production of salamanders according to the same mould, but rather allowed its whims to try something new once again. Nature is, then, undisciplined because, in addition to atoms and electrons – as the only realities – it also creates incomprehensible and unpredictable phantoms: frogs, cats, butterflies, daisies, ants, natural scientists, and so on. Art is indisciplined because it constantly creates new and unpredictable things. Both nature and art are indisciplined because they create; because they are alive, and therefore creative.

The indiscipline of nature – as long as we do not ourselves impart reason to it – is merely methodological, not moral. It is merely a certain kind of chaotic behaviour, arising from the absence of an organizing reason. An artist, however, is a reasonable being, and this is why a moralist cannot countenance art not being measured by a moral criterion. Reason makes art into a *willed* thing, a deliberate thing, and one that, therefore, is subject to moral judgement. As willed and deliberate, art is actually a certain type of technology, and this naturally assumes the relevant cognizance. For the moralist, therefore, art is in the first instance cognizance. Science is also cognizance and, as such, it is amoral. Why, then, is art not also amoral, if it is cognizance? Perhaps because art 'renounces the norms of observing and thinking' – instead of giving precedence to reason, it gives precedence to the irrational, and in this way cognizance becomes a matter of willing. How is it then: is willing connected with reason, or with the irrational? Science is rational and science *must be*, it is a matter of necessity, inevitability, not will; art, at least modern art, is irrational – it is merely *something willed*. However, without reason there is nothing willed; there is merely 'blind and inscrutable life' – that is, something that *must be*. Science, even though its precepts are not very comforting, has found mercy in the eyes of the moralist because 'science must be'. And the fact that it must be, is a guarantee of its truthfulness, and therefore we cannot deny it our trust and support. However, 'blind and inscrutable life' has not found mercy in the eyes of the moralist and, along with it, naturally neither has art. This blind life – or art – is also something that must be, something that has its own inherent necessity. However, disapproval clouds the moralist's judgement to the extent that he degrades it to a case of merely something willed; then, in his opinion, the more irrational art is, the more affected, arbitrary, untruthful, unnatural it is; in other words: the more erroneous. The irrationality of art is viewed as a symptom of the crisis and a part of the crisis. One of the conditions for overcoming this crisis is regarded as a return of art to reason, and when to reason, then directly to science. The *postulate of art as science*: that is one of the recipes for getting modern mankind out of the mess it is in. Certainly, this is what is demanded by the new social morality.

Let us say in advance: there is no more dubious recipe than this one. And moreover: there is no recipe more senseless.

Let us try to throw some light on this. The core of the dispute lies in the question of the share of the intellect in art – that is, in the question of the relation between the intellect and 'blind and inscrutable life' or, in short, nature. In *moral virtue* – we have seen – nature is in opposition to the intellect. In the matter of *truth*, a truce occurs between nature and the intellect. In *science* there is nothing other than intellect; nature takes part here only in the *process* of explanation, but not in *what* is explained. How is it in the case of art? Let us say straight away: in art there is only nature; the intellect here takes part only in the process of creating, but not in what is created. The maximum that falls to the intellect is the role of *accoucheur*, but never the role of the one actually giving birth. Science, therefore, is amoral in that it is outside of nature; whereas art is amoral in that it is only nature. If we assign reason to nature, then it ceases to be amoral. If reason was more than an *accoucheur* in art, then art would not be amoral. Similarly, science, at the moment when it leaves its ivory tower, ceases to be amoral.

In order to avoid this ivory tower deceiving us and us mistaking it for the one that we see the artist entering, we should recall that, with the scientist only pure theoretical reason enters the tower, while with the artist only 'blind and inscrutable life' enters it. For idealists of all eras, it is only a tower of theoretical spirit that decides on the being and non-being of the world, and if art also wants to have a share in this, then it must enter this tower, whether it likes it or not. Plato castigated art for not showing any willingness to enter the crystal tower of ideas, and Aristotle defended art only because he believed in this willingness. These intellectuals still had no idea what a strange creature they wanted to tame and domesticate in their abode. It was not until Hegel, who took up the process of taming with all the thoroughness and persistence so particular to him, that someone offered art the opportunity to show exactly what kind of thing it really is. He succeeded in dragging it into the chain of ideas and concepts right to the very threshold of the sanctum of the absolute spirit, but here the exotic animal perished. There was nothing else for Hegel to do that to pronounce a funeral speech over it. It is Croce himself who describes Hegel's *Aesthetics* in this way. In this Hegel writes: 'In all these respects art, considered in its highest vocation, is and remains for us a thing of the past. Thereby it has lost for us genuine truth and life.'[124] This funeral march, which still today has not ended and which is actually accompanying two deceased – art and religion – has been joined only by the so-called Hegelian left (a philosophical term, not a political one), while the Hegelian right has resisted. It has the feeling that someone is being buried alive here.

It will certainly interest us what reviving treatments these Hegelians are applying in order, on the one hand to bring art to life, while on the other hand not killing the Hegelian spirit. Primarily, why has the atmosphere of the abode of the absolute spirit had such a murderous effect on art and religion? Let us allow Croce to speak: 'Art being placed [by Hegel] in the sphere of absolute Spirit, in company with Religion and Philosophy, how will she be able to hold her own in such powerful and aggressive company, especially in that of Philosophy, which in the Hegelian system stands at the summit of all spiritual evolution? If Art and Religion fulfilled functions other than the knowledge of the Absolute, they would be inferior levels of the Spirit, but yet necessary and indispensable. But if they have in view the same end as Philosophy and are allowed to compete with it, what value can they retain? None whatever; or, at the very most,

---

124 Georg Wilhelm Friedrich Hegel, *Aesthetics*, trans. by J. M. Knox (Oxford: Clarendon Press, 1975), 1:11.

they may have that sort of value which attaches to transitory histori-cal phases in the life of humanity.'[125]

Hegel's philosophy is a philosophy of logic, conceived as meta-physics. Everything that raises a claim for realization must clothe itself in a concept. Art also, if it is not to part ways with reality and truth, has no other choice than to clothe things in concepts. This is why the task of art is 'to take what is spiritual and set it out into the immediacy of existence for apprehension by eye and ear … in connection with sensuous material and in a sensuous medium.'[126] However, this correspondence of functions renders one of them su-perfluous; if this is a case of the same thing, then one of them must have the final word; and when it has the final word, why not also the first word? And if it is a case of a concept, then it will certainly not be logic that gives way. What lesson then can art learn here? That the recipe 'art like science' is an instruction for committing suicide. Croce and Gentile took this lesson to heart. Gentile more.

What had to be done for art in the first place? To unfasten it from in-tellect, logic, and concepts. Croce led art to a place half way between intellect and feeling. Gentile descended with art right down to pure feeling. But both of them were too concerned about not parting com-pany with the Hegelian spirit. You cannot help getting the impression that Croce expounds art as unfastened without actually unfastening it, while Gentile, who really unfastened them, covers this up under a Hegelian camouflage. For Croce, art is 'intuition', 'expression', 'form'. He writes: 'The poet or painter who lacks form, lacks every-thing, because he *lacks himself*. Poetical material permeates the Soul of all: the expression alone, that is to say, the form, makes the poet. … In such moments it is, that we best perceive the profound difference between matter and form. These are not two acts of ours, face to face

---

125 Benedetto Croce, *Aesthetic as Science of Expression and General Linguistic*, trans. by Douglas Ainslie (New York: Noonday Press, 1920), p. 301. www.gutenberg.org/files/54618/54618-h/54618-h.htm.
126 Hegel, *Aesthetics*, p. 284

with one another; but we assault and carry off the one that is *outside* us, while that *within* us tends to absorb and make its own that without. *Matter*, attacked and conquered by *form*, gives place to concrete form. It is the matter, the content, that differentiates one of our intuitions from another. Form is constant: it is spiritual activity, while matter is changeable. Without matter, however, our spiritual activity would not leave its abstraction to become concrete and real, this or that spiritual content, this or that definite intuition. ... The statements repeated so often, with others similar, that art is not knowledge, that it does not tell the truth, that it does not belong to the world of theory, but to the world of feeling, arise from the failure to realize exactly the theoretic character of the simple intuition. This simple intuition is quite distinct from intellectual knowledge, as it is distinct from the perception of the real. We have seen that intuition is knowledge, free of concepts and more simple than the so-called perception of the real. Since art is knowledge and form, it does not belong to the world of feeling and of psychic material.'[127]

What is evident at first sight: a technical concept of the imaginative and artistic process. Matter and form; material and laws. The emphasis on the theoretical and cognitive character of art shows that Croce remains a rationalist and a technician even in art. In this art, there is no place for reality, because reality is not comprised in mere form; even Croce himself admits this, when he says that form without material would be a mere abstraction. But what use to him, then, is material? Nothing more than an 'impression', an inconstant changeable phenomenon.

The heart and epicentre of art is reality. A decomposition into impressions and form, into material and laws, is already the fruit of analysis and speculation. If Croce limits art merely to form, he cannot end up anywhere else than in abstraction, and if this is a case of abstraction without concepts, of an 'expressive' abstraction, then

127 Croce, *Aesthetic as Science of Expression*, pp. 9, 28, 42.

this is merely a geometrical line and outline, and therefore no less a mere map, a map without reality. Croce exhumes art from Hegel's conceptual map, only to bury it again in his own expressive map. It is evident that the guarantor of reality is rooted even deeper than where Croce sought it.

Gentile descended more deeply: 'For an artist, so long as he is an artist, art is life itself, and therefore not art, just as a dream is not a dream, for so long as a person sleeps. Quite simply, just as a dream is not thinkable without a higher form of experience, which higher form contains the dream within itself and therefore evaluates the dream and in doing so transcends it, so neither can we talk about art, until we make it the content of our judgement, which judgement however is no longer art.' (*Philosophy of Art*)

Reason can have art only at the cost that this art is actually no longer art; the absurdity of the spectator's and the theoretician's presence in artistic creation could not be expressed more clearly. Gentile also demolishes the fallacy that an artist works unconsciously: 'Art is conscious in the highest degree; in it, all the forces of the spirit are awake, present, and creative. ... Its unconsciousness is relative. It is not the consciousness which a person uses to evaluate art, but it is possible to compare it with the which a plant or an animal lives, with the way in which instinctive creation lives.' – Art is a participant; art is nature. However, when Gentile had reached this far, he recalled his Hegelian pedigree. Croce did not concede to nature a spirit, only a passive 'psyche', and this is why he hesitated to descend with art as far down as nature. However, Gentile simply declares: 'Nature is merely a feeling alongside a thought. Like every pure feeling it is unreal; its reality is comprised in the thought.' Nevertheless: 'An idea is a reality, a world; but the Atlas that bears this world is feeling.' – We should not allow this to confuse us. A book trying to achieve the impossible – to disguise as a spectator, a guarantor that it has found in a participant – must necessarily contain such a strange things. This did not escape the reviewer who wanted to make this acceptable for us. In the case of Gentile, according to this reviewer, it is not a case of feeling 'in the vulgar psychological conception, but rather in the strictly theoretical, cognitive, and philosophical sense.'[128] (Friedrich Kainz)[129]

The conclusion is this: the intellect has precisely as much place in art as feeling has in science. We could also put it this way: in art there is as much nature as there is a lack of nature in natural science. Because art is nature, art is not cognizance – that is, a producer of precepts; however, neither is it moral virtue, nor truth, because it does not stand in opposition to reason, and neither does it lie in an embrace with reason. And just as art is not truth, neither is it a flag-carrier of ideas. Art is nature and it has no any other aim than nature has: life itself. The artist may be led by all kinds of possible tendencies, but if his work is to be a work of art, then he cannot be tendentious – that is, tendencies cannot be allowed to manifest themselves here as ideas, truths, or precepts, but rather just as they manifest themselves in nature: as living concrete individuals. Nature is not tendentious; it does not lecture us on ideas and truths, but nevertheless! – What ideas and tendencies we find in it, if we want to understand with our reason! Simply anything that wants to be art must undergo a test of life, not a check of logical and theoretical correctness. If a work is to be an artistic work, then it is necessary that we do not read or hear a single word in it about the tendencies and ideas that we find in it. A work of art can hide within it as many tendencies as are hidden in nature – that is, as many as there are 'readers'. We should not require from an artist anything more, or anything less, than that he creates a living reality. However, this makes as much sense as requiring him to live. Either he lives, and therefore creates, or he deliberately engages in creation, and therefore merely forges like a technician and in his

128 Friedrich Kainz in *Časopis pro estetiku – Zeitschrift für Aesthetik u. Kunstwissenschaft* [*Journal of Aesthetics and Art Studies*], 1937.
129 Austrian philosopher (1897–1977).

internal being languishes. Such is the case with this 'exercising the will' in art. Those who see a technician in nature, also seek this technician in an artist. And just as a technician of nature depends on 'cognizance' – that is, on laws of nature, or respectively on the all-knowingness of God – so also the work of an artist is supposed to be preceded by cognition, by theory. Art should be science; art should be dehumanized. These diagnosticians have evidently mistaken the amorality of art with the amorality of science; the amorality of the heart with the amorality of the brain; sovereign ardent humanity with the lack of humanity which left to itself was transformed into an inhumanity such as human beings had never before experienced. Gustave Flaubert, the acknowledged patron of dehumanized, objective art, of art as science, writes in one of his letters: 'I expressed myself badly, when I wrote that an artist should not create with his heart; I wanted to say that he should not introduce his own person into the scene.' He did not do so, but nevertheless he did not lie, when he said: 'Bovary, that is me.'

Let us seek here for the key to the artist's 'theory', to his cognition. The fact that an artist does not cognize, does not mean that he sits in his ivory tower and simply shakes out of his sleeve what he has been endowed with by some magicians. An artist does not create from his *cognition*; he creates from his *experience*. We have already earlier indicated what a substantial difference these two words mean for us: the difference between a spectator and a participant. Quite simply: cognition is stored in memory, in knowledge; through experience a person's living constitution is transformed. In the first case, you add a new perception to a series of perceptions; in the second case, something of you dies and something new is born. There is a continuity between perceptions; you organize them, you revise them, you improve them, you connect them to the perceptions of other people and create a chain of objective cognition, of science, which continues, 'develops', is linked together in 'railings'. Experience does not develop; it is discontinuous; it perishes and a new experience arises.

In the first case, you act according to what you know; in the second case according to what you are, or to put it more precisely: according to what you are in the process of becoming. If, therefore, we say that an artist does not create from cognition, but rather from experience, then by this we mean that he does not portray what he knows, but rather what he is, or to put it better: what he is becoming. While science attempts to achieve an unchanging eternity, art – as nature – attempts to achieve something more real and more essential: an eternally living present. Art becomes real every moment; science will never become real. Science systematically continues; art constantly ends and begins.

This sounds almost as if it were copied from Schopenhauer. He also says that science, seeking causes, never arrives at its aim, while art is always at its aim. But what aim is this? It is not much different for art than it is for science; the cognition of general concepts, of kinds, of types, of Platonic ideas. Through intuition, art finds itself all at once face to face with what constantly escapes the cautious reasoning of science. It is not necessary for us to follow Schopenhauer's conclusions further. The fact that he eventually finds his own objectivized will in a Platonic idea, and thus considers the world as his illusion, as nothing, this merely provides us with a further strange piece of evidence of what awaits human beings at the end of cognition: mysticism or death. These two words can be used to describe the two focal points around which Schopenhauer's life revolved, and from this we can safely judge the truthfulness of his philosophy.

However, primarily here we once again confirm that art is one thing, and cognition quite another. Just as an artist inserts tendencies in his works only at the expense of art, so also we find ideas in his works at the expense of art. Art does not provide us either with lessons, or with truth; through art we acquire new experiences. Through science we expand our knowledge; through art we participate in life. Madame Bovary or Anna Karenina, Dmitri or Ivan Karamazov, Don Quixote or Hamlet, and many others: these are living beings whom we have met, with whom we have spent a certain part of our lives and who are truly our own experience. Of course – and we will return to this later – this experience is acquired by an artist, and also by us, under the dominance of a certain life situation which is not exclusive and unusual, which occurs constantly in everyday life. However, for us it is as though this everyday experience is broken up into chance glimmers of realization, while art concentrates this experience in a constant and intensive luminous current. A fundamental feature of this life situation – for the meanwhile let us call it *borderline* – is that it causes all human tendencies to disappear, except for an intensive relation to life for the sake of life itself. However, by this we are saying that a work of art, by evoking this borderline life situation in us, is some kind of switching point leading us away from the collective world of appearances to the individual world of reality, from the world of the spectator to the world of the participant. Art is about nothing other than laying down a direct path from the living to the living without detours through the world of appearances and knowledge. Because this detour has a high price; it costs everything: reality, life. Every person has his own real world, unchangeable for another one. If he is to come into contact with other people, then as a rule he has no other choice than to leave his own real world and enter the collective world of knowledge and conventions, into a kind of common conversation room, where mutual communication takes place on the basis of what is the same, exchangeable, 'objective' between human consciousnesses. Reality, real life, has no access here.

Certainly an artist is not guided by the thought or notion of some kind of meeting: in whatever form he creates his work, whether into the form of little gods, animals, creatures, landscapes, people, angels, things, outlines, coloured blots, verses, songs or music, this is always merely an effort to discover a living reality, which is nothing other than maximum participation. At whom or at what is this participation aimed? Reason talks about God, Life, Mankind, Nature, the Absolute, this or that Principle, but only reason has need of ideas, names and images; for an artist-participant it is enough to create an emotional speech which expresses his emotions, which speaks, which lives. To whom does he speak? To anyone who hears this, and in whom he inspires a living and intensive feeling of participation. What kind of participation? Participation with everything living. In his work, an artist says: nothing living is foreign to me. And we feel: whatever he touches, he brings to life. It touches us and through us all the things of the world. It reaches us without any detour through the world of knowledge; we never encounter it in a public conversation room, where only social persons and uniforms gather; it visits us only in the privacy of our own abode. If there is something miraculous about art, then it is precisely this. It brings together living beings without them having to give up their personalities, their realities; it gives them an opportunity to look into real faces – faces that have not been whitewashed and painted over with a collective, social morality; it allows souls to recognize one another according to an internal fellowship, not according to a ready-made uniform. An artist is assigned the task of creating in a human world means of communication of the type that nature creates when it communicates, or lovers when they understand one another. However, nature and lovers are silent when communicating. An artist should communicate, and yet he should also remain silent. He should not speak, and yet he should say everything. The solution of this Pythic enigma is an artistic work.

For the realization of art, therefore, an artistic work is necessary. Perhaps every person has moments of poetic experience in life, but only very few of them are capable of concentrating these momentary flashes into a compact and seamless current of light. Their works then act on us like a focusing lens which concentrates the fragments of our poetic experiences into an intensive living experience. An artistic work which is adequate to nature in its formation forces a spectator to come to terms with it in his own way – that is, either to utilize it in some way for his scaffolding, or to eliminate it as unnecessary, or possibly even harmful. Like nature, for a spectator art also loses its reality; it becomes a mere 'phenomenon' to which the following question is posed: Which other thing is this thing? And, as in the case of nature and as in the case of morality, so also in the case of art there is no doctrine which does not make use of art and reduce it to some atom or primordial juice or idea. In this way, art becomes a bearer and an expression of everything possible, but not a bearer and expression of itself. The strangest notions are attributed to art at the expense of its own reality. The common feature of these doctrines is that they are rational, that they are knowledge, knowledge of art, and therefore they are not art. However, on the basis of their 'cognition', their knowledge, these doctrines pose an urgent demand: an art of the rational, an art of the 'comprehensible', even art as science. Before reason succeeded in rationalizing nature into today's science, this took a lot of hard work; it would not like to have to make such an effort with art. A technician of nature is not known, and it is better not to speak about him at all, but a technician producing art, that is a creature with a brain like me, and therefore I can require from him that he supplies me with art that is nicely rationalized, classified and with labels attached. Popularly this is described as the contention that art should depict reality, nature. What an irony! We have stuck labels on nature; that means that we know it. Therefore, artist, if you do not want to deviate from reality, and by so doing also from all reasonable people, make sure you avoid depicting something that does not have a label attached to it with the appropriate name, personal details, body weight and height, and God knows what else. Just as irrational nature is collectivized in rational technology, just as individual personal morality is collectivized in social morality, so also the command that is given to art for its journey into the world of security and insecurity sounds like this: 'You must see like everyone, feel like everyone, be an obedient wheel in a collective machine. There is no art except realis-

319

tic art.'[130] (René Huyghe)[131] The requirement for comprehensibility in art – this amounts to an attempt to moralize art. To turn its fundamental element – that is, its emotional element – into a cart on which what a person feels can be loaded. Art is supposed to produce a mood for theories, ideologies; it is supposed to be served to people as a chocolate-covered candy, whose chocolate coating enables its less appetising filling also to be swallowed. We savour the chocolate candies and care precisely as little about their fillings as we cared about what the priest wrote on the blank cheque which we signed as a confession of our faith, and we thus sold our soul in return for the promise of its immortality. Thus – in spite of all the diagnoses of the obsolescence and extinction of art – an official art is being born which promises secular society no less usefulness than the calculation with immortality had for religious society. On the one hand, we assert the demise of art, but on the other hand we are trying to revive it with our rationalized and technological existence. However, just as racism is scientific kitsch, so moralized art is artistic kitsch. Václav Vilém Štech[132] aptly characterises kitsch: 'Kitsch pretends nobility, depth, feelings; it simulates an experience. ... A purveyor of kitsch ... does not want to be, but to seem. ... Kitsch is not in essence a result of not knowing. It does not arise from lack of knowledge, but rather from a distorted approach to the subject, from vulgar feeling, appearing from the outside as an insufficient feeling for rhythm, and mainly from untruth.'[133] If 'the last century did not know kitsch', then this is precisely because it did not have art as an institution, as a social morality. This is why it is not possible to agree with the opinion that art was a living form of some earlier society.

130 Dopis z Francie [Letter from France], Sborník S.V.U. Mánes (Mánes Union of Fine Arts almanac), 1939–1945.
131 French art historian (1906–1997).
132 Czech art historian (1885–1974).
133 Václav Vilém Štech, *Skutečnost umění* (*Úvaha o příčinách, způsobech a smyslu tvorby*) [The Reality of Art (Deliberations on Causes, Methods, and Meaning of Creation)] (Praha: Pražské nakladatelství V. Poláčka), 1946.

The truth is that it is only in our era that we encounter art as a form of collective existence for the first time.

Everything that is made with the intention of making art inclines toward kitsch. In a way, it is correct to assert that past eras did not have art, but nevertheless it would be more correct to say that they did not consciously think up art, they did not have it in mind; rather they had life, and therefore they also had art.

Everything that a human being creates from a living feeling, from a pressing need for emotional and irrational expression, can have the impressiveness of art. An Assyrian relief, an Etruscan vase, an African amulet, a Gothic Pietà, a military command of Jan Žižka, the ecstatic confession of St. Teresa, a child's colouring book, a fairy tale – all these have the impressiveness of art to the extent that we remain detached from the ideological and rational content of these works and to the extent that we immerse ourselves only into their irrational emotional speech, which is nothing other than a pure manifestation of life, pure participation, and a testimony of the living for the living. Untruth, from which kitsch is born, has nothing to do with logic and neither does it actually have anything to do with truth. An artist does not express precepts or propositions, and neither does he preach truth; he creates life. It is us who – if we want – draw lessons and truths from the artist's depths, just as we draw them from nature. Untruth in the artistic sense is when life is pretended where it is not.

It is evident that art is not bound to logical, material, or historical connections or – as is popularly said – to reality and truth. It does not have to describe and depict anything 'that really happened'; it does not even depend on its plot and its protagonists being physically and technically probable or even possible at all. It depends only on the human heart not being falsified. Only the heart knows what is 'nothing' and thus only it knows what is life. Only it can make art to some degree living or non-living, human or inhuman, and therefore it assesses for us, for instance a technical, utopian novel that precisely respects science as impossible, non-living, monstrous, untruthful, while on the other hand it values the most simple-minded fairy tale that is 'entirely in contravention of the facts' as living, self-evident, and truthful.

The services that we have entrusted to art in the collective world of knowledge, technology, and morality, it fulfils extremely badly. There is no end to the complaints. Not only does it not popularize and does not wrap up in sugar ideas and precepts, but it also serves us up bitter wormwood and expresses itself in a way that no one understands it. Instead of producing depictions of natural and human things in accordance with a collective card-index founded on meticulous measurement, it serves us up a reality so deformed and mutilated that it makes our heads hurt to look at this. Religion explained the curse of work by inherited sin and remunerated this curse with bills of exchange, payable after death. Science deposed religion, and the new society accused religion of making fools of people; the heavenly bills of exchange lost their validity, but the curse of work remained. Art, originally accused along with religion of feeding illusions to wretched humankind, was granted a reprieve on the condition that it assist in raising working morale. It was supposed to have the lion's share in a challenging task: to re-educate human beings in such a way that they feel something as a blessing which they had previously felt as a curse. However, the reprieved re-educator is not only failing to educate, but it is even giving a very bad example: 'Ever since the times of Ruskin there have been many attempts at introducing art back into work itself. Vain attempts. ... You are going to make an effort and possibly suffer, such is the moral law; you are going to engage in play and have the greatest experience, such is the aesthetic law. ... Artistic contemplation is the fruit, if not of laziness, at least of idleness. ... Art has never been very fond of economic or professional problems, in spite of the exceptional importance that these have in real life. ... Art lives from luxury; art cultivates luxury deliberately and for luxury's own sake.' (Charles Lalo) – Art was supposed to fulfil another delicate and vital task. As Freud has taught us, we are in the grip of dark, uncontrollable desires, which in the first instance threaten the basic cell of society: marriage and family. 'The social organism was faced with a choice: either it had to expel this undisciplined passion as a foreign body and to fight against it as something alien, or it had to organize it and allocate it some function among others. Failing to find any other possibility, it organized this passion in the form of art.' (Lalo) So, art was entrusted with an honourable living of procuring, in order to 'redeem the sexual peace of the family hearth'. However, the honourable dads and the dishonourable youths, if they go to libraries, theatres, and art galleries at all, do so not in order to notionally satisfy their libidos there, but at the most in order to gobble up a starter, which should serve to arouse the appetite for the main course later at an appropriate place. Apart from that, today it is the cinema which in the matter of such refined appetizers has no competition. There have never been so many complaints about the deplorable influence of art on morality as there are today. In the forum of collective morality, modern art has earned the epithet of perverted, deviant, degenerate, epileptic art.

Psychoanalysis has played a strange double role in this forum. On the one hand, in terms such as libido, eros, sex, the id, and so on, it presents us with an internal world as a reality which it defends against the mask of morality of the external world, but on the other hand it endows this external world with the 'principle of reality' (*Realitätsprinzip*). In art, religion, and philosophy, apparently, the human soul creates an illusory substitute for the harm to life that arises from its incapability of participating in the reality of the external world. But we do not learn a lot from psychoanalysts about exactly how this reality is a given reality – that is, a guaranteed one – or about how it could and should therefore be capable of demonstrating that this internal world is illusory and unreal. They simply talk about a person who has a sense for reality and about a person who does not have this sense, without concerning themselves too much with the nature of this reality. For instance, according to Freud, it can be said that a person with a sense for reality is represented by the person whom we have called a spectator and a technician, and S. Ferenczi[134] also states similarly that 'the sense for reality reaches its culmination in science.' According to fundamental psychoanalytic theses, you would adjudicate that 'libido', eros, instinct – simply the one who directly participates in reality, who itself actually is this reality – would have a greater sense for reality, but a logical bridge is lacking here! On the contrary, the 'reality principle' is assigned to the reality of the one who looks on and imitates, to the technician and his world. Well, if the technician as reason has reality, then what about libido, eros, sex? Israel Levine shows us the way out of this conundrum: 'It is true that the Real, or Necessity, is perceived by us as the economic, social, cultural standards, and conditions of the community in which we live. But in the last analysis it consists of something more elemental. It consists, in fact, of the 'Laws of Nature,' or, even more simply, of the properties of molecules. If I may assume for the moment a dualistic setting for the argument (which would be a matter for ultimate metaphysical justification) what is being maintained is that the essence of life is the interaction of life-urge and molecules, and that the evolution of reason is a stage in this process which reflects the effort of the life-force to control, appreciate, 'get round' the properties of molecules, in the struggle to achieve its own goal.'[135] There is no need to continue. You can easily deduce yourself that the battle between the 'reality principle' and instinct is a battle between the higher level of reason and the lower level of reason, and so the desired 'spectator' gets the last word after all: 'Alles, was ist, ist vernünftig. [Everything that is, is reasonable.]' Reason and molecules, technology, laws, and material – these are the last requisites of psychoanalytical teaching about the irrational essence of life and the world. What then can art expect from

---

134 Hungarian psychoanalyst (1873–1933).
135 Levine, *The Unconscious*, pp. 205–206.

this? Is it, then, any surprise if in the end art serves only 'illusion' in contrast to the 'reality' of morality?

Where is the borderline between the 'illusions' of the internal world and the 'reality' of the external world? If, as a result of a genetic mutation, one brown caterpillar is hatched amongst green caterpillars, and on a green leaf it is soon gobbled up by a bird, does this mean that the green caterpillars have lived by reality, while the brown one has lived by illusions? By this, I merely want to recall how our understanding of reality is technical, pragmatic; how we are inclined to prescribe to reality and truth (that is, what is created and guaranteed by life) the measure of a precept (that is, what is disproved by a loss of life). An internal equivalent as a factual equivalent is replaced here by the Darwinist principle of 'natural selection'. This principle, operating with the 'instinct of self-preservation', conceives reality as something given, as something which it is sufficient to preserve, to maintain (in the 'struggle for life'). The Darwinist 'survival of the fittest' is not a principle of nature; it is a principle of a spectator's explication of nature. Nature, for which nothing is given, which must create everything, does not dream of survival; it has a more pressing and essential concern: living. Note that this also applies literally to a creative person, and that it is a parasitical creature, one living from the given, that has the greatest concern about surviving.

Biologist Jakob von Uexküll asserts that 'the real world is built from thousands of subjective worlds'. This statement may mislead us just as the statement that talked about absolute truth as a sum of perspectival, partial truths did. The real world as a sum of subjective worlds is only the invention of explicators, a map of a spectator. The real world of an individual is not – there is no longer any need to remind you of this – a *part* of some world. It is an *entire* world; it cannot be added to, subtracted from, divided. Whatever is, is in this world. Whatever accepts its existence in your world does so through your 'here' and 'now'. And if you contend that any kind of existence is illusory, then this illusoriness is given to its existence in your world, not in another one. And everything that you feel or accept as an inconsistency, a contradiction, or a defect, no matter whether this is a case of illusion, poverty, iniquity, injustice, evil, or anything else, this represents an inconsistency and a defect of your world, and if you feel the need for rectification, then you are faced with the task of rectifying your own world. However, in this way, by taking responsibility with your conscience for your own world, you are taking responsibility for the whole world. And so the harmony of your own world is possible only as a harmony of the whole world.

As we have shown, technician-reason has torn apart this unitary and single world into two worlds – an external and an internal one – and has placed these in opposition to each other as 'reality' and 'illusion'. For the idealist technician, the 'external' world is illusory, while for the materialist technician, the 'internal' world is illusory. Both attempt to flee from the illusory half of their own world by seeking to dominate the other half, the 'real world': the idealist by systematically pursued asceticism and the spiritual techniques of the internal world, the materialist by science and the material techniques of the external world. It is logical that the hegemony of the one suppresses the other, ideologically, morally, and also physically. In the medieval era, for instance, under an idealist rule, research and natural scientific practices (alchemy, the investigation of the stars, autopsies, and similar) were viewed as diabolical and monstrous, and condemned to be carried out only as illicit, sinful, and scandalous activities. Today, under the hegemony of science, it is now the spiritual world of the idealist that is regarded as monstrous, and certain manifestations and practices are restricted to the suspicious field – closely guarded by science – of 'para-psychological phenomena'; asceticism and mysticism are pilloried, ridiculed, and despised.

Today's scientific and technical person falls victim to a peculiar self-deception when he deludes himself that his successes in transforming the external world are evidence that he is subjecting and adapting this world. But what is he transforming here? He is rather merely emptying and adapting his inner soul. He masters the material world at the price of giving up his own humanness, the entire richness of his inner soul, and becoming a slave to material and its dull mechanical psyche. He declares that he has forced nature to become a slave to him – how utterly naïve! The first and last condition of a successful science and technology is that nature does not concede one tiny bit, but on the contrary that a person must concede a lot, that he concedes everything, that he ravages and eviscerates his inner soul to the very bottom. An ancient barbarian horde, when it conquered a developed nation, absorbed its soul and became a cultural nation. We, cultural Westerners, subjecting the world of material, have absorbed its soul and become barbarians. The barbarianism of those hordes was at least vital, animal; our barbarianism is mechanical, intellectual, in its entire nature inimical to life.

Well, art protests in the name of living reality, in the name of a person who is not confined, not mechanized. It protests against a person, a being with the richest inner soul, the most creative being, reducing his life to the level of the poorest and dullest inner soul. There are primitive peoples who believe that, when they kill a predator and eat its heart or drink its blood, they gain its power, cunning, and adroitness. We do not have such a belief, but we nevertheless think that the necessity of using salt and eating rabbits binds us to reduce the reality of our being to the being of salt and rabbits. It is foolish to say that this or that person *lives* in illusions. If it were possible to live in illusions, what would be better than to hold onto the illusions?

Psychoanalysis, interpreting art as an illusory substitute for real life, cites an elderly Ibsen, who in his artistic epilogue confessed that art had robbed him of his life. The circumstance that such a confession cannot be expressed other than in the past tense – because the statement 'art *is robbing* me of my life' is absurd – evidently says nothing to the psychoanalyst. A lover never says: love is robbing me of my life; but once he no longer has it, then he says: love robbed me of my life. H. G. Wells did not accuse art all the while that he would have to have said: what I make my living by, is betraying me, but only first when he had to say: what I made my living by, betrayed me. Art, like love and moral virtue, is not an employment with a retirement pension.

Carl G. Jung, when he is not actually thinking about psycho-analysis, is capable of saying this about art and its irrational nature: 'As long as we ourselves are caught up in the process of creation, we neither see nor understand; indeed we ought not to understand, for nothing is more injurious to immediate experience than cognition. ... Perhaps art has no "meaning," at least not as we understand meaning. Perhaps it is like nature, which simply is and "means" nothing beyond that. ... It needs no meaning, for meaning has nothing to do with art.' – But the devil's foot appears, as soon as the psychoanalyst intervenes. All of a sudden a work of art 'may truthfully be called a message to generations of men. So *Faust* touches something in the soul of every German. ... Could we conceive of anyone but a German writing *Faust* or *Thus Spake Zarathustra*? Both of them strike a chord that vibrates in the German psyche, evoking a "primordial image" ... the figure of a healer or teacher of mankind ... the archetype of the Wise Old Man, the helper and re-deemer. This image has lain buried and dormant in the unconscious since the dawn of history; it is awakened whenever the times are out of joint and a great error deflects society from the right path. For when people go astray they feel the need of a guide or teacher, and even of a physician.'[136]

You are a witness, my friend, of how reason is getting into bad ways, and how the irrational will be held to account for all the havoc that reason causes. But in reality, the irrational will have as much

136 In *Collected Works of C. G. Jung, Vol. 15: Spirit in Man, Art and Literature*, trans. by R. F. C. Hull.

of the blame for this, as nature has in the fact that people kill one another with bombs, poisonous gases, and flames.

Psychoanalysis entrusts to 'irrational' art the remnants of what, as collective knowledge, has been buried for ages in the lowest layers of the human unconscious. Art here submits a certain collective, tribe, or nation to the same therapy that a psychoanalysis subjects his patient to; only with the difference that the artist is both doctor and patient. As a patient art must lie down on the operating table. We know that in this case an operation is regarded as successful in which the patient dies. Because 'a cognized feeling is not a feeling, but rather cognition'. Therefore, 'just as religious man has been surpassed, so also must artistic man be surpassed. He must change into a doctor. … Artistic works are made more and more deliberately, but precisely because of this they must finally change into science. … Because, as everywhere, here also the abnormal shows the path of freedom for the normal. A cured neurotic has looked deep into his 'psyche' and thereby also into the inner lives of all people; the illness has made him knowledgeable, because he needs knowledge – that is, the control of his subconscious – for his renewal. Suffering has perfected him. … Because the conditions for the treatment of neurosis are given, a distant view into the future of the human species opens up. Humanity can now confidently face the hysteria inevitable at the end of every cultural development, because it is capable of overcoming this end by making it into a transition; and while in the past nations have perished as a result of neuroses, now they will go through this neurosis with the benefit of knowledge. However it is only once a perfect re-evaluation of the psyche has been successfully achieved, only once the entire suppressed subconscious has become conscious, that a new type of humanity liberated from art will be able to direct and control its "urges" with a firm hand.'[137] (Otto Rank)

---

137 Otto Rank, *Der Künstler, Ansätze zu einer Sexual-Psychologie* [The Artist: Approaches to a Sexual Psychology] (Vienna: Heller, 1907), p. 58.

Moral virtue, love, truth, art – all this is merely cocooned, suppressed sexuality. Psychoanalysis and other kinds of analyses have cured us of love, truth, moral virtue, of art. Sexuality is free, conscious; but is it controlled? With the loss of moral virtue, love, truth, and art, we have also lost all the motivations to control it; there is no longer anything to impose such an obligation on us merely on account of its naturalness. The only one of these natural things left for us is precisely this sexuality. There is no reason to suppress it, and neither is it wise to do so. Neither of course is there any reason to make it into an intimate matter; after all, nature does not make it into one. However, nature is devoid of shame because it is devoid of reason. We have lost our shame, but we have not lost our reason. We have become animals with reason. This is the source of the complaints about the immorality and savageness of our era.

We have been told: civilization must give up its sacred concepts about human beings, if it is to advance forward. It has given them up and advanced. However, its dark shadow has advanced with it and overtaken it.

If I show that there is no other art than irrational art, then, my friend, you may very well ask what comprises the difference that leads us to call one sort of art – for instance, modern art – irrational, while we call other types of art rational? Well, this is connected with so-called *deformation* and has its origin in a rationalist understanding of art. A rationality which posits itself as a measure of art introduced a dualism of rational and irrational art. The usual form of this dualism is a differentiation into classical art and romantic art. An attempt to better capture this duality led Nietzsche, for instance, to distinguish Apollonian and Dionysian; Richard Müller-Freienfels to divide art into '*Gestaltungskunst*' and '*Ausdruckskunst*' (that is, roughly expressed, into art as communication and art as self-expression); K. Scheffler to classify all art into either Greek or Gothic art; and to other similar attempts.

The biggest defect of every division of art is, I would say, that it is a division. Every such division comprises a statement of reason, for which the measure of art is not art, but rather the distance that art has distanced itself from reason. Reason evaluates art by art's distance from itself, reason, and assesses this distance as a *deformation* of nature by art. ... But which nature? Nature as a rational depiction, not as a vital process. If, therefore, art deforms something, then it deforms the rational; perhaps in the same way that our view of an actual landscape deforms the map of the same landscape that is folded out in front of us.

Why does it sometimes deform more, and other times less? As we have seen, this is in essence a question about artistic styles and directions in their historical and local versions. Psychoanalysts teach us that artistic styles mirror the social morality of the period and society in question. The degree of 'deformation' is merely the degree of cocooning in which the sexual drive has to conceal itself in order to be able to make itself apparent in the given moral and intellectual regime of any particular society. Such a conception turns the entire matter upside down. If art is merely a manifestation of living reality, a creative expression of an individual, then there is nothing to be concealed, and therefore neither is there anything to deform; on the contrary, then, the real role of 'deformation' here is to make visible and give expression to what would otherwise, without this deformation, remain hidden, suppressed, unexpressed. In this sense and to this extent, an artistic style is really dependent on the moral and intellectual regime of a certain society and period. However, art is not a cocoon, a hiding place from this regime. On the contrary, it is a proclamation of living reality against the collective good outward appearance; it is a manifestation of the creative life in opposition to automatic existence; it is a vital process in contrast to a mechanical process.

The reason why one artistic style is more rational than another is because art does not reject any means of expression that enables it, in any given situation, to express its creative vitality as fully as possible. An artist can – without any danger for his art – make use of a pair of compasses and a ruler, for so long as he is almost the only person using these instruments. Using these instruments would not of itself alone make the focus of his creation rational, even if he himself were to claim this. Emil Utitz[138] writes that 'the majority of artists are radical formalists, even if their own works speak clearly against this. Form – this is precisely what they struggle to achieve; the other things come of their own accord, providing of course that they are real artists.' Artistic creation struggles to achieve reality. The problem of form and content only occurs first in an explanation, no matter whether this is a critic's explanation or the artist's own. Bedřich Václavek,[139] one of the martyrs for faith in a better mankind and in a more human mission for science and technology, regards 'the problem of the intellect in a literary work of art' as resolved, arguing that, even though the participation of the intellect cannot be excluded from poetic creation, the 'poetic conception must arise directly from experience and it cannot merely copy and beautify a previously conceived intellectual plan.' In short, we can repeat: the intellect can – in an extreme case – be an accoucheur in art, but never the one giving birth. If is a dictator, it is a bad accoucheur; it wants to give birth where it should only assist, organize, and preserve.

Without the organizing activity of the intellect, a human society cannot exist. However, to organize is not to give birth: organizations, collectives, institutions, churches, states are not the ones that give birth; in the best case, they are *accoucheurs*. If their ambitions go beyond this, then they hinder and prevent birth, instead of assisting it. In such a case, the one who gives birth does so without an accoucheur, or possibly even against this accoucheur. In artistic creation, this

---

138 Prague-born aesthetician and psychologist (1883–1956).
139 Czech Marxist aesthetician, killed in Auschwitz (1897–1943).

raculous garden where he can walk around and pick the richest and most beautiful fruits that he needs for his work. ... Art should develop alongside science; these two human expressions are mutually inseparable and both derive from a single and religious foundation, which is the beginning of the universe.'[141]

After all we have said here about the relationship between art and science, we can see that today only someone with a simplicity worthy of Francis of Assisi – or precisely of an artist – could hold such a view. For art, the cohabitation of art and science cannot end up in other way than the cohabitation of art and religion ended up for religion: one day art will become superfluous and will be thrown on the scrap heap.

It cannot be denied that there is no unified style in modern art: anarchy, randomness, impetuosity, confusion, inconsistency, and exaggeration reign in it. But this anarchy and impetuosity very much resemble that displayed by a flock of sheep when attacked by a wolf. What is decisive in such a case is not stylistic behaviour, refined manners, but rather: everyone for himself, and save yourself any way that you can. Modern art is in such a situation. It has been attacked by a wolf and the main thing is to save its bare existence. The Hellenistic idyll of paradise in which the wolf and the lamb will frolic around with each other has become a fable of times gone by. To send a lamb to pasture in a garden occupied by a wolf today means persuading it to commit suicide.

The behaviour of art in such a situation is a sign of its living nature and health. For as long as art does not wait for recipes and pieces of advice, as long as it senses danger instinctively and reacts instinctively, this means that it has not parted ways with life. Religion – it seems – has already lost this instinct for living. On the one hand, it retains its accumulated negotiating shrewdness in bargaining and exchange, its property and traditions, while on the other hand it sticks its head into the wolf's paws unwarned by any instinct that these paws

141 Gino Severini, *Du cubisme au classicisme* [From Cubism to Classicism], 1921.

are those of a wolf. And so now the task of defending the limited out-post of life against the deluge of automatons and robots is left to art virtually alone. It must be admitted that it is better suited to this role today than religion is. Primarily, art is less liable to any kind of brib-ery than any of the religious gods; it does not make any compromises or concessions. Face to face with art, no one can pretend that he is something that he is not, and this is so for the same simple reason that a corpse cannot pretend that it lives. In comparison with gods, art has the enormous advantage that it is visible, factual, evident, but at the same time it cannot be apprehended by reason. It works in open daylight in front of the sight of all; it does not oppose any control or test; it is as self-evident and mysterious as nature itself. It is a religion whose 'god' is visible, but nevertheless inaccessible to the touch of sci-ence. Its position vis-à-vis science is entirely different! While science simply denies the existence of the god of religion, it cannot dispatch the 'god' of art with a brief statement: 'I do not see, I do not hear, I do not feel'. This 'god' is here, and if I say: I do not perceive it, then I fall into the suspicion of being blind and deaf. If science has removed reli-gion, then it is now up to art alone to show science its limits.

To recommend the recipe of Leonardo da Vinci to a contemporary artist and to offer him a pair of compasses and a ruler is the most foolish advice that we can possibly give him. What can art possibly hope to achieve with a pair of compasses and a ruler, when today every secondary school pupil knows how to use these instruments? In a period when the swarm of engineers and specialists is growing, for whom the task has been exclusively set aside of bringing the use of these instruments and of calculation to the level of perfection that it is absolutely possible to achieve with them? Is it so difficult to understand what a comic, dilettantish, and hopeless figure an artist armed with a pair of compasses and a ruler is alongside an engineer? If the culmination of the use of a measuring instruments and calcu-lations is an automaton, a machine, a conveyor belt, a mechanical process, life as a process of a chemical crucible, then an artist, if blood is still running in his veins and not water, will fling the compasses and ruler onto the floor.

There are, however, some who have used this recipe and have tried to create an artistic style reflecting the period: for instance, the Constructivists. George Grosz praises them for seeing with greater clarity in the contemporary period. Their aims are free of archaic prejudices; they try to attain objectivity; they are concerned with real needs and uphold an art that can be constructed, perceived and verified. Unfortunately, according to Grosz, they commit the error of remaining confined within art. 'They forget that, as a rule, there is only one type of constructivist: the engineer, the architect, the welder, the carpenter. In a word, the technician. ... The more honest among them, therefore, put so-called art aside and focused their energy on the study of technical sciences in order to master the real basis of constructivism.'

Let us take the example of architecture. This art, bound fatally with the compass, the ruler, and calculations, found itself faced with a choice: to give up its instruments and perish completely, or not to capitulate, to give up on art, and become a mere technology. It decided for the second of these options. However, as such, it is no longer able to master any tasks over and above mere utility.

Let us take photography and film. If they do not want to be art, then they produce documentaries. And as art, they are almost pure technology and share its fate: one day is enough for them to become so antiquated that they become laughable for us.

Recently I read an appeal by a doctor to modern creative artists: apparently they should acquaint themselves more closely with pathological creation. If 'they got to know this creation in all its interestingness, but also its repulsiveness, then they would certainly evade morbid problems and motifs. Today's science is capable of leading an artist through this bleak labyrinth safely and without exertion.'[142] (Milada Lautererová)

142 Milada Lautererová in *Věda a život* [*Science and Life*], vol. XIII.

As is known, it was precisely psychiatrists who classified not only some artists, but art as such, as a pathological phenomenon. The author of the appeal has evidently failed to notice that the most problematic, the most dubious, and the 'most repulsive' creations are produced precisely by those artists who take an interest in pathology, by those who study it scientifically and base their own artistic theories and programmes on it.

For instance, from a study of psychopathology, an artist can gain the insight that he has an unconscious. In every other case a finding means an instruction for a conscious, deliberate activity. However, for an artist who is enthusiastic about science, a finding is an instruction – what a surprise! – for an automatic, spontaneous, 'unconscious' activity. The only problem is that in the course of this unconscious creation, he has the bad luck – as Josef Čapek says – that he knows all too much about this unconscious. And therefore his 'irrational' creations merely reflect an illogical linking of a chain of rational objects and elements.

No matter where you turn, you can see over and over again that science is capable of leading an artist 'safely and without exertion' away from art, but not of leading him to art. If there were not other deliverance for art than in doctrines and theories, we could have read out the funeral rites over it. If we are able to talk about any task and purpose for modern art at all, then only about the one that art has always had: to manifest life – that is, creation – and to fight against illusion, against the illusion of the 'given'. There is no other illusion than the illusion of the 'given'.

One negative phenomenon that must be ascribed to this illusion is the detrimental and misleading separation of work and creation. H. G. Wells writes in his *History of the World*: 'Has there ever in the history of the world been a human society that gave precedence to creating over conspiring?' Society cannot give precedence to creation for the simple reason that it is not creative. This is why it can exist only from the 'given' and must give precedence to security ahead of creation. Science is a prospector of the 'given' and technology is the gold-digger that extracts it. This is the source of the life-and-death connection between society and technology. People expect from technology a liberation from hard labour, while society expects technology to secure and increase its power. For as long as human societies exist, there will most probably be no end to competition for power. And as long as competition for power does not cease, no machines or organizations will alleviate mankind in his mournful and arduous lot. The dependence of society on technology has today taken on a monstrous character. Modern material technology is a reflection of a despotic regime in which one person knows and commands, while the others do not know and blindly obey. The most monstrous thing about technology: that one or a very few individuals require an army of robots. On one side is the inventor, the theoretician, the engineer; on the other side are gangs of human automata at a conveyor belt, stupefied by five or six unchanging movements that they are doomed to perform the whole year long. Technology, which was supposed to liberate humankind from menial work, has deprived him of creation. Social morality has found itself confronted with the task of instilling in the minds of humans as a blessing something that it promised to eradicate as a curse. It pays him for this more justly – that is, proportionately to the feeling of harm, of loss in life that his arduous labour brings him. It assigns this labour a place on the ladder of human activities and allocates it as an honourable duty, as a moral obligation – that is, it elevates and praises this labour precisely because it is a 'sacrifice', a harm suffered in life, and thus flatters humankind's inclinations towards martyrdom and cults, and reckons with these inclinations. Current social morality goes so far in this effort that it pronounces any activity which does not have these features – that is, any activity which does not bring with it a feeling of harm to life, because it is creation – as luxury and indolence, but closing its eyes to the fact that a person, an artist, carries out this activity even under conditions under which not even the lowest kind of errand-boy would lift a finger. In this way, art becomes a fruit of indolence and luxury and a producer of 'illusions'; in this way, art 'isolates itself from life'; in this way, it actually for the first time becomes 'art' as separate and distinct from 'work'.

But: if earlier periods did not have art, but rather only work, then this was because this work had not yet parted ways with human creativity: creation enabled; it did not disable. If today machine production does not offer human creativity any possibility of individual creation, then it can be understood that, on the other hand, art has also had to set aside a place for itself as an essential vital counterweight. The 'isolation of art' is not, therefore, an expression of art parting ways with life, but rather of work parting ways with life. The degree of artistic 'deformation' can be a measure of this parting of ways.

It is grotesque when social morality, which classifies art as a deserter from life, recommends it to us as a recompense for the harm to life that has been caused to us by all-day arduous labour. However, in truth it is necessary to say that art, as it is, is not suitable for social morality. If it is to be granted mercy, then it must be allocated to 'work' – that is, it must be performed as something that is assigned from outside, as something that is a duty, an order, something which is itself a sacrifice, a harm to life, something which is worthy of its reward, money, titles, and honours. How is art to be allocated to 'work'? By assigning it the role of producing entertainment, alcohol, 'oblivion, precious and golden happiness' (Wells) in a world of arduous labour. This is symptomatic: we want to know, and when we know, we make forgetting the condition of our happiness.

But art has just about as much in common with alcohol as a sleepwalker with a drunk. Being enchanted does not mean being saved, says George Santayana. If it is a case of crossing over a tightrope, then sleepwalking is the best state, and drunkenness the worst. While a sleepwalker makes his way across a narrow rope without losing his balance, not even a broad highway is wide enough for a drunk to cross safely. While in the first case we can talk about a state of greatest concentration, the state of the second is one of greatest dissipation. Alcohol vitiates reason; its aim is to distance us from reason, from knowing, to make us forget. However, we have shown that art does not consist in distance from reason, in a vitiation of reason. The irrationality of art cannot be measured by its distance from reason, because its irrationality does not consist in this. Drunkenness, on the other hand, is defined by this distance. In art, there is a maximum of life guarantees, in drunkenness a minimum. There is no art without an effort to be someone, to be a guarantee; drunkenness, on the contrary, is a desire not to know, not to guarantee, to be no one. In a world of entertainment, people do not have names. A person who is drunk loses his name, while someone who is getting drunk ceases to acknowledge his own name. However, the world of art is a world of guarantors; their names mean obligation.

Picasso offers us a key to modern art when he says that art is ceasing to be *production* and becoming *creation* (viz. previously cited Mánes almanac). In an era of photography, film, and precise machine production, an artist no longer produces faithful documents, but rather makes visible the living human hand during the creation of a work of art, and it depicts the creative process itself rather than things. It disdains models, because today a model has become a prototype for mechanical imitation and serial production. Modern art does not create any style nor found any schools, because it is repelled by the normalizations, formulas, and standard techniques that are typical for the requisites of today's depersonalized factory products.

Simply Picasso's entire work springs from a deep and intensive feeling for the human and the living, and therefore he finds it all the more painful to bear when he is not understood precisely by those people to whose efforts to achieve a new man he feels so close and to whom, for the most part, he openly declares his allegiance. After all, precisely because his moral and artistic conscience feels solidarity with this effort, it should not be necessary for this effort to stoop to promoting the moralization of science and the moralization of art.

As is always the case, in being misunderstood, today's artist also pays the price for penetrating further and deeper into human affairs than the rest of us. For a person not to be enslaved by another person: this is something that has always been fought for. The artist can also count to his credit that the conscience of the world has finally been aroused. However, a just wage and transfers of ownership are not yet sufficient to change menial work into creation. The issue that especially perturbs an artist today, what he urgently confronts us with in his work, the thing without which there will be no new human being, no human being in the full sense of the world, is this: How to liberate a human being internally – that is, how to change work into creation? To those utopians who expect this miracle merely from science and technology, and from them alone, from the very same science and technology that provides states with the most powerful weapon in the struggle between states for power by depriving the human individual of creation and subjugating him instead to work, to these utopians the modern artist replies with all the unyielding 'irrationality' of his work: no! The entire human tragedy lies in the fact that the path to humanness intersects with the path to power and security. If you set out on the first path, you commit a crime on society; if you set out on the second path, then you commit a crime on nature. An artist is highly suited to experience this tragedy. 'The state,' says Georges Bernanos,[143] 'fears only one opponent: a human being. An autonomous, free human being.' The fact that this does not in any way depend on the form of social regime is evident from Flaubert's words, written during the flowering of the 'individualistic era': 'Individuality is a crime. The eighteenth century denied the soul, and the work of the nineteenth century will probably be that it will kill the human being.'

143 French Catholic author, (1888–1948).

What is to be done? For art, there is no choice. Art – this is the sovereign distinction of something that defends life and the human being. Therefore, art cannot change creation into 'work'. It cannot constitute a harm to life, since it stands and falls with allotting the highest value to life. To compromise means to die.

In society, we are building institutions of security. However, we are not building institutions of life, because it is not possible to build such an institution. Life consists in individual guarantees. The world of art, moral virtue, and truth – this is the world of individual guarantees. Therefore, it cannot be guaranteed by laws, decrees, required reading texts, money, or rifles; it is guaranteed by free beings who do not bow when confronted either by required reading texts, by money, or by rifles.

Beauty is one circle and art is another circle, and the two circles more or less overlap. The two circles overlap most in the case of 'rational', 'comprehensible' art. Greece and the Renaissance represent a classic, supreme type of beauty. In contrast to this, the impressiveness of the Gothic does not consist in beauty, and it seems that modern, 'irrational' art's break with beauty is complete.

Therefore, we should not be surprised that there have always been attempts to reduce beauty to rational elements, represented in an extreme form by numerical and geometrical relations. In this extreme case, the so-called deformation, and thereby the 'irrationality', of a work of art is then determined by the degree to which constant numerical relations are violated. Leaving to one side the fact that this rationality contains a good dose of Pythagorean mysticism, this attempt to reduce beauty to rational elements comprises the same error as when rationality attempted to appropriate moral virtue. Moral emotion is provoked by practical reason and stands in opposition to it, or respectively to the egoistical instinct that reason represents. Beauty is not provoked by reason, but rather enters into a complementary relationship with it – that is, they are mutually bound together, but at the same time are mutually exclusive. And it is precisely on account of this capability or characteristic that beauty can contribute greatly to art, and the more rational art is – that is, the more faithfully, as one says, it depicts reality and conveys ideas – the more heed it pays to beauty. Beauty is an emotion that arises in that particular life situation that we have called *a threshold one* and which is marked – as we have briefly noted – by the fact that in this situation all practical and theoretical tendencies disappear and all that remains is an intensive relationship to life for its own sake. In other words, if a certain event – whether depicted, narrated, or acted – is to be accepted by a person as art, and not as a mere report serving this or that tendency, or as a history attempting to describe 'what really happened', then it must evoke in a person that threshold life situation when all practical and cognitive tendencies disappear and all that remains is only an intensive participation with everything living. In order for art to achieve this, it 'makes itself beautiful'; and the more rational it is – that is, the more tendencies it has to overcome and reduce to one single tendency: to live – the more beautiful it must make itself.

On the other hand, of course, 'irrational' art, which has had to renounce the production of 'faithful portrayals' (or – as in the case of primitives and children – it has a different measure of rationality, and thereby also of 'faithful' portrayals, and thereby also a different conception of beauty), can no longer actually reckon with a full contribution of beauty in our assessment of it. Such an art must search for another path to our feelings than an aesthetized rational notion. If it succeeds in this, then by doing so it also influences our relationship to 'beautiful' art. For instance, we know that a classical Greek statue or tragedy is beautiful, but we no longer feel this. This is why we call its beauty cold. If someone were to create it today, then it would not even have this beauty for us. What makes the art of antiquity beautiful for us, is the era of its creation.

What, then, does beauty consist in?

Let us look closer at that living situation that manifests itself in the experience of the beautiful. F. X. Šalda says: 'Beauty is first given by a perspective from afar. ... Beauty is only the poetry of the past and the melancholy of recollection.' Similarly, Jean-Marie Guyau:[144] 'Poetry is in essence a part of what we call the poetry of recollection.' Primarily, then, we must make an essential differentiation between memory and recollection. While the first belongs to the realm of cognition, knowledge, and the intellect, the second appertains to lived experience. Memory attempts a 'faithful' maintenance and reconstruction of the past; through memory a person is transferred to the past and tries to secure it 'as it was', and not as it is now – that is, in a recollection. Memory is a spectator, while recollection is a participant. Memory has an analogous relationship to a recollection as a document has to a poem. A recollection treats memory in the same way as an artist treats so-called reality. And it is precisely this aesthetic emotion that changes a memory into a recollection.

Memory, on the one hand, returns me to the place of an event and, through reconstruction, tries to produce a document, while in a recollection, in contrast, I do not return. A recollection does not place me back into the event, but rather, on the contrary, shifts me away from the event. A recollection puts me in that threshold life situation in which my relation to beings and things is freed of all tendencies and intentions, and there remains only the feeling of a living bond with them. Memory reconstructs; it does not revive. Events and persons are no longer; there is only I, who 'know' the past. In a recollection, things and beings live, but I am separated from them for ever; for them I have already perished. Death as a phenomenon of the external world and as a fiction of the future is the knowledge of death; it is the memory of death. However, a recollection is an experience of death; a recollection is the reality of death, its presence in my inner soul.

So, if beauty is the poetry of recollection, then this means that beauty is an experience of death. Through recollection, our heart finds itself in that critical, limiting, concluding position in life, in

144 French philosopher and poet (1854–1888).

which we feel that we are leaving and will no longer return. Beauty is that intense embrace with being and things, when we feel that we are saying goodbye for ever. Things are beautiful not because beauty is one of their characteristics; they are beautiful because the eyes that are enraptured are mortal. Death lives in us from our birth, and looking through its eyes, we see beautiful things and beings worthy of love. Beauty is an inaudible harmony in which the mortal in things converses with the mortal in us. There is no beauty in things themselves; only if we touch them with a certain intimate caress, with an ingenuous soul, with a brave heart, do they induce us to turn away toward departure. Beauty is the heart's speechless, intimate understanding with things about the highest certainty, about the final truth. Beauty is life intensified to its limit by the experience of death.

However, the experience of death is not only beauty. There have been mystics who have unveiled the experience of death in love. And there has also been a morally virtuous being who – giving himself away – lived the experience of death. This is why we can perhaps say that the entire world of participation and reality grows out of the experience of death. And if the world of reason and the given, the collective world of security and insecurity, is built on the appearance and fiction of death, then the world of participation and creation arises from the experience of death.

While reason declares a human's ownership of the things and beings of this world, love and beauty are a feeling of a fleeting encounter with them. Love and beauty, kindling with death, take away our ownership of things and beings; they liberate them from us. An owner does not know beauty; a slave-owner does not know love. Anything that you appropriate, you lose for your heart; the more you engage in subjecting things in the material and logical world, the more these things are lost to your heart. Why is the beauty of a landscape not discovered by its owners, the local people? And why do prospectors and gold-diggers also fail to recognize this beauty?

We will go some way to clarifying the artist's share and our share in the beauty of a work of art, if we try to give a reply to the old question about the difference between an aesthetic emotion aroused by a work of art, and an aesthetic emotion aroused by nature. What is the difference between a landscape and a picture of a landscape as 'aesthetic objects'? In essence, none. The presence of beauty indicates that in both one case and in the other this here is a case of an aesthetization of a rational notion, or respectively a 'realistic' notion; in both cases, an aesthetic emotion arises through the inducing of a borderline life situation. The only question here can relate to how this process of inducing comes about in nature, and how it comes about in front of a picture. How is it that a picture is almost always capable of stimulating in us what a landscape only rarely and accidentally succeeds in doing?

When we were building the cable-car in the mountains, it used to happen on Sunday mornings that the workmen, getting ready to dress in more festive clothes, would come out onto the doorstep of their cabins, and looking up at the ridge of mountains and at the fresh meadows spreading out into the distance, could not stop themselves from shouting out: How beautiful! And meanwhile – you will say – this was no other landscape than the one for which on workdays, when they toiling away with pillars and steel cables, they had no other words than 'damned terrain'. Why this difference? This is clear, Charles Lalo would say: the cause is Sunday, the day of emptiness and idleness. It is true that many of them spent the day lying in bed or sitting in the tavern, but these were not the ones who admired the beauty of the landscape in the early morning. These people, on the contrary, on many occasions made long and demanding hikes into the mountains, and when I inquired about what drew them there on a Sunday, to a place that on weekdays they spent their time with distaste and only because forced to do so, I discovered that they do so out of a need for some kind of other relationship to this undisturbed nature, a more intimate and free relationship, a relationship – I would say – that is vital and living, rather than technical and lucrative. They no longer thought about how they would 'get the better of it', how they would 'outwit it', subjugate it, harness it. They felt a kind of need to wash their hearts of the tricks and stratagems of the weekday, and to bring their hearts back pure and guileless to the place where they have so far brought them calculating and avaricious. Do we capture this difference if we say that Sunday is a day of idleness in contrast to a day of work? Those for whom Sunday was merely a day of idleness remained just as untouched by the beauty of nature on Sunday as on a weekday. They did not even go out into nature at all on a festive day. In other words, in order for nature to be beautiful, it is primarily necessary to bring the soul of Sunday to it. But that is not enough; it depends additionally on what Sunday is for you. It is similar with art, only with the difference that – while you must bring the soul of Sunday with you into nature – an artistic work, in contrast to this, welcomes you with the words: today is Sunday. This is the entire difference. The rest depends only on you. Here it is a case of what purpose you have reserved for Sunday. What you request of Sunday, you will also request of art. Doing nothing, entertainment, alcohol, pleasure; or merely rest; or meetings, camps, political agitation, proclamations, celebratory toasts, congratulatory telegrams. This would be a Sunday conceived, so to speak, in a modern way – that is, biologically, macro-economically, politically, scientifically.

But there is also a Sunday in a non-modern, original, festive, or to put it better sacramental, sense: a Sunday of the 'ultimate, final' – that is, the main – matters of a human being, Sunday as a day on which the salvation of the soul and life is decided. This does not mean that Sunday is a day of festive, fine, and noble tales and deeds. Sunday is a day of a different perspective, a perspective from a distance, a day of reincarnation and transubstantiation, a day which places our heart on the sharp edge of life and death and makes it feel the only thing necessary, without which life falls into emptiness. Sunday is a day of beauty and love, a day of the challenge: be reborn, so that you do not perish; give yourself away, so that you can live; live, so that you can create; pass away, so that you can be born again.

Such is the recipe of salvation which art offers and which is the recipe of nature: free yourself of the future; free yourself from the phantom of death and live the reality of death!

If a weekday is a day of work, then Sunday is a day of creation, of creation on one's own self. 'I create, therefore I am. ... A creator is not an organized worker who works for six days and rests on Sunday. Sunday is the Lord's day, a great creative day. A creator does not know any other days. If he was to cease to create, even for a second, then he would die. The void is greedily lurking.'[145] (Romain Rolland, *Le Voyage intérieur*) The name of Romain Rolland[146] is a guarantee that this is no haughty person who is speaking here, but rather an artist whose highest aim and life-long programme was: the human being. And the words that he speaks here also express a commitment and a programme, a truly human, truly social programme.

My dear friend, you have been seeking for Robert's nature according to the method of your science. Just as you sought to come to an understanding of certain things through other things, you also hoped to find Robert through other beings. However, just as every one of those things answers only for itself, so each person in the tight circle of those keeping vigil over Robert has also answered only for itself. From these replies, you have compiled a vessel which was supposed to produce Robert's form. However, when you opened up this vessel, all that appeared there was a dark hollow, a maze of lines and forms turned inside out, where precisely what was at stake – Robert – was missing. I have attempted the opposite approach. I did not form a similitude of Robert according to the vessel, but rather formed the vessel into the shape of Robert. In Pirandello's play *Six Characters*

---

145 Romain Rolland, *Le Voyage intérieur* [The Interior Voyage] (Paris: A. Michel, 1942).
146 French author and pacifist (1866–1942).

in Search of an Author there is a scene in which the precise outline of a non-existing character is created. This character subsequently really appears embodied in a concrete person, and this as a simple consequence of that fact that all the other beings and things of this miniature cosmos are in their proper place. If we forget about the dramatist that created the character and breathed life into it, then we are really inclined to believe that mere form, a mere outline, creates reality. I recall how you portrayed a rainbow to me: you said that if we take away everything that is not a rainbow then we will have a rainbow. This is as if you had said: if you take five things, you will have six of them. But I know that, in addition to all those things that were not a rainbow, I also had to take a rainbow, in order to have one. And, therefore, I had six things, because I had taken six of them.

You say that every thing is a function of the entire remainder of the universe. A human being, for instance, is therefore the sum of everything in the universe that is not a human being. T. G. Masaryk opines that if theology is the science of God then science (in the true sense of the word) is the science of mankind, and for this science, mankind is the measure of all things and also the first and last subject of research. Let us try once again to assemble a human being from what is provided about him by individual sciences. For a physicist, a human being is merely a whirl of electrons; for a chemist, he is a conglomerate of chemical reactions; for a mathematician what is, he is a+b=c; for a biologist, an aggregate for the production of primordial juices; for a psychologist, a complex of senses or something similar; for a sociologist, a point of intersection of actors of interaction; for a theologian (let him also have his say), an angel, a depiction of God, and so on. What can we do with all these replies? Let us try to present to individual experts the replies of the other experts so that they can express their opinions about them and advise us. And here we will hear: I as a physicist cannot in truth say anything other than that a human being is ...; I as a chemist cannot in truth say anything other than that a human being is ...; I as a biologist cannot in truth ...; and so on. However, I do not understand why a human being should be only a cluster of atoms, clay, slime, or only algae, a guinea pig, an ape, or possibly even all of these put together, when he is quite evidently something unique and autonomous apart from all of this. I started my quest in search of answers from experts of various specialized sciences about whether a human being is respectively a piece of clay, an animal, or an angel, without really holding out much hope that I would understand any of the possible replies. Now, I end with the answer: *a human being is a human being*. And I think that I understand this seemingly Delphic reply; I certainly understand it much better than the reply that a human being is only a piece of clay, an animal, an angel. And while an expert knowledge of the properties of clay, animals, or angels is needed to provide the evidence that a person is merely a piece of clay, an animal, or an angel, then the evidence that a human being is a human being will perhaps remain only the prerogative of dilettantes. From time immemorial, artists have always stated their allegiance to this principle; this is why scientific experts always find the mark of dilettantism on artists' foreheads.

The truth is that for science a human being is not the measure of all things, but rather the contrary: all things are the measure of a human being. Science has compiled a vessel from all the things that are not a human being, and offered this vessel to us as a witch's casket, from which – when we open it up – a living human being will step out no differently than in the play by Pirandello previously mentioned. However, we have opened up the casket and found it empty. We see only an unclear cavity, a tangle of lines and distorted surfaces, but the essential thing is missing. There was no creator to create the body and breathe a living soul into it.

Nevertheless, there is a way in which we may even say that a human being is the measure of all things for science; that is, not a human being, but rather only human reason. Reason – this is the only thing that differentiates a human being from nature, and apparently it is this reason that makes him into a person. This, then, means that to rationalize nature means to anthropomorphize it, to humanize it. But what a surprise! This anthropomorphization means a complete removal of anything human; we have then cast this vessel for the depiction of a human being from such an anthropomorphized and dehumanized nature; and all of a sudden we are massively shocked when it is not human and when not being human means exactly the same as being inhumane.

At the beginning of the modern era, Spinoza mixed up a strange medicine for the suffering human being: *amor intellectualis Dei*. Perfect cognition and knowledge was supposed to lead us from self-love to love for God and all things. However, systematic use of the medicine brought unexpected consequences: first of all, God died, and then so did moral virtue, love, beauty, and finally humanity – the human being himself. Spinoza expected that the cognition of laws of nature would inspire us to a love of all mankind. Kant was more modest: cognizance of the law was supposed to inspire us at least to respect and a feeling of duty. But he also demanded a lot; it was necessary to go right down to nothing. Cognizance of laws relieved us of all inspiration; we know everything and we feel nothing. And because we feel nothing, we are no one, we are nothing. We are an empty vessel, a form, an abstraction. And losing our human essence, evaporating in less than steam, in a mere silhouette, a formula, we grasp at the last piece of living tissue, at the last drop of hot blood which is still left to us, and in order to prove to ourselves that we are still alive and real, we rage and go wild around until we collapse. However, apparently we are going wild because we are overflowing with life and boiling over with hot blood; because there is all too much nature in us. In reality there is all too much anthropomorphized and dehumanized nature in us. For us to become people once again, it is necessary for there to be more nature in us – that real nature. This is why Bergson seeks deliverance in a new mysticism, Huizinga in a new asceticism, and Whitehead in art; or respectively in love, moral virtue, and beauty not as sacred concepts, but as something natural, as the way in which a human being is a part of nature, and not as what differentiates him from nature – this is what makes a human being a human being.

We have understood Robert's behaviour as deranged, extreme, abnormal, and as deviant from what is natural. However, what deranged him was not nature, but rather our social morality, professions, bigotry. This was an extremity such as the behaviour of someone who was striving for internal fullness and perfection appears in the eyes of those who are striving for external security. However, reason, by dividing life into a dual conditionality – the one self-sacrificing and the other parasitical – has allotted perfection to the realm of fairy tales. However, if it shows us a parasitical conditionality on one side of the relations and connections on which life and the world stands, then it also shows us self-sacrificial and creative conditionality on the necessary other side. However, by this it is saying: even if the world of saints themselves is a fairy tale, then there remains the effort to be a saint, an effort at reality insofar as and as long as the gorging animal has the upper hand. Well, look. We are raising an obelisk of life and each of us is clasping in his hands one of the ropes which are attached to the top. The obelisk is leaning substantially to one side, but a majority of us linger precisely on this side in the fond contention that it is safer there, because we have to make less effort; the rope is not even tense, let alone excoriates our hands. There are only a few isolated simpletons on the opposite side and they are pulling on their rope and straining their limbs for all they are worth. These are the ones who are striving to be perfect. They know very well that, even if they exert themselves to death, then they will save their lives. Let us have no illusions about the nature of this world: life always needs help from the side on which there is a minority; life is always most threatened by the majority. But saints will always be in a minority, because the majority will always go the way of least effort. The thing that requires the least effort of all is a fall. A human being feels most happy and most safe when life is plunging into the void. In the moment when he cares for nothing other than his own safety, he is the most dangerous for life. The paradox of this world lies in the fact that those who are striving to be angels, beings that are unreal and unrealisable, are fighting for reality. William James speaks about saints as those who 'know the secret of the world'.

This is the reason why, in searching for an answer to fundamental human questions, we are attracted to the life and works of those uncategorised and uncategorisable beings that stand and fall unsupported by anyone or anything else than themselves, or at most loved by one or two faithful adherents. What is the truth of their fates, their lives and ends?

This: a human being is mortal, just like everything else in this world; his life is a currency that should be expended, never stored away. The less that you expend and the more that you save it, the harder you make your departure. When you have given everything away, then death does not come as a destroyer, but rather as a good housekeeper, who is keeping order in his affairs. When you store your life away like a treasure in a safe chest, then death comes as a thief, a robber, and a murderer. This is the entire secret of a full life, a life that is not afraid of death: giving more than taking.

If we request from death immortality, then apparently we are not asking for a reward, but rather only for justice. What kind of justice? If we have not lived, but rather have merely loaned out our entire life at an exorbitant, non-Christian, interest rate, then certainly immortality. However, if we have paid in cash and given away until nothing remains, then what kind of justice are we going to demand from death? This, and no other: not to know anything any longer. Not to know that I have been eliminated from the battle, recalled from the building site, relieved of my task, deprived of creative effort and work. What are soul and consciousness still good for, when there is nothing left to guarantee for, nothing to be responsible for, to strive for and to struggle for?

I conclude, my dear friend, my deliberations about Robert in order not to try your rare patience any longer. It is strange how clear the reasons for Robert's end were to all of us. We drove him into isolation and poured onto him the plug of our social moralities and orders, and we thinned out the air under this plug into a state of unbreathability. And when he fell and lost consciousness, we expressed our beneficent willingness to grant him as much air as he wished, on the condition of course that this would be air from our bellows. In this way, we treated the 'ill person'; in this way we re-educated the 'deranged person'. And when totally out of the blue the blow came, all of us without embarrassment said to ourselves: incorrigible, incurable. Otherwise, after all, it could not have ended in this way. And of course: it ended thus, because he refused to breathe my air, to accept my religion, my moral, economic, scientific, social, human principles! How grotesque! Such is the truth of Robert's end: He breathed in all too much of our labelled, artificial air. We truly cured him and reformed him. Our rationalistic, moral, and economic therapy functioned in such a way that every motivation for creation, for life, dried up in him. Robert killed himself: How evident and simple this was! But it is not evident and simple. The question must be posed in this way: What killed Robert? He said: I do not want to merely eke out a bare existence just for its own sake; I am not going to trudge along with a corpse. So, he did not, therefore, kill himself: he merely cleared away a corpse. Who killed Robert? If, my dear Melin, you have read these pages carefully, then you will nod your head: a surfeit of our moral and analytical interest, and absolutely zero human interest on our part.

Robert's true likeness is in his work; let us search for it there. And what is more: our true likeness is also there, because this is the likeness that captures us in our position on the high-wire. And let us not forget: there are still Roberts living among us.

BIBLIOGRAPHY

Bavink, Bernhard, *Science and God*, trans. by H. Stafford Hatfield, London: G. Bell, 1933

Bergson, Henri: *Creative Evolution*, trans. by Arthur Mitchell, New York: Henry Holt, 1911

Bergson, Henri: *The Two Sources of Morality and Religion*, trans. by R. Ashley Audra and Cloudesley Brereton, London: Macmillan, 1935

Brožek, Artur, *Nauka o dědičnosti* [Theory of Heredity], Praha: Aventinum, 1930

Croce, Benedetto: *The Philosophy of the Practical: Economic and Ethic*, trans. by Douglas Ainslie, London: Macmillan, 1913

Croce, Benedetto: *Aesthetic as Science of Expression and General Linguistic*, trans. by Douglas Ainslie, New York; Noonday Press, 1920

Deussen, Paul, *Allgemeine Geschichte der Philosophie unter besonderer Berücksichtigung der Religionen* [General History of Philosophy With Particular Reference to Religion], Leipzig: F.A. Brockhaus, 1915

Dratvová, Albína: *Problém kauzality ve fyzice* [The Problem of Causality in Physics], Praha: Česká akademie věd a umění, 1931

Driesch, Hans: *Man and the Universe*, London: G. Allen & Unwin, 1929

Durkheim, Emile: *The Rules of The Sociological Method*, trans. by W.D. Halls, New York: The Free Press, 1982

Eddington, Paul: *Space, Time and Gravitation: An Outline of the General Relativity Theory*, Cambridge: Cambridge University Press, 1920

Engels, Friedrich: *Ludwig Feuerbach: The Roots of the Socialist Philosophy*, trans. by Austin Lewis, Chicago: Charles H. Kerr, 1903

Engels, Friedrich: *Landmarks of Scientific Socialism: "Anti-Duehring"*, trans. by Austin Lewis, Chicago: Charles H. Kerr, 1907

Engels, Friedrich: *Dialectics of Nature*, 1939

Faure, Elie: *History of Art: The Spirit of the Forms*, trans. by Walter Pach, New York and London: Harper, 1930

Fiske, John: *The Destiny of Man, Viewed in the Light of his Origin*, Boston, New York: Houghton, Mifflin, 1884

Freud, Sigmund: *Leonardo da Vinci: A Psychosexual Study of an Infantile Reminiscence*, trans. by A. A. Brill, New York: Moffat, Yard, 1916

Freud, Sigmund: *Beyond the Pleasure Principle*, trans. by C. J. M. Hubback, revised by Ernest Jones, London and Vienna: International Psycho-Analytical Press, 1922

Furnas, Clifford C.: *The Next Hundred Years: The Unfinished Business of Science*, New York: Reynal & Hitchcock, 1936

Georg, Eugen: *The Adventure of Mankind*, New York: E. P. Dutton, 1931

Habáň, Metoděj: *Psychologie* [Psychology], Brno: Edice Akordu, 1937

Haldane, J. B. S.: *The Marxist Philosophy and the Sciences*, New York: Random House, 1939

Hegel, Georg Wilhelm Friedrich: *Aesthetics*, trans. by J. M. Knox, Oxford: Clarendon Press, 1975

Huizinga, Johan: *In the Shadow of Tomorrow*, trans. by W. H. Huizinga, New York: W. W. Norton & Company, 1964 (orig. Dutch, 1935)

James, William: *The Varieties of Religious Experience*, New York: Longmans, Green, 1902

Jeans, James: *The Universe Around Us*, Cambridge: Cambridge University Press, 1929

Jeans, James: *The Mysterious Universe*, Cambridge: Cambridge University Press, 1931

Jeans, James: *The New Background of Science*, New York: Macmillan, 1933

Jeans, James: *Physics and Philosophy*, Cambridge: Cambridge University Press, 1943

Jordan, Pascual: *Anschauliche Quantentheorie* [Illustrative Quantum Theory], 1936

Jung, Carl Gustav: *Collected Works Vol. 6: Psychological Types*

Jung, Carl Gustav: 'Psychological Aspects of the Mother Archetype' (1939) in *Collected Works Vol. 8: The Structure and Dynamics of the Psyche*

Jung, Carl Gustav: *Collected Works Vol. 15: Spirit in Man, Art and Literature*, trans. by R. F. C. Hull

Kallab, Jaroslav: *Trestní právo hmotné* [Criminal Law], Praha: Melantrich, 1935

Keith, Sir Arthur: *Concerning Man's Origin*, London: Watts, 1927

Kozák, Jan Blahoslav: *Přítomný stav ethiky* [The Current State of Ethics], Praha: Dědictví Komenského, 1930

Krejčí, František: *Positivní ethika* [Positivist Ethics], Praha: Jan Laichter, 1922

Le Bon, Gustave: *The Crowd: A Study of the Popular Mind*, New York: Macmillan, 1896

Levine, Israel: *The Unconscious; an Introduction to Freudian Psychology*, New York: Macmillan, 1923

Linhart, František: *Úvod do filosofie náboženství* [Philosophy of Religion], Praha: Sfinx, 1930

Lichtig, Ignaz: *Die Enstehung des Lebens durch stetige Schöpfung* [The Origin of Life Through Constant Creation], Amsterdam: Noord-Hollandsche Uitgevers Maatschappij, 1938

Nachtikal, František: *Technická fyzika* [Technical Physics], Praha: Spolek posluchačů inženýrské chemie, 1931

Nietzsche, Friedrich: *The Antichrist*, trans. by H. L. Mencken, New York: Alfred A. Knopf, 1923

Niklitschek, Alexander: *Technik des Lebens* [Technology of Life], Scherl: Berlin, 1940

Pascal, Blaise: *The Thoughts of Blaise Pascal*, trans. by W. F. Trotter, New York: P. F. Collier, 1910

Rank, Otto: *Der Künstler, Ansätze zu einer Sexual-Psychologie* [The Artist: Approaches to a Sexual Psychology], Vienna: Heller, 1907

Robinson, James Harvey: *The Mind in the Making*, London: Jonathan Cape, 1923

Rolland, Romain: *Le Voyage intérieur* [The Interior Voyage], Paris: A. Michel, 1942

Russell, Bertrand: *Problems of Philosophy*, London: William and Morgate, 1912

Sabatier, Auguste Louis: *Outlines of a Philosophy of Religion Based on Psychology and History*, trans. by Rev. T. A. Seed, London: Hodder and Stoughton, 1902

Šalda, František Xaver: *Boje o zítřek* [Battles About Tomorrow], Praha: Volné směry, 1905

Sauerland, Kurt: *Der dialektische Materialismus* [Dialectical Materialism], Neuer deutscher Verlag, Berlin 1932

Severini, Gino: *Du cubisme au classicisme* [From Cubism to Classicism], 1921

Smuts, J. C.: *Holism and Evolution*, Macmillan: London, 1927

Sorokin, Pitirim Alexandrovič: *Contemporary Sociological Theories*, New York: Harper and Brothers, 1928

Štech, Václav Vilém: *Skutečnost umění* (Úvaha o příčinách, způsobech a smyslu tvorby) [The Reality of Art (Deliberations on Causes, Methods and Meaning of Creation)], Praha: Pražské nakladatelství V. Poláčka, 1946

Tolstoy, Leo: *Anna Karenina*, trans. by Constance Garnett (1901), revised by Leonard J. Kent and Nina Berberova, New York: Random House, 1965 (Modern Library edition, 1993)

Tvrdý, Josef: *Nová filosofie* [Contemporary Philosophy], Praha: Nakladatelství Volné myšlenky, 1932

Uhlíř, Antonín: *Sociologická idea* [The Sociological Idea], Praha: Otakar Janáček, 1932

Úlehla, Vladimír: *Zamyšlení nad životem* [Thoughts About Life], Praha: Život a práce, 1939

Wells, H. G., Huxley, Julian, and Wells, G. P.: *The Science of Life*, New York, The Literary Guild, 1934

Whitehead, Alfred North: *Science and the Modern World*, Cambridge: Cambridge University Press, 1926

Woodger, J. H.: *Biological Principles*, London: Kegan Paul, Trench, Trubner, 1929

Part-Written Letter to Melin
Ivan M. Havel[147]

147 I made partial use of one of my essays on science and my obituary for Josef Šafařík in *Vesmír* magazine in 1992.

December 28, 1992

Dear Melin! – Well, well. Just look what has slipped off my pen! Melin, a name forgotten and left behind in some high school class, a nickname. God knows where it came from...

Once upon a time I discovered this name, in the preceding sentence, in a book on the table of my grandfather. It was lying there, mysterious, full of strips of paper inserted and stuck in it with notes in German and Czech, written in your (now legendary) small handwriting. I, a curious and inquisitive schoolboy, tried to read: 'The Tightrope Walker Over the Void', 'The Tightrope Walker Gets Vertigo', 'The Tightrope Walker Dances'.

That was quite a long time ago. Now the name Melin, unforgettable, belongs to you.

*

At that time you entered into my life, at a distance, and in your way you remain in it inconspicuously and at a distance to this day. Powerful like Merlin.

I wanted to become a natural scientist and circumstances led me down a path that was, so to speak, Frankensteinian. I still have a vivid memory of how you tested me on the successes of artificial intelligence and how you did not bat an eyelid, when I thought up how the human mind arises from matter, and how in turn this human mind then thinks up how a human mind arises from matter. I will never forget your roguish smile, when you asked: 'And what about death? What about the consciousness of one's own death?'

I have spent many years among scientists and sciences, and insofar as I have been capable of maintaining a distance at important moments, this has been with your help. I ascertain with surprise how few other scientists do this. Apart from that, I regret that my grandfather's translation of '*Seven Letters*' [into German] was never published abroad. (To this day I still do not know why.)

Your verdict on the stance of a science (we scientists would say: on the stance of scientism) has in the meantime become exceptionally current and relevant, and many people would read you. Many people should read you: there are still quite enough scientists who research atoms and molecules in the belief that they will find out something about, for instance, a frog. And molecules and atoms reply as much as they are capable of replying: that a frog is nothing other than a dance of atoms and molecules. If, on the contrary, we ask a frog what it thinks about molecules, it will say that they are dwarf-sized frogs.

*

Do you miss your study room? I cannot even imagine you without it. A typewriter surrounded by books. A painting by Jiří Kříž[148] on the wall. (Later on, a television was added, but in my view it never really fitted in.) Your wife Anyna [family nickname for Anna] brought tea and stretched out on the sofa. (In more difficult years you always sat me down in the kitchen – perhaps because of some suspicion about your neighbours or concerning possible wiretapping – but I did not feel so good there: I had become all too accustomed precisely to your study.)

How is it possible that our conversation was never banal? How is it possible that I was never diffident to speak with you about out-of-the-ordinary things?

Sometimes Jirka[149] also dropped by. Possibly because he wanted to hear the latest news from Prague, but he hardly ever let me get a word in, and when he did actually ask me about something, he did not wait for an answer. For me, he also, in a certain way, belonged to your study. As did the scene visible through the window, gradually

148 Czech painter (1945–1993).
149 Jiří Kuběna, poet and art historian (1936–2017).

growing darker as the evening set in until eventually it disappeared entirely in the light of the street lamps.

Once you let me have a look behind the scenes of your work. You even showed me those legendary pieces of notepaper on which for many years in your small handwriting you noted down various observations and ideas, passages copied from books, thoughts. I envisage how you perhaps compiled ornaments on the table from these small pieces of paper, the seeds of your books and essays.

*

Why, Melin, does it irritate you, when someone calls you a philosopher? The fact that you do not intend to share this term with university departments, institutions and professionals? I know that it is more agreeable for you when you are regarded as a writer (and it is also true that it is writers who regard you more highly). However, your time cannot be measured in the number of sentences written. Rather your sentences can be measured by the number of thoughts in them, concealed in every one of them. These sentences are metaphorical, aphoristic, and ironic – just like your life. Sentences whose authorship cannot be mistaken: 'The less you are, the more you have.' 'Is a human being a self-deception of an animal, or an animal a self-deception of a human being?' 'On the gallows of Golgotha power wanted to put an end to a human being, but on the cross of Golgotha a human being put an end to power.' 'I die, therefore I am.'

You died almost on the same day as your second and final book, *On the Path to the Ultimate* (*Cestou k poslednímu*), appeared on your desk … still with the fresh aroma of printer's ink. All of those of us who knew you felt in some way that the fate of this exceptional – constantly almost finished, constantly revised – work was your personal fate. We did not differentiate between you and your book, and neither did your wonderful Anyna, who said to us over your grave: 'Don't be surprised that I am not crying!' The theme of your book is death. Death and mankind, death and power, death on the cross, death as a verdict, death as an entreaty.

*

Science does not recount truth about the world; it merely recounts what the world would be like, if it possessed truth. Science does not fascinate us with truth, but with power. Science and technology are generally viewed as instruments that can be used to the benefit of life and also to its detriment. As far as human beings are concerned, what is more decisive is how they behave toward their death. And here science in its very principle robs human beings of death as a personal challenge for self-identification through values transcending death; it thus creates an insuperable antagonism between mankind and power, between the cross and the gallows.

In both your books you are not very flattering to science. However, it would be necessary to read them in their entirety for us to recognize that this is merely a part of your frontal denial of power in any kind of form, and that you appeal to us – who alone among living creatures bear the burden and challenge of our mortality. If science describes death, then it most probably describes it as the cessation of some kind of process. Perhaps it is appropriate to stop defective processes. However, in between this general assertion and the concrete stopping of a concrete process there is an intermediate element: a human being who should decide on this. It is his decision and his responsibility; neither science nor the law can remove this from him.

We humans have the privilege that we know that death is treading behind us. One specific death, behind each of us, his own. You cited Dietrich Bonhoeffer: 'Not external circumstances, but we ourselves make death what it is: a death of which we are voluntarily aware.' To take life away from a person means stealing his death. About this science is silent.

AFTERWORD

Hrádeček (V. Havel's cottage, near Trutnov),
from the left: Olga Havlová, Ondřej Hrab,
Václav Havel, Jiří Kuběna, Josef Šafařík,
Anna Šafaříková, Zdeněk Urbánek, Josef Topol

A VOICE CALLING IN THE DESERT –
SEVEN LETTERS TO MELIN AS INITIATION BOOK

And only where there are graves are there resurrections.

Friedrich Nietzsche

A philosopher worthy of the name has never said more than a single thing; and even then it is something he has tried to say, rather than actually said. And he has said only one thing because he has seen only one point; and at that it was not so much a vision as a contact. This contact has furnished an impulse, this impulse a movement, and… this movement, which is as it were a kind of swirling of dust taking a particular form, becomes visible to our eyes only through what it has collected along its way…

Henri Bergson

If you are struggling in vain to recall from where exactly you know the name of the author of this book, then do not be embarrassed – neither in the Czech cultural milieu is Josef Šafařík a widely known personality. However, even today it can happen that a curious reader can come across one of his books in an antiquarian bookshop, become engrossed after starting to read it, and then leave with a book by an author whose name means nothing to him. Only later does the reader uncover the half-secret and half-forgotten tale of Šafařík's life.

However, if you know the work of dramatist, dissident, and former Czech President Václav Havel – in great detail – you may have encountered Šafařík's name, albeit only in a couple of mentions. Even in the consciousness of specialists, in many cases the name of Josef Šafařík and his works live on only as a footnote. Let us start from one of these few fragments.

An attentive reader of the interview conducted by Karel Hvížďala with Václav Havel could notice this assertion: 'The very first Czech philosopher to have some influence on me was Josef Šafařík, a reclusive philosopher from Brno. Thanks to my grandfather, I had known him since my childhood and his *Seven Letters to Melin* was my personal philosophical bible in my early youth.'[150] Let us search further: if we had in our hands an original edition of Havel's third play *The Increased Difficulty of Concentration,* we would see that the dramatist dedicated the play precisely to Josef Šafařík (at that time essentially unknown outside of a narrow circle of close friends). Šafařík even wrote a philosophical deliberation for the play's program and an afterword for the printed edition. Havel also refers to precisely these texts by Šafařík in the 92nd letter of his famous *Letters to Olga,* which concerns Ionesco and the Theatre of the Absurd (that is, authors presented in Czechoslovakia in the 1960s who were a major inspiration both for Havel and Šafařík), when he paraphrases: 'Šafařík correctly distinguishes between truth and information: information is portable and transmissible, whereas it is by no means as simple with truth.'[151] However, such a brief mention hardly captures the deep relationship between the two over many years. In interview and television documentaries Havel occasionally talked about Šafařík's influence on him, but in his own essays he never cited Šafařík. Commentators have thus been inclined rather to see a connection with the philosophy of Jan Patočka, who was one of Havel's fellow spokespersons for Charter 77, or to examine Havel's links to well-known European philosophers, such as Heidegger, Kant, and others.

Nevertheless, Šafařík is present somewhere in the background. Even in Havel's last book, the self-ironic autobiographical collage

---

150 Václav Havel, *Disturbing the Peace: A Conversation with Karel Hvížďala,* New York: A. Knopf 1990, pp. 18–19.
151 Václav Havel, *Letters to Olga: June 1979 – September 1982,* (London: Faber and Faber, 1991), p. 224.

To the Castle and Back, this friend, mentor, and spiritual teacher has his place:

Hrádeček, December 9, 2005

I remember my friend, the great but little-known Czech philosopher Josef Šafařík, who spent about twenty years writing his last book – it was called *On the Path to the Ultimate*. He wrote it, you might say, in blood; he was always rewriting it and he was never finished. His other friends and I tried to persuade him to let it go, that it was important that it exist and circulate, but he wouldn't listen. Meanwhile conditions changed and his book was actually able to be published by a proper publisher. On the very day that they brought him the first copy from the publisher, he died. Clearly, the moment he had completed his life's work, his life lost its meaning. Perhaps unconsciously, he had held back from completing it, so that he would still have a reason to live, and therefore he went on living. (pp. 336–337)

It is noteworthy that Havel does not talk about the topics of Šafařík's final work, but rather about his creative approach – about the mysterious connection between his life and his work, which really led to him dying, at the age of eighty-five, three days after the book's publication. It evidently attests to a deep affinity, when Havel, at the conclusion of his life, in a book taking stock of his own life, posits a link precisely between the conclusion and completion of Šafařík's work and his life's journey. However, what Havel neglects to mention, out of modesty, is that Šafařík managed to add just one more dedication to the finished printouts of the book – precisely to Havel: 'To an old friend and a young president.'

These are only a few brief mentions, about which it is sufficient to write a short footnote. However, this does not clarify Havel's fascination with Šafařík, a fascination shared by many of Havel's friends, including dramatist Josef Topol and poet Jiří Kuběna... Who, then, is the personality hiding behind these brief mentions? And how was it that *Seven Letters to Melin* had such an influence on Václav Havel – and not only on him?

A LIFE IN SECLUSION

The attempt to ascertain at least some basic facts is complicated by the legendary private disposition of the subject of our inquiry: Josef Šafařík never sought admiration and above all else valued the peace and quiet that enabled him to concentrate on reflecting and deliberating on words. In 1948, when his first work was finally due to be published, after it had won a competition held by the Družstevní práce publishing house for an original philosophical essay, he lamented in a letter to a friend: 'They want some information about my life and work, and I feel as though my blessed privacy is starting to crumble. I do not want to even think about what is going to descend on my head now. God have mercy on me, the jury and Družstevní práce! You, who know to a large extent what is in the book, will believe me that this is no pose. If the book does not encounter people of good will – and I do not suppose that is very likely – then I am in for a right circus. Apart from that, God protect me from good people as well. They are the most difficult to protect yourself from.' Šafařík's scepticism was well justified.

The basic facts at least are known. Josef Šafařík was born in 1907 – just like Jan Patočka, but fate took him down a completely different path in life than that of the world-famous philosopher. Šafařík grew up in the family of the owner of a prosperous engineering firm, and it was taken for granted that as the oldest son, and thus the firm's future inheritor, he would study engineering. Although he did not do badly in his studies at Brno's University of Technology, where he completed a degree specializing in hydro-engineering, nevertheless since secondary school he had longed to pursue a literary path. A definitive decision was not made until 1938, shortly after he turned thirty. Shortly after his father's sudden death, he decided to liquidate the family firm and attempt to make a living in the field of art. He was supported in this risky gesture for life by his future wife Anna. (They had met in 1936.) She was also instrumental in his decision to give up his post at the city construction office, which was a guaranteed job for life. From then on, he lived practically without a source of regular income. For the meanwhile, his wife, who believed in his talent, ensured a living for the household. (One of the paradoxes of the life situation of Josef and Anna Šafařík: they did not get married until 1946, after twenty-one years of acquaintance. Before the war, she – as an employee of a health insurance company – would have been immediately dismissed after marriage, while during the war marriage was impossible because Šafařík was in hiding to escape being sent for forced labour by the Nazi authorities.)

It was while in hiding during World War II, under the Nazi protectorate, that Šafařík wrote the first pages of his essay that would eventually appear as *Seven Letters to Melin* – apparently while sitting on boxes of coal in the cellar. Ten whole years filled with unsuccessful attempts at writing a play, a novel, and short stories lie between his fateful decision to devote himself to literature and the eventual publication of his first book: ten years in which Šafařík took part in all kinds of literary competitions, without ever asking for advice or for anyone to put in a good word on his behalf. At the time, his wife, not without bitterness, wrote in her diary: 'He says that in this way at least he will not be indebted to anyone.' It was not until the competition held by Družstevní práce publishing house in 1947 that the anticipated breakthrough occurred. The specialist jury was shocked and taken aback: an unknown engineer-philosopher, an autodidact, had written a wide-ranging, erudite, and indubitably original essay.

However, events were already heading relentlessly in a different direction: in February 1948 the complicated and dynamic changes in the political situation of post-war Czechoslovakia culminated in a communist putsch. The Communist Party took hold of power, and for a further forty years Šafařík was doomed to live in a totalitarian state – with occasional thaws and relaxations. This made itself felt very quickly. The book was published in September 1948. In November one single critical review appeared in the official Communist Party newspaper *Rudé právo*, which concluded that the book evidently did not correspond with the officially propagated Marxist-Leninist philosophy and was absolutely unacceptable: the book was apparently 'superfluous, even harmful', contained 'reactionary ideas', and defended a historically superceded bourgeois relativism. Commenting on the further creative aims of the author, the reviewer even states: 'We are afraid that he will not be given any opportunity for this!' Symptomatic of the mood of the time is in particular the admonishing conclusion of the entire review: 'However, we must also pose the question of what aim the Družstevní práce publishing house was pursuing by issuing this thoroughly bad book? Unfortunately, books like this are not infrequent here in our country. In the future it is going to be necessary to control our book market much more carefully and to remove in advance such superfluous and harmful books, which are in essence alien and inimical to the interests and needs of our people.' These words were no mere rhetorical questions: the Družstevní práce publishing house, one of the key cultural firms of interwar Czechoslovakia, was confiscated, and Josef Šafařík's book was *de facto* banned and unsold copies were destroyed. Nevertheless, some copies were successfully sold, and so for the next forty years curious readers would be able to find it in family libraries or on the dusty shelves of a second-hand bookshop.

Šafařík reacted to the political situation with an 'internal emigration'. However, after 1948 it was no longer possible to live as an independent author of his own will. (He would have to have been an official member of the Federation of Authors and in this way legalized his status.) In order to avoid an accusation of social parasitism, which was often used by the ruling regime to criminalize persons attempting to lead an independent life outside of the system, every year he always tried to find a temporary job for a few months. In 1959, when he was once again involuntarily spending time in manual labour, he fell into a deep concrete pit in a sugar factory. As a result of the accident he suffered long-term injuries (impaired and double vision), which led to him being granted a disability pension. However, the commission stated: 'He has not done much to contribute to building socialism. We will award him the lowest possible pension.' Thus, Šafařík, without ever seeking one, gained a minimum, but regular, income. More importantly, he obtained the official status of a disability pensioner, which enabled him to survive without being further persecuted by the system as a parasite. He later ironically declared about this: 'In a period when authors were granted well-paid creative holidays, were able to leave their places of employment and towns, and escape these distractions to stay in well-heated castles or villas with all comforts, I had to fight for a minimum of peace and quiet, and if it had not been for the injury which made me into someone – that is, a pensioner – whereas previously I had been a no one, because I did not have a regular job, I would never have had any peace from snoopers, zealots, the envious, and state offices.'

It was only in the 1960s that the thinker was drawn out of his isolation by some people who, in spite of the severed ties and oppressive atmosphere, found their way to him. So, poet Jiří Kuběna, playwrights Václav Havel and Josef Topol, and many others gradually appeared in his small apartment in Brno. It became apparent that, even though it was only possible to obtain a copy of *Seven Letters to Melin* with great difficulty by searching around second-hand bookshops, for many people the book had the significance of an initiation – and led many to seek out a personal meeting with the unknown, half-forgotten thinker. (Some of them were even surprised to learn that the author of this strange and difficult-to-categorize book was still alive.)

In the context of Czech culture, the 1960s represent a major upturn. A relative easing of the regime takes place: censorship is limited; books appear by authors hitherto banned; new theatres and literary magazines are founded; relations with foreign countries are strengthened. We sometimes speak about this period, possibly somewhat exaggeratedly, as the 'Golden Sixties'. The fact is that, between the years 1948 and 1989, this period was the freest and culturally richest. Culture, which had been centrally directed, standardized, and censored in the 1950s, bloomed for a period of almost ten years.

It was also during this period that the most spectacular event of Šafařík's life took place. A circle of young admirers and friends founded – perhaps a little bit satirically – the Society of Friends of Josef Šafařík, which succeeded in organizing a public lecture for him in Prague, in the hall of the Mánes art gallery, a centre of cultural life at that time. Šafařík presented a new essay, later published as 'Man in the Machine Age' (*Člověk ve věku stroje*). The lecture was delivered in spring 1967 in the presence of the intellectual elite of the time: among those present were poet and artist Jiří Kolář, art theoretician Jindřich Chalupecký, literary historian Václav Černý, philosopher Jan Patočka, and many others. The interest shown by creative artists, literary figures, and people from the theatre world confirmed that the book and also its author – even though they had been expelled from official culture – were very well known in certain circles. In retrospect Havel said about this: 'I noticed some kind of echo, or reverberation… in response to this book, and what was interesting was that many artists with whom I was in contact in the 1950s – unofficially of course – and also people connected with art in one way or another, such as Jiří Kolář, Jindřich Chalupecký, and others, knew this book well and held it in high esteem, while philosophers did not take it seriously. They regarded it as the work of some kind of weird amateur.'

At this time Šafařík published several short texts in magazines and theatre programmes. After August 1968, the invasion of the Warsaw

Pact forces and the violent suppression of the so-called Prague Spring, he once again withdrew from public life. There followed the period of so-called 'normalization', which lasted for the whole of the 1970s and 1980s up until the Velvet Revolution. The atmosphere of this period was incisively captured by Václav Havel in his so-called "Letter to Gustav Husák" from 1975, addressed to the then Czechoslovak president. Šafařík maintained contact only with his friends, the number of whom however decreased. He himself refused to be a teacher to anyone; he wanted to be only a companion or a guide. He also remained detached from the majority of dissident activities and refused to sign Charter 77, stating that as an artist and thinker he was obliged to express himself exclusively through his work, and that he did not intend ever to become mixed up in politics. The ageing man concentrated his efforts on his final and comprehensive work, the first version of which he finished in 1984, but which was not published until spring 1992. Three days later Josef Šafařík died. The monumental essay of more than six hundred pages bears the revelatory title On the Path to the Ultimate (*Cestou k poslednímu*).

These are merely the outlines of someone's life story, but in this case more than any other what Šafařík wrote in a letter to Josef Topol applies: 'However, I now know that silence is depth, and that words and deeds are merely superficial, fluttering in the wind. In silence there is a fundamental encounter. I recall Georges Bernanos, who says that a person comes from the inside and returns to the inside.' The description of events about a man who truly and consciously detached himself from public space does not say a great deal about very much. We must look into his works, look inside...

LETTERS WRITTEN TO HIS ALTER EGO

Šafařík first book does not begin like a systematic philosophical tract, but rather as a novel in letter form: as a philosophical deliberation in letters. We can only speculate about exactly what the first version of the text was like, but from surviving literary attempts (unpublished by Šafařík) we can conclude that for a long time he was searching for a way in which to give a persuasive literary form to his deliberations. His dramatic attempts at plays of the Ibsen type suffer from overcomplicated plots and rather unconvincingly created characters, but they also contain noteworthy dialogues in which the characters try to solve existential questions. These early plays are also possibly too autobiographical. The first version of *Seven Letter to Melin*, which has not survived, was apparently in the form of a novel – about several friends who go for a trip to the countryside and engage in debate. When we read the definitive version, we can still find some traces of novelistic structure: all of the deliberations are developed around a story, around a crucial, personally felt situation – the suicide of an artist, the motivation for which the writer attempts to understand and explain to the letter's recipient. Fragments of novelistic narration, snippets of concrete situations, are thus continually anchored in Šafařík's thinking and constantly impart a personal level to it: after all, this is a case of the suicide of a friend, of trying to comprehend the sense of this suicide, and thereby also of the sense of our life. Šafařík's search for a literary form is thus a case of a search for a balance between personal expression and capturing a process of thinking; it is a search for his own voice – a personal, personally guaranteed voice.

In contrast to systematic, 'academic' philosophy, Šafařík places a fundamental emphasis on form, on literary quality, on style. We can understand Šafařík as an 'essayist', but by this we are not saying very much – the philosophical-literary essay is an unclear category. However, if we seek for parallels and comparisons in history, then we can perhaps say that Šafařík is closer to Platonic dialogue than to Aristotelian system-building. He would certainly have got along with Montaigne, and among novelists he highly esteemed Flaubert – precisely for the refinement of his style. A forerunner in literary stylization is, for instance, Kierkegaard. Šafařík did not make use of pseudonyms and literary masks, but one of his significant texts from the 1970s, Nightmare (*Noční můra*), is once again composed as a dramatic dialogue, in which the author remorselessly counterbalances the arguments of both sides, and it is as though he himself is hidden behind both masks. And it is worthy of note that Melin, the name of the person addressed in the letters, is actually Šafařík's nickname from secondary school, and some of his close friends (for instance, Havel and Topol) addressed him using this nickname. When we consider this detail, *Seven Letters to Melin* appears to us as a refined construction: the author is actually writing to himself; or to be more precise, the author, who gradually defines himself as a thinker or an artist, is writing to his friend, a natural scientist, whom he addresses by his own nickname. It is rather as though this is not a case of letters, but rather of an internal discussion between two aspects of one personality – the artistic and the scientific; a discussion that reflects Šafařík's own path in life as an engineer who wants to become a man of letters. It is a case of an internal dialogue (in the form of letters), which is actually one of the oldest philosophical approaches, associated already with Socrates. The question also arises of whether this Robert who committed suicide is a real person, or whether he is merely a further projection of the author's I. Šafařík is talking with himself about himself... To formulate this in terms that are those of Šafařík himself: a spectator and a guarantor inside a person engage in a dispute about the person himself...

Already in his unpublished juvenilia Šafařík circled around the theme of suicide, and many of his idealistic heroes choose suicide rather than acceding to the values of provincial small-town society. Artist Robert, therefore, is an embodiment of an extreme, borderline situation in which – according to Šafařík – a person is confronted with his or her own mortality and has to confirm the values by which he or she lives. In reply to a question from one of his friends about what was the biggest temptation in life for him, Šafařík apparently replied simply and without hesitation: 'Suicide.' The theme of mortality, of the finality of human being, is a lifelong theme of Šafařík, and in his *On the Path to the Ultimate* this theme is transformed into a discussion on the sense of sacrifice (and the sense of tragedy). However, in the form in which he formulates this problem in the pages of *Seven Letters to Melin*, Šafařík – unconsciously, and thereby all the more surprisingly – agrees with the opinion of Albert Camus that the only really fundamental philosophical problem is... suicide.

Even though it may seem at first sight that the core of the book is the conflict between an artist and society, Šafařík gradually shifts his deliberations to a more general level – he is concerned with the conflict between authentic being and hypocritical society. This conflict also has an autobiographical basis arising precisely from Šafařík's attempts to make his way as a writer in the face of opposition from those around him, who viewed him at best as an idealist, and at worst as a down-and-out failure and a dangerous social malcontent. His later wife complains in her dairies several times about how unbearably her relatives behaved toward Šafařík, whom in essence they never took seriously, because as a man without a regular income and a reputable profession he could therefore simply never be a 'good catch'. Šafařík makes use of this personal, specific level only as an inspiration; he interprets it as a general problem, the analysis of which appealed to readers in the 1950s and can still be current and topical today.

He was not of course the first person to raise this theme in modern society. We can also formulate this differently: Šafařík wants to unify his work and his life, but the hypocrisy of society (whether small-town interwar society or post-war totalitarian society) prevents him in this. In the Czech context this premise about an existential unity between the work of a creator and his or her fate or personality is associated primarily with the modernist literary critic F. X. Šalda. In the 1890s, inspired by Nietzsche among others, Šalda became the spokesperson who formulated the tenets of Czech modernism. His approaches and critical judgements were formative for several generations. There were two cornerstones of Šalda's programme:

style and precisely the unity of an artist's life and work. For Šalda, the very personality of a creative artist was the real and essential result of creation: 'Such works are almost immaterial. They are only a symbol and a trace of the dark and grand military campaign of the soul, mere disembowelled erratic boulders, twisted pillars, and abandoned cremation grounds – when the lightning has gone out and the voice has faded away in the dark and the night.' (F. X. Šalda, *Osobnost a dílo* [Personality and Artwork])

From F. X. Šalda it is only a step to one of the most distinctive persons who had an influence upon Šafařík – Friedrich Nietzsche. Anyone who has read *Seven Letters to Melin* in detail may be surprised now – Nietzsche's name appears only several times, when Šafařík polemicizes with Nietzsche's concept of suicide and self-sacrifice. Nevertheless, Nietzsche is more present in *Letters to Melin* than it may seem at first sight: it is Nietzsche's impulses that Šafařík recasts and personally transforms, and thus he does not cite Nietzsche, but rather proceeds forward in Nietzsche's spirit. Sometimes we can easily detect cases where Šafařík has been inspired by Nietzsche: we should be aware that the central metaphor of a person as a tightrope walker who proceeds uncertainly over the abyss of nothingness, but then begins to dance when he finds internal certitude, is actually a thorough development of the comparison that we find in *Thus Spoke Zarathustra*. (Several times a person is compared to a tightrope walker, and Zarathustra – in the states of his greatest mental composure – moves around on the Earth as a dancer or appears as a dancing star.) In *Twilight of Idols* Nietzsche puts this forward with his typical brevity as a principle in one of his aphorisms: 'To enter only those situations where you cannot have any counterfeit virtues, where instead, like the tightrope walker on his tightrope, you either fall down or remain standing – or come away.'[152]

---

[152] Friedrich Nietzsche, *The Anti-Christ, Ecce Homo, Twilight of the Idols: And Other Writings*, (Cambridge: Cambridge University Press, 2005), aphorism 21, p. 158.

It makes no sense here to talk about plagiarism or epigonism. It is simply typical for Šafařík that he aligns so strongly with some authors that he accepts their thoughts, but then transforms them, and constructs from them his own – entirely personal and distinctive – universe. Meanwhile, Šafařík affirmed his esteem for Nietzsche very often, and we could add him to those few people in the Czech context who were influenced by the great destroyer. (I have in mind the already mentioned F. X. Šalda, as well as translator Otakar Fischer and philosopher Ladislav Klíma.) Once Šafařík wrote among his working theses: 'Nietzsche once said that life without music has no sense. I would express this more broadly: life without art has no sense.'

This entire thought structure of the book is sustained by the author's attempt at a pregnancy of style. However, style here is not merely a literary category, but rather an existential one – in the sense formulated by one of Šafařík's inspirations, F. X. Šalda: 'Style is nothing other than organized pain, desire, and anxiety, and the necessity of the era, an expression of necessity, and not external coquetry and attractiveness, speculation for cheap applause.' (F. X. Šalda: *Boje o zítřek - Duše a dílo* [Battles Over Tomorrow – Spirit and Artwork]) This is precisely the reason why the book is structured as a personal meditation: it develops from a concrete, existential situation – and precisely the refined style imparts to the book its personal urgency, sense of entreaty, mesmerism, and sometimes even belligerence and irony. In some ways Šafařík is a poetic philosopher or a philosophizing poet (and let us recall that Nietzsche is also talked about in this way, as also is his dark inspiration Heraclitus). The precision of his style sometimes leads to aphorisms – some statements in the book have a terseness, a forcefulness, and a poetry: 'Death is a shadow thrown by a soul blinded by reason.' (*Melin*, Chapter 6, p. 262) With this citation we have touched upon one more of the central themes of the book, which is the overcoming of nothingness. In view of the fact that, for Šafařík, reality is primarily an internal matter, nothingness (and death) is not a physical experience concerning absence or emptiness, but an existential angst from the transitoriness of the world and an absence of sense – and, therefore, this sense must be created over and over again.

Jiří Kuběna, one of Šafařík's close friends and affiliates, who was also a propagator of his works, said that in its diction the book reminded him of the poems of Karel Hynek Mácha, the most significant Czech poet of the nineteenth century and a leading figure of Czech Romanticism. Let us recall one of the most striking passages: 'So, if beauty is the poetry of recollection, then this means that beauty is an experience of death. Through recollection, our heart finds itself in that critical, borderline, concluding position in life, in which we feel that we are leaving and will no longer return. Beauty is that intense embrace with being and things when we feel that we are saying goodbye forever. Things are beautiful not because beauty is one of their characteristics; they are beautiful because the eyes that are enraptured are mortal. Death lives in us from our birth, and looking through its eyes, we see beautiful things and beings worthy of love. Beauty is an inaudible harmony in which the mortal in things converses with the mortal in us. There is no beauty in things themselves; only if we touch them with a certain intimate caress, with an ingenuous soul, with a brave heart, do they induce us to turn away toward departure. Beauty is the heart's speechless, intimate understanding with things about the highest certainty, about the final truth. Beauty is life intensified to its limit by the experience of death.'[153] It is merely a question of taste whether we detect echoes of Nietzsche here (and his deliberations on forgetting) or precisely Karel Hynek Mácha (who in his famous poem *Máj* [*May*] was the first Czech poet to demonstrate the close affinity between beauty and the terrifying nothingness of death) or we allow ourselves merely to be swept away by Šafařík's voice itself.

---

153 *Melin*, Chapter 7, p. 346.

If we were to attempt to characterize *Seven Letters to Melin* in general, then we could say that stylistic refinement is conjoined in it with an attempt to create an existentially personal, subjective conception of morality, of personal responsibility: the conflict between an artist and society, but actually in fact between a human being and society, leads to a radical emphasis on the personal guaranteeing of a person's actions and on personal authenticity. This radical moral individualism also manifests itself in Šafařík's explication of a 'classic' philosophical case – the death of Socrates. For Šafařík this 'first' philosopher is worthy of being followed not on account of his ideas, but on account of the thoroughness with which he personally guaranteed these ideas – even as far as his own death. Therefore, in the end Šafařík – in a somewhat utopian fashion, possibly even anarchically – dreams of a world of authentic human beings. He formulates this simply in his last essay: 'even if a world made up of saints alone is a fairy tale, then there remains the effort to be a saint, an effort at reality insofar as, and as long as, the gorging animal has the upper hand.'[154] This combination of subjectivism and style is also typical for the other thinkers whom we have already mentioned previously. This was critically, but aptly, characterized by Roger Scruton: 'Kierkegaard's brilliance as a writer and critic more than makes amends for his magnificent philosophical failure. A study of a philosopher with whom he has often been compared suggests that this ethic of subjectivity will always require literary gifts of a high order. These Friedrich Wilhelm Nietzsche (1844–1900) certainly possessed.'[155]

---

154 *Melin*, Chapter 7, p. 353.
155 Roger Scruton, *A Short History of Modern Philosophy*, (Routledge 1995), p. 185.

A BOOK WHICH APPEARED
AT THE WRONG MOMENT

In order to understand at least part of the enchantment that the book held for Václav Havel, Josef Topol, and Jiří Kuběna, or for other artists and literary figures who discovered the book for themselves in the darkest 1950s in communist Czechoslovakia, we must clarify the exact context in which the book appeared.

The brief post-war interlude from 1945 until 1948 was characterized in Czechoslovakia not only by a power struggle, but also by an attempt to restore severed cultural ties. A great deal was done in this direction by art theoretician Jindřich Chalupecký, who attempted to introduce existentialism – by then already relatively established and coming into fashion – into the Czech context. Chalupecký carried on the work started by Group 42 (Skupina 42), a loose association of poets and creative artists formed during World War II. In their artistic works, the members of this group attempted to transcend avant-garde principles and *de facto* moved in the direction of a kind of form of 'existentialism'. In 1947, one issue of the quarterly literary journal *Listy*, edited by Chalupecký, was devoted exclusively to existentialist thinking and literature. As well as short stories by Franz Kafka, the quarterly published essays by Sartre, Camus, and Lev Shestov for the first time in Czechoslovakia – and for a long period also the last time. At the same time, literary critic and historian Václav Černý was giving lectures on existentialism at Prague's Charles University. These lectures resulted in the publication of a collection of studies entitled First Booklet on Existentialism (*První sešit o existencialismu*), which was published at the beginning of 1948. Within a week the book was sold out, and extra copies were immediately ordered. However, already in autumn of the same year, publication of the second volume, entitled Second Booklet on Existentialism (*Druhý sešit o existencialismu*), was not allowed, and Chalupecký's *Listy* was likewise banned.

Šafařík's book was also published and subsequently banned in this period.

We can, therefore, only speculate about whether – if there had been the possibility for an appropriately erudite critical reflection and reception of Šafařík's first work – features close to existentialism would have been recognized. In his book Václav Černý wrote: 'There are truly as many existentialisms as there are existentialists,' when he tried to represent the variety of existentialist thinking. And it would certainly have been possible to include also Šafařík in some such thing. However, in the *Second Textbook on Existentialism* (which was not published until 1989), when Černý seeks for a specific Czech existentialism, he judges that the typical feature of this is a 'moral focus of existentialist feeling' and praises in particular the poetry of Jiří Orten as the most striking example of this. He concludes his interpretation of Orten's poetry with these words: 'If every creative artist has himself as an extreme limit, toward which he is consciously or unconsciously heading, this is certainly the case of Jiří Orten. For me there is no doubt about the ideal extreme limit to which he was inclined: it is a saint without God. The age little understands just how terribly characteristic this type is for it.' We can only shudder when we realize that Šafařík's appeal for a guarantor, for an authentic being, is in its way an appeal for undogmatic and non-institutionalized personal sainthood. Consider this statement – already cited here once before – by Šafařík: 'even if a world made up solely of saints is a fairy tale, then there remains the effort to be a saint, an effort at reality insofar as, and as long as, the gorging animal has the upper hand.' The similarity of Šafařík's words to Václav Černý's formulation is striking. It is as though Černý wrote a review of *Seven Letters to Melin* without knowing he was doing so. However, unfortunately, as far as the reaction of Černý, Chalupecký, and their contemporaries is concerned, in practice we have to depend only on indirectly reported responses. In connection with Šafařík's lecture at Mánes in Prague in 1967, Anna Šafaříková wrote: 'A crowd of people before eight o'clock. Václav Černý, Jindřich Chalupecký, Josef Palivec, and so on demonstratively announced their presence.' She also noted this comment made by Šafařík: 'One sentence from Václav Černý ('We must go to Šafařík's lecture to demonstrate our support') or Jiří Kolář ('We lived for twenty years from *Seven Letters*') gives me more than they can possibly guess.' Unfortunately, we cannot cite any more evidence.

However, we can perhaps imagine the way in which Šafařík's book, begun in the 1930s, resonated in the 1950s. The book's emphasis on the authenticity and free expression of an artist, and on the freedom of a human being, was terrifyingly concrete at that time. Similarly, Šafařík's rejection of a reductive natural-scientific view of reality, and of the objectification and bureaucratization of the human world, became a criticism of so-called scientific Marxism or scientific communism, of all efforts to govern the state in a centralized, totalitarian, and allegedly scientific way – and not only the state, but almost every aspect of human existence. In those dark times Šafařík's anarchic emphasis on the individuality of being was a defence of the very right of a creative soul for bare existence. At a time when the communist regime was persecuting many poets and even imprisoning some of them (including Catholic poet Jan Zahradníček), Šafařík's words must have been a revelation for those creative artists who had been driven out of the public arena into the seclusion of their studies and their workshops.

WHITHER TO PROCEED ON PATH TO THE ULTIMATE...

In spite of the fact that a circle of admirers developed around Šafařík in the 1950s, no school formed around him such as that which was created – despite all obstructions on the part of the communist regime – by Jan Patočka. Šafařík did not shut himself off from anyone, but he refused to be a teacher in the sense of leading anything in an organized way (for instance, the 'apartment seminars' held in people's homes). He was rather sought out as a spiritual adviser and friend. He strictly refused to take responsibility for other people's lives: in his opinion, every person had to resolve him or herself the question of guaranteeing for his or her own authentic life.

Because of this approach, in the 1970s and 1980s, during the years of so-called normalization, Šafařík found himself partly outside of dissident circles, even though he was always in contact with them. It was this – in some ways radical – emphasis on personal responsibility that led to him declining to sign Charter 77: on the one hand he insisted that an artist should not enter into any kind of relationship with politics, and on the other hand he was more and more sceptical toward power as such. In the end, in his final work – in a very absolutist way – he did not see anything positive at all in power. Now, in addition to the beginning of Šafařík's thought, let us also take a look at its conclusion.

In *On the Path to the Ultimate* his lifelong polemic with society and power was reflected in this fatalistic assertion: 'Contemporary free-thinking democracy has a propensity to gravitate of its own accord toward dictatorship. Democracy is merely an interregnum on power's path to totalitarianism.' (*Cestou k poslednímu*, p. 275) With a hindsight of almost thirty years since the book's publication, we should think once again about why Václav Havel described this essay as a 'book of the future'. I fear that, for the current state of the world, the following sentence is more and more apposite: 'Bureaucrat-ism is the senility of power; democracy a mere interregnum' (*Cestou k poslednímu*, p. 260). Šafařík's absolutized scepticism is here directed at society in general. Here the conflict between the individual and society, first put forward in *Seven Letters to Melin*, is also updated. However, over the course of time Šafařík's criticism of society has now become much harsher. In the optimistic mood of building a new free society in Czechoslovakia in the early 1990s, shortly after the Velvet Revolution, the scepticism of the old thinker seemed excessive – possibly even like the bitterness of old age. Among the targets of criticism in the book, Šafařík also takes aim at some activities pursued in dissident circles for the promotion of human and civic rights: he reproached them with being ultimately concerned with these civic rights as a share in power, while the essential human values remained to one side. This is a problem that has accompanied the question of political engagement since time immemorial – where is the border between public engagement and collaboration with the system?

It was evidently precisely this scepticism of Šafařík's, his withdrawal from public space, and his distance toward dissident circles that led to him remaining a lonely figure on the margin of cultural events. Thus, thanks to his engagement in Charter 77, Václav Havel is primarily associated – among Czech philosophers and thinkers – with Jan Patočka. In the view from abroad, Patočka dominates quite inevitably – firstly, because he is a philosophical personality in his own right, and secondly because Šafařík's works have so far been almost exclusively available only in Czech. Meanwhile, both Šafařík and Patočka have their significance for the formation of Havel's philosophical outlook, but each in an entirely different way. While Patočka (but also Heidegger, Kant, and Husserl) are primarily creators of ideas with which Havel felt a need to engage, Šafařík is a personal friend, a guide, a creative personality – that is, a non-academic philosopher, in contrast to those university, systematic 'classics'. Šafařík, on the contrary, was outside of all systems and thereby provoked and inspired. However, so far Šafařík's obstinate voice, insisting that an artist should not have anything to do with power, has had no place in interpretations of the life story of Václav Havel as a literary figure who became a politician. Nevertheless, I dare to contend that, for Havel, Šafařík's scepticism and his doubts had their significance: they could have reminded him of the limitations of any kind of secular or godly power. We know that, even though the dispute regarding Charter 77 divided the long-term friends politically, there remained a great human respect between them. Even though he did not agree with Havel in many things, Šafařík nevertheless regarded Havel as 'his' president.

Many of the themes that Šafařík formulated at the turn of the 1940s and 1950s in the hermetic seclusion of his study-library in Brno have since become a common part of public discussion and sometimes even only a banalized phrase – today every commentator can berate technology, and to defend individuality in the post-liberal world is perhaps superfluous. However, in precisely those places where the poet speaks more forcefully than the philosopher, the thinker, Šafařík's texts speak powerfully still today: a short paragraph encapsulates the core of a problem with passionate emphasis. Such places in his works are worth seeking out. And thus, as for many it may once have been a lone voice crying in the desert, Šafařík's voice – placing an emphasis on fundamental existential questions and implacably demanding a personal reply – can be a challenge for today's globalized, bureaucratized post-... world.

David Drozd

The Václav Havel Series

aims to honor and extend the intellectual legacy of the dissident, playwright, philosopher, and president whose name it proudly bears. Prepared with Ivan M. Havel, and other personalities and institutions closely associated with Václav Havel, such as the Václav Havel Library and Forum 2000, the series focuses on modern thought and the contemporary world – encompassing history, politics, art, architecture, and ethics. While the works often concern the Central European experience, the series – like Havel himself – focuses on issues that affect humanity across the globe.